Rik Mayall

Comedy Genius

also by the author:

Al Pacino: The Movies Behind The Man

For my mum

Contents

The Oxford English dictionary defines the word Genius as:

1. Exceptional intellectual or creative power or other natural ability.

   'she was a teacher of genius'

2. An exceptionally intelligent person or one with exceptional skill in a particular area of activity.

   'a mathematical genius'

Arguably, Rik Mayall embodied both strands of this definition. He had a natural ability for comedy, whether on the stage, on TV or on film. But most importantly, he knew what made great, and edgy, comedy. He was a master practitioner. His comedic intellect was greater than 99% of his contemporaries. He was a comedy genius.

Mayall was such a household name that almost everybody has their own unique memory of him. Whether it be the anarchy of *The Dangerous Brothers*, *The Young Ones* or *Bottom*. Or the politically satirical characters of Kevin Turvey or Alan B'Stard. Some may even remember Mayall best for his more serious work in the likes of *The Bill*, *Jonathan Creek* or *Rik Mayall presents...* There was humour in some of the episodes but it was greatly toned down in favour of Mayall showing a more dramatic side to his acting. Comedy was his bread and butter though. Whether on-screen or behind the microphone Mayall revelled in comedic energy. Listening to his voice work on audiobooks where you can feel the sweat pouring down his face as he goes full-tilt radical while reading some of the dialogue. Mayall in the vocal booth and Mayall in-front of the camera was one and the same. He always gave his all.

His crude, lewd anarchy was exactly what youngsters, and adults, revelled in. When he was on TV you never knew what he would do next. His crazy energy wouldn't have worked in mainstream light entertainment. Mayall was dangerous and edgy and raw. The occasional instances in which he appeared on a chat shows were awkward because he had to present himself as Richard Mayall, and that simply wasn't him when cameras were rolling. His co-star from *The Young Ones*, Alexei Sayle, told me: "He didn't do chat shows. He couldn't do chat shows. He couldn't give good interviews. Rik couldn't be serious." One such occasion saw Mayall and his comedy partner Ade Edmondson appear on a live phone-in segment on the kid's TV show *Going Live* to promote their forthcoming *Bottom* tour. They struggled to suppress their anarchic sides even when taking phone calls from kids at home; double entendres were uttered. The pair were unsuited to be on pre-watershed TV, it felt wrong. Mayall and Edmondson were at their best when smashing each other in the face with a frying pan or the refrigerator door or dropping a TV on their heads. It was cartoon violence performed by real humans; a real-life Tom and Jerry.

Mayall was rarely photographed or interviewed away from his work. He chose to keep his personal and professional lives very separate. His personal life only featured in the headlines on very specific occasions such as the aftermath of his horrific quad bike accident. It was the one time we saw behind DR. THE RIK FUCKING MAYALL persona and actually saw Richard Michael Mayall. This was a trying time for his legions of fans and must have been almost unbearable for his family, as it did, at one stage, look like we might lose the people's poet. Thankfully he recovered and the accident only fuelled his anarchic nature as he would for the rest of his life go around declaring he was better than Christ as he had died for a longer period of time than the son of God before being resurrected. Typical Mayall.

So, this is it, a commentary on the works of Rik Mayall. He had such a wide and varied career (even though he was predominately known for his comedy roles) that it was difficult to uncover absolutely everything he did. Hopefully I've covered/uncovered as much as is currently possible and maybe you, lovely reader, will discover a new piece of work via this book you were not aware of. If you want to complain about something missing however, then in the words of Richard Richard "Fick urf you sad, pathic winker."

1958 - 1979

(When Richard became Rik)

Matching Tye is a quaint village in the wilds of Essex. It is the type of picturesque location that reminds you of the beauty in the English Countryside. It is a quiet and peaceful place where life moves at a slower pace. Yet it was the birth place of a human ball of energy, a person so electric he could fry the entire British power grid.

Richard Michael Mayall was born on 7 March 1958 to John and Gillian who were both drama teachers. He was the Mayalls' second child after Michael (sisters Libby and Kate would arrive later). Richard was a tantrum thrower from an early age. He would wail loud and long as his parents tried to placate him.

The Mayall's continued to live in Matching Tye until Richard was three and then moved Droitwich Spa in Worcestershire. John and Gillian continued to teach drama, and John would regularly put on plays for the local community at the Norbury Theatre. One of those plays, Bertolt Brecht's *The Good Woman of Setzuan*, featured Richard. His performance as a little peasant boy amounted to him climbing into a dustbin and eating chocolate stowed inside. Whilst appearing in his parents' plays, Richard started to gain confidence, and a cheeky streak. When he attended Rashwood County Primary School, Richard was included in the school's Christmas Carol service. However, a teacher told him beforehand: "Don't sing – I want all the children to sing but not you because you've got a horrible voice. So just move your mouth to look like you're singing." Richard did exactly as he was told – he didn't sing. But he did mouth the words in an overly dramatic and comedic way that started to draw laughs from the adults in the audience. He then proceeded to waggle his bum around as well. Howls of laughter came from the mums and dads in the audience, however the teacher who had previously told Richard not to sing wasn't laughing. Mid way through the concert Richard was pulled off stage by the teacher and told to stand in the corner of the room as punishment. This backfired spectacularly for the teacher as Richard continued to mime along with the words and waggle his bottom. The audience were more focussed on the little boy in the corner than the group of children on stage.

Richard wanted to be a trouble-causer but was too afraid, so he would seek out the kids who had already been labelled as troublemakers and suggest naughty things for them to do. For all his acting out in school, at home Richard was in a safe middle-class environment where his parents were, in his words, "beatnik." John continued to put on plays and included Richard in his production of *Waiting For Godot* as the Boy Messenger.

By the time Richard was eligible to attend secondary school he had won a day-scholarship to attend the prestigious King's School in Worcester. During his seven years at the school Richard was "thoroughly sociable, well-liked and an influential member of his year" his housemaster John Turner told the *Worcester Observer*. He studied History, Geography and English at A Level. Peter Diamond was Richard's English teacher who found him to be a pleasant boy who happened to be very funny: "I'd love to tell you that Rik was a riot in class, but it was a marked trait of his character that he was a conformist." Richard's love of acting grew dramatically while at King's School and he featured in many school productions including *Rosencrantz and Guildenstern Are Dead* and *The Two Gentlemen of Verona*. Yet Richard wasn't all work and no play as he regularly spent the mid-morning school break in the churchyard next to the school smoking with his friends. During these times he would act out little skits and characters while his mates looked on, puffing on their cigarettes.

By the fourth year of King's School, Richard was writing his own plays and performing them in his drama class. He threw himself into drama work but his other schoolwork suffered badly. By the time he was ready to leave King's School he had messed up his A Level's so badly (Two C's and an E) that he couldn't attend University on his grades alone. Fortunately he was rescued by the Clearing system, a process where Universities fill any spaces they have left. He was given the chance to attend Manchester University for a drama course. It was around this time that Richard decided to change his name, not legally, to Rik Mayall. Some say it was because he loved the comic strip of *Erik The Viking*. Others suggest it was because he noticed a boy at school called Rick who was popular with the girls. The newly-named Rik Mayall had new educational horizons.

It was 1975. The Labour Party were in power. Margaret Thatcher became the leader of The Conservative Party. The IRA detonated a succession of bombs in London. A jury returned a verdict of wilful murder against Lord

Lucan, who had disappeared from view. Charlie Chaplin was knighted and *Monty Python and the Holy Grail* was released in cinemas. This was the backdrop to Rik Mayall, with his long hair and flared trousers, first stepping into Manchester University.

The B.A. Drama course on which Mayall had been offered a place consisted of around 30 like-minded individuals, all keen to hone their talents in the hope of venturing into the entertainment business. Mayall's first year there was quite reserved. He studied hard and worked well with each individual on the course. However, he never fully showed his flair for acting. By the second term Mayall had joined a small comedy group called 20th Century Coyote set up by fellow classmate Lloyd Peters that including friends Mike Redfern and Mark Dewison. The troupe became a lunchtime resident at The Band on the Wall jazz club in Manchester. Here they would perform short improv sketches that were "anarchic slapstick mixed with a large dose of Monty Python's Flying Circus." Late in the academic year, an additional member joined 20th Century Coyote: "I can remember the seminar when Rik asked me if I would do some stuff with 20th Century Coyote." Adrian Edmondson told *The Independent* in 1994 "I said: 'Well, I'll have to have a contract, luv.' And he wrote me out a contract during the seminar which said something like: 'I promise it will be horrible and nothing will ever go right. La de da. Rik Mayall.' He was true to his word."

Bradford-born Edmondson hated school and he was constantly caned for breaking school rules. The one adult he liked at school was his English teacher who encouraged him to pursue drama and cast him in several school plays including Shakespeare's *Hamlet*. Edmondson managed to secure an audition at The Royal Academy of Dramatic Arts in London but was too scared to attend it. Instead he opted to go to Manchester University as it was easier: "You just had to go and tell them you were clever" Mayall told *The Independent* years later.

Mayall and Edmondson hit it off immediately and soon they were writing their own material: "At college everyone was doing either real political material or heavy arts stuff and we kind of developed a don't-give-a-toss philosophy" Mayall told *The Independent* in 1994. They began selling the *Morning Star* newspaper for extra money and between sales they would work on their material including a bit where one shouted *"Morning Star!"* the other would respond with "Morning luv." They also regularly put on their own comedy stage productions for the drama course's weekly Studio Night residence.

Mayall was living in a shared student house called Lime Cottage in East Didsbury. Legend has it that Edmondson would turn up on his MZ150 motorbike and try and ride it up the stairs. The sad reality is that never actually happened, not even once. However, Mayall did bunk lifts off Edmondson to get to University on time: "I remember the first time I decided to go on the back of his motorbike, and thinking: 'I can either go along with this and probably die, or catch the bus.' I got on." The third and final year of the B.A. Drama course proved to be the spark that Mayall needed to breakout of solely acting in University plays. *The Guardian* theatre critic gave him the Boris Karloff award for the most outrageous ham on view thanks to his performance in *Sherlock's Last Case* at the National Student Drama Festival. 20th Century Coyote continued, without Peters, and started to pick up a following and some positive reviews. It was a conversation Mayall struck up with someone in the first year of the course that would prove to be one of the most fruitful friendships he would have.

Ben Elton, the son of a teacher and professor of educational research, grew up in the suburbs of London before moving to leafy Surrey. He attended college in Stratford-Upon-Avon before taking up a place at Manchester University. During his first year Elton was writing plays that were putting some of the third year students to shame. Mayall saw something in Elton that convinced him they could be great pals and even better writing partners. Mayall also struck up a friendship with his drama teacher's daughter Lise Mayer. She too had a comedic streak that Mayall found hilarious. Mayall and Edmondson stayed friends with Elton and Mayer through their last year at Manchester University.

After graduating in 1978, Mayall took up an offer to tour America for three months in the Oxford and Cambridge Shakespeare Company's production of *The Comedy of Errors*. He played Dromio of Syracuse: "It was great training – trying to make Americans laugh at Shakespearian comedy." His impressive turn in a dramatic role lead him to start looking for serious acting jobs upon his return. However, they were in short supply, especially as he was back living with his parents in Droitwich.

Mayall bounced through a series of dead-end jobs to bring in some money and ensure that his partnership with Edmondson continued. They toured their half hour comedy shows around The Midlands (Edmondson was, at that time, living in Tamworth with his first wife). One play was called *The Joke* and it consisted of them failing to do Knock Knock jokes and finished with a long piece about the setting up of a joke culminating in laughter recorded on a tape player. The duo received at first good responses. This shifted to great and then to outstanding the more they toured.

Eventually, in 1979, the two friends took 20th Century Coyote to the Edinburgh Festival to perform a new play they had written called *Death On The Toilet*. Mayall played Death and God who both spoke to Edmondson's Edwin who was stuck on the toilet. In the audience one night was soon-to-be best friend and comedic actor Alexi Sayle: "It was theatre, it had comedy, cruelty and jokes, lots and lots of jokes. There had never been anything like it on the Fringe." He recalled to *chortle.co.uk* about seeing *Death On The Toilet*. The forty-minute play was a hit! From the box office returns Mayall and Edmondson had saved enough cash to move to London and seek their fortunes at Soho's Comedy Store.

The duo decided to write new material and came up with a play that satirized Ken Campbell's *The Warp* – a twenty-two hour journey through gurudom and post-1960s mind expansion. Ever the jokers, Mayall and Edmondson called their play *The Wart*. It toured for ten days around London's smaller comedy venues. Total attendees for the whole tour numbered twenty. However, one of those in the audience at The Tramshed in Woolwich was James Fenton, *The Sunday Times* drama critic, whose review said Mayall was: "a very talented young maniac." By the end of 1979, Mayall and Edmondson were performing at The Comedy Store, a newly formed comedy club that was fast becoming known as the place to see "alternative comedy." The fast turnover of comedians meant that Mayall and Edmondson had to quickly and constantly write new material in order to keep appearing at The Comedy Store. Their approach to comedy also changed and they found themselves having to write and perform material that they classed as Cabaret – talking directly to the audience. New sketches and characters appeared in their sets including their now infamous Gooseberry sketch, The Dangerous Brothers and Rick The Poet. These, and other Cabaret sketches, made them stars in waiting. Mayall wouldn't have to wait too long though because as a new decade began offers were flooding in to his agent. The British public were about to be introduced to Rik "fucking" Mayall.

Mike Redfern: I first met him [Mayall] at school. Our first year at secondary school. We were very close at school and when I was sixteen my family moved abroad. My dad was working in Belgium and the school wouldn't take me on as a boarding pupil. My folks didn't know what to do about it until one day Rik's mum just turned up on our doorstep and said: 'I hear you are moving and Mike has nowhere to live. Why doesn't he come and live with us?'. I lived there for two years. One year Rik was there and one he wasn't as he had gone to university. I was part of that family. It was lovely.

Lloyd Peters: It was 1975 and we shared a hall of residence at Sellafield in Manchester and we bonded straight away because we shared a similar kind of irreverent, kind of rude non-PC sense of humour. He had a party trick where he would fold the flap of his ear into his earlobe and I could spit water through my teeth. We thought we were going to make a fortune out of that.

Redfern: Rik was the driving force in putting together 20th Century Coyote. Lloyd named it.

Peters: When we moved into a cottage in the second year, so 1976 onwards, is when I registered the name 20th Century Coyote. I actually filled in the wrong piece of paper. I registered it as a theatrical agency rather than a theatre company. But it was still in my name in the cottage at Didsbury. That is where 20th Century Coyote started and the document I have got is in my name to that address.

Redfern: We performed in Band on the Wall at lunchtimes to an audience who had no interest in anything but Guinness. It was a real hard school to grow up in as a performer.

Peters: It was either very later '76 or very early '77 when we started to perform at Band on the Wall. We were kind of the resident company there for three months. We didn't really have a script. We just had key lines that we had to say and the structure of the plot. As it was there wasn't much plot to it. We did rehearse though. We took it seriously. We rehearsed quite solidly and then performed three dates a week at Band on the Wall at lunchtimes.

Redfern: At the end of their [Mayall, Edmondson and Peters] second year and my first, the university, for the first time ever, took a team to the Edinburgh Fringe. All of us went as performers in mainstream-ish productions but we also had a 20th Century Coyote production that we took up there called *My Lungs Don't Work*. It was pretty good but we didn't get the audiences. The Fringe club invited Rik to perform there one evening and he delivered an absolutely barnstorming show. He took bits out of the show we had been doing. We were in the audience performing but as audience members and he absolutely took that venue by storm.

Peters: We did a couple of gigs outside of Band on the Wall. We marketed it. We had a leaflet and charges and contact names. We were trying to get the Equity card. We had to look like a kosher organisation.

Redfern: They [Mayall, Edmondson and Peters] went down south and worked very hard at getting any form of comedy work. They started to make contacts through the energy.

Peters: It was only after university, when we moved to London, that him [Mayall] and Ade did some shows as 20th Century Coyote. They asked me if they could use the name, which was good of them. I was doing drama. Doing *Boys from the Blackstuff* and working with Mike Leigh. I was on a different kind of path. They [Mayall & Edmondson] did a tour before that and they asked me to be their roadie but all I remember is I trapped my finger in the door of the car. I did the sound for them. It was very depressing at that time as nobody understood what they were doing. There was about twenty people in the audience and I think I even had to pay [laughs]. Then it all just kicked off.

1980s

(A young one, a dangerous brother and a politician)

While Rik Mayall & Adrian Edmondson continued their assault on the live comedy circuit, Mayall was slowly breaking into film and television. His first appearance on TV screens was uneventful in a blink-and-you'll-miss-it role as First Supporter in new TV show: *The Squad*, a programme about young cadets being put through police training. The show aired on 1st October 1980. Mayall had also secured a scheduled BBC Two appearance in an adaptation of The Velvet Underground's *The Gift* alongside Edmondson. The show had been adapted by one of their university friends but was pulled at the last minute as the producer felt it was too punk to be shown on television. University buddy Lloyd Peters also filmed Mayall in a parody adaptation of *Un Chien Andalou* called *Le Chat in the Loo*. It wouldn't be until 1981 however that Mayall really started to make his mark in film and television.

His appearance in the first ever British mini-series *Wolcott* as the sneering, racist PC Fell was a very different piece of acting for him. *Wolcott* was the first British police drama to feature a black actor in the lead role, played by George William Harris. The broadcast over three consecutive nights in January 1981 drew heavy criticism from both left and right-leaning members of society. Mayall, thin to the point of appearing gaunt and sporting a close-cropped hair cut, gives an aggressive performance. His copper is a nasty piece of work that is more interested in giving a hard time to the black officer on the force than any of the criminals he is meant to be chasing. His performance showed very early on that he had the talent to play straight roles.

However, it was comedy he loved and comedy he couldn't escape. Documentary filmmaker Julian Temple was hired to make a short film about the rise of alternative comedy, specifically the underground Soho comedy club The Comic Strip. A thirty-minute piece that is a narrative driven by Jennifer Saunders lost in Soho looking for her sister. Down dark alleyways and passages she bumps into all manner of strange folk (played by the stars from the club). Eventually the film's plot gives way to showing live stand-up sets from Alexei Sayle, Arnold Brown, The Outer Limits and The Dangerous Brothers. It was meant to be a tongue-in-cheek look at what went on behind the scenes of the club, but, in truth, it was more of a promotional video for the entertainers themselves. Mayall and Edmondson's on-stage screen-time consists of them telling a knock knock joke followed by a joke about a Gooseberry in a lift. It is anarchically manic and frenetic, and for anyone who didn't know who The Dangerous Brothers were this short screen-time would certainly make sure you never forgot them. While possibly seen as the first episode of what was to eventually become *The Comic Strip Presents...* this short film played in cinemas in-front of screenings of the punk music film *Urgh! A Music War*. Most of those comedians featured in the short film also appeared on the song Pop-Up Toasters from Alexei's Midnight Runners (Sayle on lead vocals and Mayall, Edmondson, Planer and Richardson on backing vocals). Released as a 7" single that featured excepts from 20th Century Coyote and The Outer Limits performances from the club on the B-side.

Alternative comedy well and truly arrived into mainstream television when the series *A Kick Up The Eighties* appeared on British TV on the evening of 26th September 1981. The show was created by Tom Gutteridge, the mind behind the Russell Harty chat show for the BBC. The show featured a series of contemporary sketches and musical parodies from existing and new comedians such as Miriam Margolyes, Tracey Ullman, Richard Stilgoe and Roger Sloman. However, it was the weekly appearance of Mayall that ensured the show was talked about up and down the country. Playing investigative reporter Kevin Turvey from Redditch, he would spit out long monologues about such subjects as sex, death and sex Again. Dressed in a flowery shirt, stonewash jeans and a blue parker coat with a mess of hair, Turvey's rambling speeches would veer rapidly off topic. He would also frequently discuss Theresa Kelly, a young lady back in Redditch with whom he was in love. The first series ran for six episodes every Monday night on BBC Two at 9pm and the end credits listed Kevin Turvey as himself. This kept the viewers guessing as to whether or not this was a real person. Mayall told *The Oxford Student* newspaper how Kevin Turvey came about: "I phoned up Alexei Sayle and said, "Are you going up for that telly thing next week?" and he said, "Rik! It's fucking tomorrow!" I hadn't written a fucking bean, I hadn't written anything, so I was shitting myself and I thought, well what am I going to do? I know, I'll do it Brummy, and

I'll call him Kevin, and I know, I won't write any material, I'll just talk like he's the most boring man in the world."

Mayall's performance as Turvey is a riveting piece of work because the audience is unsure where he will take the monologue next. In the short segments he was given he created a fascinating (and slightly eccentric) character who held the viewers' attention simply by sitting in a swivel chair and talking directly to camera. It was bravado of the highest order for any comedian to do that let alone one who had only been on TV a couple of times before. Due to the phenomenal reception Turvey received on *A Kick Up The Eighties*, he agreed to participate as a guest on the Russell Harty chat show several weeks later. If the chat had been rehearsed beforehand then it certainly didn't seem like Harty was prepared for Turvey to walk off set mid-interview after being asked about his girlfriend Theresa Kelly. The camera panned to Harty struck with a look of sheer panic as he tried to figure out what happened, and what to do next. Turvey returned to the stage midway through Harty's interview with musician Elvis Costello. It caught both of them off-guard and they just sat there as Turvey shouted at Harty and then left. Kevin Turvey was a game changer for Mayall.

His next project - A TV short film called *Couples and Robbers* – was one that Mayall was proud of appearing in. It told the story of newly-weds Morris and Wendy who have a life-changing chance encounter with a gay couple. The film was a light and fluffy piece that turned darker as the story progressed. It's a fascinating performance by Mayall as he bickers and barks at Frances Low's Wendy, who gives as good as she gets. This is the portrayal of a couple who love and hate each other in equal measure. This performance offered more evidence that Mayall was just as adept in straight roles as he was in comedic ones. Even in something like *Couples & Robbers* that has nastiness coursing through its veins. It premiered at the New York Film Festival on 7th October 1981 before being released in UK cinemas in the summer of 1982.

Graduating from short film to full-blown feature film, Mayall's first appearance in a feature length movie was in the twisted comedy musical *Shock Treatment*, Richard O'Brien's follow up to his cult classic *The Rocky Horror Picture Show*. Brad and Janet (played this time by Cliff De Young and

24

Jessica Harper) are entered into a gameshow where they find themselves kidnapped by the TV network and imprisoned in the local mental hospital Dentonville run by brother and sister Cosmo and Nation McKinley (Richard O' Brien and Patricia Quinn respectively). Mayall appears as one of their colleagues called "Rest Home" Ricky, who is in charge of wheeling Brad and Janet away in strait jackets and into the care of the McKinley's. As with O'Brien's previous movie, *Shock Treatment* has several quirky musical numbers and Mayall gets to partake in a couple of them. However, for a film that is high on energy and might be described as camp, Mayall is decidedly restrained in his performance. He never takes it to the levels of full-blown crazy, instead he simply skulks in the background with that slightly twisted and maniacal smile that he could produce on a whim. The film was a critical and commercial failure upon release, but it didn't help that it never received a full cinema release in most countries. Over the intervening years it has gained a huge cult following and is now seen as one of the films that preceded and, possibly predicted, the rise and rise of reality television.

Mayall also appeared in a blink-and-you'll-miss-it performance of a policeman in the weird and quirky British thriller *The Orchard End Murder*, which first appeared in cinemas in the North East of England on 1st November playing as a double bill with D*ead And Buried* before being shown as a stand-alone feature the following year. Mayall appeared in a second feature film in 1981.He put in a brief performance in John Landis's horror *An American Werewolf in London*. His character, known only as "2nd Chess Player", featured prominently in the scene where the two leads venture into a pub for some respite from the weather. While Brian Glover's "1st Chess Player" tells a joke, Mayall sits on the opposite side of the table, laughing at his Chess playing partner. The scene was shot in The Black Swan pub, Martyr's Green on the outskirts of Surrey not in Yorkshire as the film suggests. Mayall's appearance in the film came about because of a hilarious set of circumstances that even he must have laughed at. Director John Landis spoke to *The Guardian* in 2009 about it: "Frank Oz and Jim Henson were in London making *The Muppet Show* and they took me to the Comedy Store on a night off and there was this act on, two guys called Rik Mayall and Ade Edmondson. They were basically just screaming at each other, but it was hilarious. I went to meet them afterwards and, I don't know why, I just offered them a part in the movie. I don't think they really believed me, because Ade didn't turn up but Rik did."

Mayall's next film role was another brief appearance. This time it was opposite Hollywood megastar Donald Sutherland in the World War II drama *Eye of the Needle* based on Ken Follett's novel, *Storm Island*. Mayall Played one of the three sailors that Sutherland's character Henry Faber shares an overnight train carriage with. This time, Mayall did get a line of dialogue: "Fancy a game of poker mate?" directed at Sutherland. It was a small step up in the world of feature film acting for Mayall but it was the stage that still held the magic for him. The Comic Strip club in London's Soho had become a mecca for alternative comedy for those living in the south. Not everyone however, could get to London to see the alternative comedy revolution and consequently a UK tour was organised by Peter Richardson towards the end of 1981. First stop on the tour? Glasgow. Venue? An old porn cinema. A big bus carted the performers, including Arnold Brown, Dawn French, Jennifer Saunders, Adrian Edmondson, Alexei Sayle, Rowland Rivron, Mayall and others, around the country to equally "alternative" venues. On 20th December 1981 BBC Two broadcast a highlights show of Fundamental Frolics, a special one-off charity event in aid of MENCAP. The gig showcased the talents of a mixture of stand-up comedians and musicians including Alexei Sayle, Mel Smith, Griff Rhys Jones, Neil Innes, Rowan Atkinson, Chas & Dave, Elvis Costello and Ian Dury. Mayall alongside Adrian Edmondson, appearing under the name 20th Century Coyote, performed a six-minute set that was an early precursor to their Dangerous Brothers work as they bickered and fought before Edmondson stormed off stage and left Rik "The Poet" to read some of his new work including a piece called *Theatre* that is both philosophical ("What is theatre?") and surreal ("why don't you ask Vanessa Redgrave? Because I don't know Vanessa Redgrave"). It was over to BBC One on New Year's Eve for a thirty-minute comedic look at the events that unfolded during 1981 on a TV show called *81 Take 2*. "Due to stocktaking literally dozens of mint and previously unseen 1981 jokes must go before midnight" read the description in the *Radio Times* magazine. Cast members included Robbie Coltrane, Celia Imrie and The Hee Bee Gee Bees. Mayall's appearance came at the end of the show as a "Live From Vegas!" sketch. The majority of the jokes were at the expense of Americans. He also had a troop of dancing girls with him. It was a rare cabaret/end of the pier style segment from the alternative comedian.

1982 started with Mayall making a brief appearance on a TV show hosted by another comedic duo. *Wood and Walters* was a short-lived British sketch show created and starring Julie Walters and Victoria Wood. It showcased both comedians performing sketches with each other and/or special guests, and while it may have only lasted one series it set the mould for what both women would mainly be known for in their later work. After an initial pilot episode in January 1981, the order was given for a full six-episode series to be broadcast a year later. Mayall appeared twice in the show. Firstly, as a character called Mitch: a chauvinist pretending to be a feminist who monologued about why we should treat women with respect. The performance broke the fourth wall as Mitch wandered around the sets talking directly to camera. For this role, Mayall dressed in a green silk shirt which he'd left open to the navel accompanied by silk waistcoat and trousers. It is a very confident and impressive performance, especially considering it is one long five-minute monologue without a cut away or break. His second appearance was in a brief Game Show parody opposite Wood. It is a quick-fire guessing game that saw Mayall's character fail to get any of the correct words except when Wood said to him: "I'm one of these" and his reply was: "Twat." It is a richly frenetic piece of comedy and, based on this skit alone, it is a shame that Mayall and Wood never worked together afterwards.

Mayall's first venture into the world of TV adverts came as he advertised the chocolate bar *54321* in a blink-and-you'll-miss-it appearance as an astronaut trying to eat the snack through his helmet.

2nd November 1982 saw a huge change in TV comedy as *The Comic Strip Presents...* was commissioned by British TV's Channel 4. It was to feature performers from The Comic Strip comedy troupe based in London including Mayall, Edmondson, Alexi Sayle, Jennifer Saunders, Dawn French, Nigel Planer and Peter Richardson. The first series was to consist of six half hour episodes. Mayall's first appearance in series one was during the second episode *War*. Playing three different characters in tiny roles. His U.S. commander character offered a brief glimpse of Mayall doing a respectable American accent. *The Beat Generation* episode (third in transmission) was a British pisstake of the French New Wave films from the likes of Jean-Luc Godard and Francois Truffaut. Set to a jazz infused soundtrack and shown in black and white this episode had the whole gang playing hip characters who smoke and have sex. Mayall is, at first, an aggressive and angry man, yet after a "snog" with an American (played by Jennifer Saunders) he becomes completely relaxed and all of his anger fades away. It's a fun yin yang performance from Mayall who sports a chiselled jawline beard and short spikey hair.

His appearance in the fourth episode called *Bad News Tour* was almost against type. His character Colin Grigson is a subdued, pot smoking guitar player of few words. He prattles about in the background swishing his long hair and fine tuning his guitar. It is a very laidback performance from Mayall. However, it is worth viewing the episode just to see Mayall prance around onstage wearing skin-tight leopard print trousers. Director Sandy Johnson remembers what it was like making that episode: "We felt we were doing something new, something quite original. But while we were working somebody came up and said 'Hey! There is this film being made in America called Spinal Tap about a rock band' and we were like 'Wait a minute! That's what we are doing.' They were both being made at the same time." *Bad News Tour* aired sixteen months before *This Is Spinal Tap* hit cinema screens.

Playing a toff-turned-caveman in the episode titled *Summer School* saw Mayall crawl around on all fours in a makeshift outfit that resembled a rug rather than a loincloth. Sandy Johnson was also the director for this episode: "When we did *Summer School*, Rik's character was almost like his character from Bottom. This sort of manic character who was very obsessively trying to have sex and he ends up bumming a corpse in a tent without knowing what he is doing. It was quite edgy at the time." This was the last episode of the first series of *The Comic Strip Presents*. The show brought The Comic Strip into British homes and began to make stars out of those involved. Sadly, the sixth episode of series one was never made. It was to be a spoof on the chat show format called *Back to Normal with Eddie Monsoon*. The script, written by the whole cast, was deemed too vulgar and possibly libellous as well. Channel 4 decided it was too dangerous a prospect to go ahead with that episode (The script for it was eventually published as part of *The Comic Strip Presents...* book in October 1983). The Comic Strip troupe took part in an Australian tour during the spring of 1982. Bringing alternative comedy to a new country proved successful and they emerged as one of the big breakouts of the Adelaide Festival.

ITV commissioned satirists Andrew Marshall and David Renwick to write a six-part sitcom for the channel called *Whoops Apocalypse*. It was set during the weeks leading up to the apocalypse and the global political situation that caused it. The show starred Peter Cook, John Cleese and Richard Griffith, amongst others, it also featured a brief cameo from Mayall as a Southern states of America country music star called Biff who is brought into U.S. President Johnny Cyclops's office along with some strategists who want to unleash a new and all-powerful nuclear bomb. Mayall says very little throughout the sketch until the end where he plays the guitar and sings a song called "Johnny Cyclops never started World War III". It is a fairly basic and uneventful appearance from Mayall apart from revealing that he could actually play the guitar.

In May 1982, Mayall appeared in a light-hearted Television play produced by Scottish TV called *Northern Lights*. Celebrated theatre and television actress Judy Parfitt played the lead role of Dr. Baverstock, an unmarried woman who falls for a member of a touring mime troupe, played by Mayall. The material was slightly whimsical. Some light dollops of humour are sprinkled throughout but this isn't classic Mayall, more a documentation of an actor trying new directions whilst still keeping his foot in the comedy door. Even he was slightly sheepish about the play telling *The Face* magazine "I misread the script and said 'Yes'." After that, it was back to comedy quick sharp. Due to the almost instant success of Mayall's creation Kevin Turvey on *A Kick Up The Eighties*, the BBC commissioned a special one-off forty-minute show called *Kevin Turvey: The Man Behind The Green Door* about a week in the life of Redditch's own investigative reporter. Airing on the 13th September 1982, it took Turvey outside of the usual confines of a studio and followed him around as he investigated local issues. The episode also introduced his mum and their lodger Mick (played by Robbie Coltrane). Turvey, the sociably unsociable rent-a-gob wandered the streets, canals and libraries of Redditch conducting his own unique brand of investigative journalism. As much as Turvey's appearance on *A Kick Up The Eighties* is fun, this one-off special showcased much more of the character's larger than life personality. His snotty, busy-body antics make for entertaining viewing throughout. Peering behind the (green) door of the Turvey's, it shows a 1980s single-parent family struggling with bills and everyday life. Still, the teenage Turvey finds fascination in the every-day life around him. It is a shame that Mayall stopped portraying Turvey as this part held so many more possibilities, either through continuing his investigations in Redditch, or sending him further afield (imagine Turvey on an 80s package holiday to Spain).

Turvey gave Mayall a comedic platform all to himself. It was a strong character. But it would be nothing compared to another character he created that would appear in a sitcom alongside his mates, one that was to be the first defining piece of work for Mayall.

"Darling we're The Young Ones"

The genesis for *The Young Ones* was simply three friends watching television and not seeing anything that reflected their interests or those of the wider, twenty-something demographic. It was all fuddy duddy comedians that had been on television for decades. Bruce Forsyth, Jimmy Tarbuck, Des O'Connor. The same tired faces doing the same tired routines. Television channels were afraid to show the newer, edgier comedians that were coming through in the early 1980s. So, Manchester University friends Ben Elton, Lise Mayer and Rik Mayall set about to change that, and *The Young Ones* was born.

Mayall recalled to *Kerrang Extra* that they wanted to give the viewers "the kind of stuff we'd really like to see on the telly, the kind of stuff that made us laugh." Initially Mayall had the idea that it should be four unemployed people living in a flat together, but he felt that would be too political so changed it to four students living together in rented accommodation. Having appeared on stage at The Comic Strip club in London with their act *The Dangerous Brothers*, Mayall and Edmondson became friends with two other stand-up comedians who performed on the same stage. They were Nigel Planer and Peter Richardson who called themselves *The Outer Limits* (a homage to the 1960s TV show). Part of their routine involved Planer coming on stage as a sluggish hippy called Neil who would try to play his guitar and sing, only to be interrupted by Richardson in different guises. According to reports (and the actor himself) it was Mayall who had the idea to write a sitcom about a group of students flat-sharing. He mentioned this to his girlfriend Lise Mayer and they set about writing a sitcom that would feature various characters that had been part of Mayall and Edmondson's stand-up act. Planer and Richardson were asked if they would be interested in appearing in the sitcom as well, and they both jumped at the chance.

When Mayall and Mayer pitched the sitcom idea to up and coming BBC TV producer Paul Jackson, whom Mayall had previously met in a club one night while performing his poetry, he jumped at the chance of making a TV show that featured the some of the stars of the alternate comedy scene. However, there was a problem. Richardson and Jackson had previously fallen out when Jackson commissioned a series called *Boom Boom Out Go*

The Lights which was also to feature stars from the alternative UK comedy scene. This new show was designed to feature solo performers and Jackson asked Planer to reprise his Neil character but didn't cast Richardson: "It was a silly thing of me to do. I was just going for the stand-ups. I made a mistake." This threw early production of *The Young Ones* into a tailspin as Richardson was to play Mike. Quickly Mayall and Mayer scrambled for another actor and almost employed Timothy Spall as he gave a script reading that both writers loved. But it was felt Spall and Planer had the same facial expressions and would be too similar on-screen. By chance Mayall and Mayer found their Mike when they went to see a play in London's West End. It starred Christopher Ryan, an actor who had played more serious and dramatic roles than comedic ones. However, that play – *Can't Pay Won't Pay* - showcased his comedic talents and both Mayall and Mayer knew they had found their new cool guy Mike. Also drafted in was The Comic Strip club compere Alexei Sayle to play landlord Jerzei "Jeremy" Balowski, alongside several other characters including members of the Balowski family. This was a direct request from Sayle because he didn't want to be stuck playing just one character in the show.

As Mayall and Mayer started to write the pilot episode they realised that they wouldn't be able to write as speedily as first planned, and asked Jackson if they could bring in another writer. Jackson agreed and they pulled in their friend from university Ben Elton. Suddenly, the threesome found their groove and knocked out the pilot script overnight. The pilot was filmed mainly on a soundstage at BBC Television Centre with the exterior scenes shot in London. When the finished version was shown to BBC Executives it was met with disbelief and they asked Jackson to write a thesis on why the show was funny. They didn't know what they were watching as it wasn't a sitcom in the traditional sense, and as such they put the rest of the series production on hold with a view to cancelling it. A lifeline appeared in the form of Peter Richardson. Channel 4 had commissioned a series of episodes, via Richardson, to feature members from The Comic Strip club. When the BBC executives found out they reignited *The Young Ones* idea and put six episodes into production to compete against Channel 4.

Each episode took two days to film. Thursdays would be filmed on a closed set for all the bigger, more elaborate stunts (Alexei Sayle told *The Express*: "This was usually the day when Rik (and sometimes Ade) went to hospital") and Fridays would be filmed in front of a live studio audience. But because the cast struggled not to break into fits of laughter during filming a lot of the Friday evening shoots ran over. The BBC, at that time, had a strict 10pm curfew on filming but very rarely did *The Young Ones* finish before or even on time. Then negotiations had to take place between crew members for an extension of ten or fifteen minutes at additional costs. Occasionally, they would not allow them an extension and if they hadn't finished filming the episode then there was nothing else to do except use what was already in the can. Money to produce *The Young Ones* was always tight, however Jackson had hit on the unique idea of including music acts in each episode. This enabled them to request additional money for production as it qualified as variety rather than just light entertainment and the variety department had more cash to splash. Music acts that appeared included Madness, Motorhead, Dexy's Midnight Runners and The Damned (who reformed specially to appear on the show). Music acts appeared in eleven of the first twelve episodes. The episode that didn't feature a music act (series 1 episode 6) instead involved a lion tamer performing to Tight Fit's *The Lion Sleeps Tonight*.

The lion tamer was used instead of a band so that the production could secure even more budget money as the he fell under the remit of Variety entertainment. During the editing of the second series the idea was hit upon to throw in flash frames, one in each episode. The episodes provoked a strong audience reaction because at that time there was controversy surrounding the use of subliminal messages in TV shows. This being *The Young Ones* the subliminal messaging didn't promote a particular meaning, instead it consisted of random images including a frog, a tap and a western shoot-out scene. Word of these subliminal messages got back to Bill Cotton, who was the managing director of the BBC, and he instructed Jackson to remove them for all subsequent re-runs (however they are viewable on the VHS/DVD releases). Exterior filming had moved from London to Bristol for reasons unknown. For one episode the crew had to spray fake snow across two houses on the street where *The Young Ones* were supposed to live. However, production manager Ed Bye had got the wrong houses and when the homeowners returned they were not best pleased.

The first episode of *The Young Ones* was shown on 9th November 1982 on BBC Two and as expected, it was a huge hit it and found its core audience almost immediately. It wasn't however, the audience the writers thought it would be. The fanbase turned out to be school children, quite young school children at that. The parents weren't so keen on their children watching *The Young Ones*, so they bombarded the writers and the cast with irate letters. *The Young Ones* ratings, while not huge, held its own for both series constantly hovering between 2 – 2.5 million, which wasn't bad for a show that is alternative in every way.

The Young Ones did continue after the show had finished. Two books were written by the cast and released. Planer put out a prog-rock album called *Neil's Heavy Concept album* and it spawned a number 2 hit for the track *Hole In My Shoe*. There was also a live tour but without Ryan or Sayle. The Fox network in America decided to try and create their own version of *The Young Ones*. Only Planer signed on to reprise his role. The pilot - called *Oh, No! Not THEM!* - was filmed but the network chose not to pick it up. Actor Robert Llewellyn said Planer had told him that they had "managed to make *The Young Ones* into a sort of grubby *Benny Hill Show*." Possibly most famous of all *The Young Ones* spin-off stuff was their duet with Cliff Richard for the Comic Relief charity, it was a cover of Richard's original 1959 release *Living Doll* (featuring The Shadows). It was released two years after the TV show had finished on 8th March 1986 and spent three weeks at the top of the UK singles chart. There was something rather poetic and beautiful about Cliff Richard the clean-cut pop star joining forces with the anarchistic enfant terriblés of television and it gave Richard his first number one single in nearly seven years.

"That was Bwwwilliant" and with those first words spoken on *The Young Ones* came another comedic revolution. Much like the *Monty Python* gang before them, Ben Elton, Lise Mayer and Rik Mayall didn't just usher in a new era of comedy but smashed their way through with a brick, a lá Vyvyan, and then proceeded to hit the viewers repeatedly over the head with a pot full of hot lentils. Binge watching episodes of *The Young Ones* is akin to having a pneumatic drill buzzing around in your head. There is no rest from the non-stop barrage of insane stunts, surreal characters and hilarious dialogue. The entrance of Vyvyan is all those things in one – he crashes through a brick wall, lands on the dinner table and then shouts at everyone before smashing Rik's head into the table. The central cast of characters could not be more different from each other if they tried yet that is the beauty of *The Young Ones*, as it becomes a story of opposites attract. Underneath all that fighting and swearing is four flatmates who do care for each other, they just have a hard time showing it.

Take the example of when the TV licence inspector turns up, Vyvyan, sensing his mates are in trouble, decides to eat the television. Any normal person might have put a table cloth over the TV but not Vyvyan, instead he decides to cram it down his gob. Underneath all that blunderbussing lurks a heart of gold, and that principle can be applied to each of the five central characters. The premise behind *The Young Ones* was that they were in essence a nuclear family with a surreal edge. Neil is mother, Mike is father, Vyvyan is the eldest child slowly going off the rails but can't leave the home for fear of being cut off and Rik is a boy that has just reached puberty so doesn't want to leave home or his bedroom. They are the neighbours who flick the V-sign when you say "Good morning" and leave their reeking rubbish in the driveway for weeks on end. They are the family everybody on the street fears. They live in their own bubble where being respectful and cordial to others is replaced with kicking someone in the balls or smashing their head into the television. It is a family without rules and viewers were not expecting that.

Elton, Mayer and Mayall were expecting mainstream audiences who liked Jimmy Tarbuck and Des O'Connor and Bruce Forsyth to dislike their show and they consistently poked fun at those viewers by never settling for the safe sitcom format. Instead they threw energy and chaos and, most of all, politics into the show. If Rik wasn't screaming "FASCIST!" then Mike was talking about why he voted for the Conservatives. This was a comedy show that spoke to young people about how life was not a bed of roses and in fact the government had almost completely forgotten about their generation. There is an outstanding cut-away scene in which Elton is fronting a TV show "aimed at young adults by young adults" and as he dances his way through the monologue to camera he really sticks the knife into the government about how they are leaving behind an entire generation and they are all forced onto the dole because there are no jobs. That underlying message was, beyond the anarchy and slapstick, what brought younger viewers to *The Young Ones*. They found a connection in one or all the characters that they had never seen on television before. It was uncompromising and never had BBC programming been so forceful.

Anyway, back to the fighting and foul language. *The Young Ones* took the slapstick violence from the likes of Charlie Chaplin, Buster Keaton and Laurel and Hardy, and turned it up to 11. They thought nothing of having Vyvyan smash Rik in the face or Neil jump out of a second storey glass window. This was Punk Rock anarchic violence with a comedic edge. Viewers knew that it wasn't to be replicated and didn't need to be told that (apart from one scene where a message flashes up about not locking people in fridges). By the second series the style of the show was established and each character had their own specific role to play within the group. It also meant that the writers could let the more eccentric elements of each character loose. Vyvyan became more violent while Rik became more perverted. Neil became more vocal and Mike oozed sexuality.

The second series is much more coherent in terms of storyline (if there ever was such a thing in *The Young Ones*) and it breathed life into the characters by allowing the actors to delve deeper into their characters for a continued period. *The Young Ones* ripped up the TV sitcom rule book. They included musical guests, broke the fourth wall by talking directly into camera, created characters who were obnoxious, had surreal cutaways and were anti-establishment. It was a show for young people that adults simply didn't understand and just as it was starting to be talked about in the mainstream the writers did the very clever thing of killing off *The Young Ones* phenomenon by having them drive off a cliff (literally) and then explode. There was no coming back from that. Two series and out. As they say in showbusiness: leave the audience wanting more.

The dated clothes, the music acts that didn't make it big and the occasional racist joke aside, *The Young Ones* is still as energetic, chaotic and anarchistic as ever. It's a comedy sitcom that was a game changer.

Paul Jackson (producer/director): We did a second *Boom Boom Out Go The Lights* and somewhere around that time they [Mayall, Mayer & Elton] brought me this script of *The Young Ones*. The first script I read was the one with the actual coffee stain on the front.

Nigel Planer (actor – Neil): The characters were based on our own stage acts. I did Neil in my live act so in this sense the TV part was written for me.

Alexei Sayle (actor – Jerzei Balowski): I very much had the sense that I needed *The Young Ones* because what I had done on TV hadn't really worked. *OTT* had been critically panned, and quite right. I thought if I'm going to be a big star then I need something that artistically chimed with what I was doing. When I read the first script of *The Young Ones* I realised that was it.

Christopher Ryan (actor – Mike): I remember the first meeting was in the basement room at BBC Television Centre. Paul Jackson was there. Rik was there. I think Ben Elton was there. Lise Mayer was there. Nigel was there. Ade wasn't there that day. That was the first meeting I had with them. We read things and did a couple of improvisations.

Jackson: I thought it would be something new and different and fresh and would appeal to a very specific audience. Which is what, at that time, BBC Two had to be. We had the wonderful Brian Winham running BBC Two at the time and that is what he wanted as well. He wanted it to be a different voice.

Ryan: They had said to me that he is an English Fonz. But I didn't want to do a Fonz because that was Henry Winkler and I had to find something different. So, I tried to take it from the words. I was finding the character as I went along.

Jackson: I just read the script and thought 'this is brilliant. This is really funny'. I had heard most of the voices because I knew the people, so it was easier for me, and because I could hear Nigel and Rik and Ade in my head it made more sense.

Ryan: There was a lot of pressure to get the thing done. Even when we did the series it was about a week per show. First a read through and then start to block it in the rehearsal rooms. Rehearse for a couple of days and then what they call a producer's run where the technicians and producers come in and make their notes. Then a couple more run throughs and then you are in the studio for the pre-record on one day, which is all the technical and effects stuff. It is all to do with time. That helps with the nerves because you don't get a lot of time to even think.

Planer: It was exciting and funny, sometimes a bit frustrating because like in any group you each have your role to play.

Sayle: Most of my pieces to-camera were my stand-up of the time. They would clear a space. My memory is that often the script would just be blank and it said 'Alexei comes on' and then I'd do part of my stand-up. I knew what would work and what wouldn't.

Jackson: I remember showing some ideas to my visual effects and sound guys and they said: "We'll find a way. We'll make it work." So I had that confidence behind me as well.

Bob Warns (properties buyer): I had to go to a sex shop at one stage because they were doing something about S&M. I remember taking myself off to this shop called Great Expectations in the East End [of London] all on my own, and don't forget I was quite young and naïve at that time, and I remember going to this very elegant shop. Down in the basement it was full of rubber gear and there were all these businessmen down there trying stuff on. I explained to the shop staff what I wanted and they hired me a load of stuff. It would have cost a fortune to buy so I hired it all. Some of it got nicked from the studio. God knows who had that [*laughs*].

Michael Redfern (actor – Policeman): I went straight to *The Young Ones* from doing a couple of episodes of *Crossroads*. The stuff they were doing in *The Young Ones* I though would never be allowed to be shown on television.

Carla Mendonça (actress – Valerie): My first ever television job was *The Young Ones* and I was so overwhelmed. I walked in and I was 21/22 and I was overwhelmed with… there was Alexei Sayle, Ben Elton and all the gang plus Maggie Stead and Pauline Melville. It was a very physical comedy show so you had to rehearse some of it.

Rupert Bates (actor – Peasant): I remember the medieval one where they go back in time. I had a speaking line in that. It was great fun. It was anarchic.

Mark Lambert (actor – Bank Manager): They gave me the very last episode where I played the bank manager. It was good fun. *The Young Ones* was more chaotic and unstructured.

Norman Lovett (actor – The Guy from the Penny Arcade): I remember being in the make-up room and Rik was being made up and he saw me in his mirror and said: "Look at you Norman, you're so relaxed." I said to him: "Rik, I've got one fucking line."

Roger Sloman (actor – Henry/Guard on TV/Right Bleeding Bastard): *The Young Ones* was a very exciting project to be involved in. Their energy chimed with me. I liked the anarchic side of it."

Helen Lederer (actress – Bank Teller/Gwendolyn): It was very exciting but I kept my head down and got on with the job. They were the stars so I didn't do anything other than say the lines correctly and obey.

Planer: I've no idea about a fifth member [housemate].

Sayle: I think it was someone they were at Manchester University with.

Warans: The scripts were changed constantly because they would go into rehearsal and it all changed. So, I would get halfway through making a sofa and then they would tell you they have to cut it and need something else instead.

Lambert: Some of it was definitely on the hoof. Writing it before the next shot.

Ryan: They were the ones on the receiving end or instigating the violence. I was fortunate in that respect. I remember one episode I had to hammer a nail through a plate into the table and to my leg. All that was very well sorted out by the effects team. There were injuries to others though.

41

Sloman: Paul Jackson was, every now and again, running up to the offices at the BBC because the bosses were worried about it.

Mendonça: Paul Jackson was very hands-on. He would go around while they were rehearsing each bit and make suggestions. Rik knew exactly what he wanted. There wasn't really any point in changing what he did because it was all innately brilliant.

Jackson: Recording was fantastic. It was a committed crowd because we had advertised it at The Comedy Store and The Comic Strip. So they were a partisan crowd. It was like a rock concert. The audiences in the studio were begging to come back each week. A lot of people saw all twelve shows. We gave certificates out at the end of the second series to people who had watched all twelve. There were about forty or fifty of them.

Mendonça: I remember it being very industrious and people did laugh and people did find things funny, especially when Alexei did his bit because that was all brought in by him.

Redfern: The work ethic that went into it was amazing. It looked like chaos but was so well rehearsed.

Jackson: The night the first episode of the first series went out we all got together and watched it. Then we went for dinner, and what we were saying while we were making it and while we were in the edit and that night was at least we set out to make what we wanted to make.

Bates: For Rik and Lise and Ben they just hit upon a market. The absurdity and the violence and the grotesque. It was just brilliant.

Sayle: I used to say in interviews 'If people share our sense of humour then this is going to be huge'.

Sloman: When we were doing it I thought they were on to something. It had a feeling about it that I thought 'This is going to be very popular'.

Jackson: We were getting messages that the kids were really liking it. Strangely, Chris Dunkley in the *Financial Times*, totally not who you would expect at all, gave us our only really good review.

Lovett: I was so excited to have been a part of the final episode.

Sayle: I remember going to see *The Young Ones* [live show] in Oxford. I remember having to be taken home. I suddenly had these symptoms of malaria because I was so jealous. I was just consumed with jealousy.

Sloman: I have a very funny story about *The Young Ones*. One of the characters I played was called Right Bleeding Bastard the TV repair man. I was going up an escalator in Tottenham Court Road tube station and this bloke was coming down the other way and he shouted: "Bastard!" I said: "You hat?" He said "I've just been watching you. You're a right bleeding bastard" [*laughs*].

Ryan: We had fun and we had laughs. There was never any animosity. They [Mayall, Edmondson and Planer] were very warm towards me and I won't forget that. As for a third series, it was never mentioned and I don't think anyone wanted it.

Sayle: I always thought it was foolish that obsession with only making twelve [episodes]. I thought it was insane. I'm not somebody who normally cared about that stuff but I was intensely frustrated that we hadn't done at least a couple of Christmas specials or another series.

Bates: It was one of those little adventures that I feel proud to have been a part of. It was a real snippet in time.

Lambert: The Young Ones was a phenomenon and very exciting to be a part of.

Sayle: It was hard work and I think the second series was more fun in some ways. We did love each other.

Planer: It was like a rather dysfunctional but basically sound family.

Jackson: Above all else, it was funny. Whether you are a director or a producer the first thing you want is funny. They were really funny people.

1983 started with Mayall appearing in the BBC comedy series *The Black Adder*, written by *Not The Nine O'clock News* alumni Rowan Atkinson and Richard Curtis. His performance owed more to Adrian Edmondson's Vyvyan from *The Young Ones* than the usual Mayall characters. Playing Mad Gerald (in the credits Mad Gerald is played by himself), an over-the-top prisoner who happens to share a cell with Atkinson's Black Adder, it is an upbeat-yet-aggressive performance that see's Mayall in a massive, dirty, back-combed wig as he attempts to make nice with his new cell mate. His non-stop gabbing is only broken when Black Adder asks if there is a way to escape to which Mad Gerald laughs for several years (literally) before immediately returning to what he was previously talking about.

Mayall went out on tour by himself during the early part of 1983. Well, not so much himself. He went as Kevin Turvey and his support was from The Bastard Squad. Which was essentially Adrian Edmondson and Nigel Planer. The show included a segment by the trio as their characters from *The Young Ones*. All for the bargain price of £4. Mayall returned to the Edinburgh Festival in 1983. His support consisted of Ben Elton and Andy de la Tour. Mayall told *Blitz magazine*: "People have heard a lot about us but haven't seen that much, and certainly not that much live. I feel a certain pressure, that people are coming along with the view 'Okay, let's see how good you really are'". The show proved to be a hot ticket as the trio played three sold-out weeks at the Assembly Rooms. One audience member who saw the show was musician Tracey Thorn (a student at the time), she told *thenewstatesman.com*: "I laughed till I thought I might injure myself, and I loved him [Mayall] unreservedly from that day on." The show lasted about an hour with each comedian doing a twenty-minute slot. The idea of rotating the slot order was discussed but quickly squashed when de la Tour and Elton said it should be Mayall who went on last as he was the best-known. The show was so popular, even the director of programming for the BBC, Brian Wenham, struggled to get a ticket. Andy de la Tour recalls: "Rik, Ben and I went to the Edinburgh Festival in 1983 to do a show together called "Stand-Up Comedy" because people weren't use to stand-up comedy back then so we had to call our show "Stand-Up Comedy". That was a huge success at Edinburgh. We had a monster success at the festival, which was great." Mayall clearly loved being on stage as he took part in the *Too Hot To Handle* music & comedy concert in April. The stage show was to raise funds for a public enquiry into another reactor at Sizewell nuclear power station. Alongside Mayall and his co-stars from *The Young Ones* (They performed a rousing rendition of *My Generation*) were comedians Michael Palin, Terry Jones, Neil Innes and Pamela Stephenson. Music was provided by Madness, UB40, Hazel O'Connor, Chris Difford and Glen Tilbrook. There was also a brief appearance at the An Evening For Nicaragua benefit concert that had been arranged by his friend and touring buddy Andy de la Tour, who also served as the host for the evening as well. Mayall performed as Kevin Turvey and finished on a joke dedicated to "Nick Ragua – whoever he is." The show was staged at the Shaftesbury Theatre in London and later edited for television broadcast. Those who couldn't see Mayall live on stage could listen to his comedy routines on a double LP that Panic Records released called *Let The Children Play* in June. It was an anti-nuclear compilation which featured music on the first LP from acts such as Peter Gabriel, Madness and Bill Bragg. While the second LP included comedy skits from alternative comedians from the likes of Alexei Sayle, Andy de la Tour and Mayall. All the comedy skits are listed as untitled. There was a slight change to Mayall's on-stage appearance towards the end of 1983 as he appeared in a production of *Man Equals Man* at the Contact Theatre in Manchester. Playwright Bertolt Brecht touched on themes of identity and war in his story of four army squaddies who loot an Indian temple, but one is left behind. An Irish dockworker is forced to take his place when they return to face their sergeant. Mayall played the squad leader under the direction of Richard Williams, who recalls: "Rik was terrific to have around and was a very positive member of the company. He was a name by then and we did well at the box office."

Mayall could still be found on TV though as *The Comic Strip Presents...* had a second series commissioned by Channel 4. The first episode of the second series debuted on 2nd November 1983 but didn't feature Mayall. The second episode took until 7th January 1984 to air. Titled *Dirty Movie*, it saw Edmondson playing Postman Bean in the style of Eddie Hitler, stupid, clumsy and slightly aggressive opposite Mayall's cinema manager Terry Toadstool who was aroused by watching a dirty movie on the big screen (a film which consisted mostly of Dawn French cavorting around in a negligee). Written by Mayall and Edmondson, it had all the hallmarks of their Bottom characters some seven years before Eddie Hitler and Richard Richard arrived on screen. Director Sandy Johnson believes this episode was a personal project for Mayall: "Whereas he was just playing a part in the other episodes, with *Dirty Movie* he was much more involved with me. He loved all the squirming characters. His emotions would be part of it, trying to burst out. He named Jennifer [Saunders]'s character after June Whitfield."

Episode four *A Fistful Of Travellers Cheques*, broadcast on 21st January 1984, was written by Mayall, Peter Richardson and Pete Richens as a pisstake of the classic Sergio Leone Westerns. Mayall and Richardson took the lead characters of Carlos and Miguel who, dressed as classic cowboys, stumble into a near-deserted town in the middle of the Spanish wasteland. Producer Simon Wright recalls what it was like working on the episode: "We shot that in Almeria, Spain. It was an absolute riot. We took over a small village and we rented various houses there and every night we would all go to the bar. There was a real genuine community. They [Mayall and Edmondson] used to mercilessly rip the piss out of Bob Spiers, the director. They used to do what they called wank patrol. They'd wait until everyone went to bed around eleven/eleven thirty then they would burst into people's rooms trying to catch them wanking. There was one very famous night where they claimed to have caught Bob Spiers wanking. The next day… I have never known Bob Spiers to be in such a bad mood." The episode veers wildly between slapstick and subtle humour which only adds to the hilarity. Mayall is quite subdued throughout, opting to play Carlos as a sinister, snivelling and shifty cowboy. It's a change of pace for Mayall in terms of acting and one that he seems to relish as he looks to ape Clint Eastwood's The Man with No Name with added English sarcasm. It is arguably *The Comic Strip Presents...* finest episode ever. Possibly one of the worst episodes of *The Comic Strip Presents…* aired the following week. *Gino: Full Story and Pics* featured Keith Allen's hoodlum Gino on the run from the Police. He steals a London taxi, picks up a hitchhiker called Angie (played by Jennifer Saunders) and goes on a car chase around Essex. One scene see's Gino and Angie arrive at the home of Tim and Fiona (Dawn French and Mayall respectively) to seek shelter and food. Tim, confined to a wheelchair, is a bad-tempered P.E. teacher who talks a mile a minute at Gino and Angie, while his wife receives the brunt of his putdowns. That is until she stabs him to death. It is only a brief scene but one that lacks any humour.

The beginning of 1984 also saw the return of Kevin Turvey to TV screens. A second series of *A Kick Up The Eighties* was commissioned, albeit only a four-episode series. The programme screened every Tuesday night at 9pm on BBC Two. Subjects Turvey monologued on included the supernatural, depression and nasty little sticky things. The show never returned for a third season. Mayall was still putting in cameos, while he continued to push his alternative comedy on and off screen. A brief appearance on the first series of *The Lenny Henry Show* in 1984 saw Mayall play a slightly psychotic fan called Martin who wrote jokes for Henry to read during airtime. Breaking into the televised show, Martin forces Henry to read some of his unpublished, and unfunny, work. It is a strangely underwhelming performance from Mayall, who resorts to shouting at Henry a lot. It is one Mayall cameo that is instantly forgettable. He put in a better cameo on the evening of 3rd November 1984 as he appeared on the hugely successful *Cannon and Ball Show* as an incredibly infuriating tourist/hotel information clerk. At only five minutes long the sketch starts out with some very safe, mainstream humour (well it was on one of the most watched mainstream comedy shows at the time). That is until Mayall goes full-anarchic on Cannon and Ball. There are brief moments where both of the light entertainers cannot keep up with the alternative comedian's comedic energy. It is a skit that contrasts manic energy (usually from Mayall) and relaxed comedy (Cannon and Ball) centring on a chaotic story in which the two hosts want to go on holiday while the tourist clerk tells them that his shop is closed. At one-point Bobby Ball grabs Mayall and pretends to smash his head in with a counter top. After several bashes to the head Mayall rises up and says to Tommy Cannon: "It is a good job you stopped him then because I could have killed your wife." This is both a frenetic and dead-pan performance from Mayall. There is something delightful about seeing an alternative comedian appear on a light entertainment programme and steal the show in just five minutes. Cannon and Ball do get the last laugh but it is Mayall's energetic performance that made the skit so hilarious.

When Rock band Lionheart released their single "Die For Love" on Epic Records, the accompanying video featured Mayall as a wheelchair-bound mad professor about to inject a beautiful blonde woman.

The Big One - an anthology book of original sketches, poems, cartoons and songs on the theme of peace - was released with a contribution from Mayall, Edmondson and Lise Mayer in the form of a short play called *Distance*. A very simple, yet wonderfully written play about two men sat in deckchair's looking out to sea, commenting on the height of people from different countries. It is a two-hander very much in the spirit of Peter Cook & Dudley Moore. The mentioning of legendary comedy actors such as Cook & Moore, Monty Python star John Cleese roped in Mayall to appear in a business training video called *Oh What The Hell*. The video aimed to promote the idea of safe attitudes in the workplace and to not dwell on the negatives or resort to 'shock-horror' tactics. The video could only be purchased by businesses for use in training seminars. Mayall featured alongside his *The Comic Strip Presents...* colleagues Dawn French & Robbie Coltrane, and Rowan Atkinson appeared as The Devil.

Mayall returned to Channel 4 with a made-for-TV documentary called *Weekend In Wallop* that screened the night before Halloween. Set in the tiny village of Nether Wallop, Hampshire the documentary's premise was to showcase a new Arts Festival that would hopefully compete against the Edinburgh Festival as a purveyor of up and coming UK talent. Performers included Rowan Atkinson, Mel Smith, Peter Cook, Jenny Agutter, Hugh Laurie, Stephen Fry, Arthur Smith and Billy Connelly. Mayall was incredibly lucky as he managed to blag two separate performing slots. Firstly, as Kevin Turvey, in a rather basic stand-up performance discussing crisps and ending with a classic: "What do you say?" joke, and secondly performing Elvis Presley's hit song "Trouble" as himself with Jools Holland on piano and Bill Wyman on guitar. However, Mayall changed a few of the lyrics to showcase his own style of comedy, including the line: "I once showed my willy to Princess Anne." This performance was much more like the anarchic, energetic Mayall that was making waves around the UK. He pulled snotty, wide-eyed faces while singing and danced in huge steps as the audience roared with laughter. Bill Wyman looked comically puzzled as to what he had been part of as Mayall ran off stage just as the music finished. Holland and Mayall had become good friends by this stage and occasionally the anarchic comedian would appear on *The Tube*, a Friday teatime music TV show co-hosted by Holland that featured live bands and the occasional comedian. It was a ground-breaking show in many ways. It went out live at 5:30pm on Channel 4 and the pop acts that appeared on it were as diverse as Tina Turner, Elton John, Frankie Goes To Hollywood, Bon Jovi, Madness and Ian Dury. The show was always receiving complaints from the general public. None more so than one of Mayall's appearances where he introduced the show by saying "It's Friday, we're live and the pubs are open" and then vomited onto the camera. Years later Holland told *The Guardian*: "One man in Northampton was so appalled he called the police."

Continuing the enjoyment of being onstage, Mayall set out on another stand-up UK tour through 1984/85, supported by Manchester University buddy and *The Young Ones* co-writer Ben Elton. The duo also took their show to the white isle of Ibiza for a handful of shows. Playing to the newly christened 18-30 holidaymakers in clubs, the show was as crazy as expected. Mayall was playing Kevin Turvey dressed as a rabbit. Wearing two layers of clothes (Turvey's and the rabbit costume) Mayall ripped through the material in the hot and sweaty club atmosphere and temperatures of up to a hundred degrees. The support in Ibiza was from Peter Bennett-Jones (who would go on to become a TV producer and talent manager). He told *The Independent* that it was high-up on his most embarrassing moments: "The punters seemed keener on Kevin Turvey and Motormouth than me for some reason." Mayall clearly loved being on stage, and continued to push himself in stand-up while also taking on serious stage work, appearing onstage at The National Theatre in a production of Nikolai Gogol's darkly comedic story of mistaken identity *The Government Inspector*. Jim Broadbent and Tim McInnerny appeared alongside Mayall for the ten-month run (Jan-Oct 1985). Mayall was singled out for praise in the majority of reviews including *The Guardian*, who said he was "Outstandingly funny."

1985 brought wedding bells for Mayall as he married Barbara Robbins. They had met while Mayall was performing on *A Kick Up The Eighties* as Kevin Turvey. Robbins was the make-up artist for the show and helped him become Turvey. They eloped to Barbados for their nuptials. TV soon beckoned Mayall back as he was offered the chance to appear in Ben Elton's new sitcom *Happy Families*. It starred some of the *Comic Strip Presents...* brigade including Jennifer Saunders, Adrian Edmondson, Dawn French and, of course, Mayall. However, Mayall only appeared fleetingly in episode three of the six-episode series as a French priest. With a sweaty comb-over haircut, Mayall smokes his way through the scene while watching, and describing, how he wants to kill renowned poet Dalcroix (played by Jim Broadbent). It is a Mayall performance that lacks physical energy yet has plenty of outrageous humour including the line: "He is a pubic hair stuck to a bar of soap." The series wasn't well received by critics and audiences alike. A second series was budgeted for by the BBC but never commissioned (the money went to fund the first series of *Red Dwarf* instead).

At the beginning of 1986 Mayall was back on TV with his Comic Strip Presents... buddies in two specials. *Consuela (Or 'The New Mrs Saunders')* was broadcast on the 1st January. Mayall's Richard, a flat-cap and wax jacket wearer with a posh accent, was very much a secondary character until the end of the episode when there was only him and Saunders's Jessica left.

The same cannot be said for *Private Enterprise*, which was broadcast the next evening. Mayall appeared in only a small scene as Ali Kiston, the lead singer of a pop group who bore a striking similarity to the band Culture Club. Donning a wildly large white wig with tassels, a beauty mark on his left cheek and brightly baggy clothes, Mayall looked like a cross between Boy George and Marilyn Monroe as he sang into the microphone before having an argument with one of the band members. If that wasn't anarchic enough, then Mayall was about to bring chaos (and complaints) to the BBC.

The Children's TV Show *Jackanory* began life in 1965. It was designed to encourage children to develop an interest in reading. The BBC produced around 3500 episodes during its thirty-year run (it was cancelled in 1996) and some of the stories read were from such celebrated authors as the Brothers Grimm, Beatrix Potter and Michael Bond. These stories were read to camera by a famous actor seated in an armchair. The show would be broadcast Monday to Friday in fifteen-minute episodes and the reader would usually finish the book by the end of the week. These episodes were quaint and quintessentially British with a laidback style to the storytelling. That was until the first week of January 1986 when the producers of *Jackanory* enlisted Mayall to read Roald Dahl's novel *George's Marvellous Medicine* about a young boy trying to kill off his horrible Grandmother. Viewers didn't know what had hit them. No longer was the actor simply sitting in an armchair gently reading the book, instead Mayall twisted around on his chair and enunciated every naughty word (his pronunciation of "Dogs Bottom" is a special delight). As he voiced Grandma's lines he morphed into Rik from *The Young Ones*, screwing up his face while snivelling and snarling the lines. By the second day Mayall was out of his seat and walking around the kitchen set. As he goes to throw some face cream in a melting pot the camera stays on the shelves behind him and when it returns the cream is all over Mayall's black suit jacket. Shortly after he wipes his cream-covered hands all over his top and then proceeds to spray hairspray into the melting pot. Day four's episode had Mayall still covered in cream, but this time he was filmed sitting on top of the kitchen table. The finale of episode five had Mayall stare into the camera and offer a serene "Goodbye". The performance provoked outrage amongst parents who sat and watched it with their kids. They didn't like the sadistic nature of the book or the anarchy of Mayall's storytelling. However, ask anyone who knows of *Jackanory* what their favourite episode is and it is highly likely to be Mayall's *George's Marvellous Medicine*. Mayall told *The Record Mirror*: "I did it really because it was so unlike what you'd expect. Although I enjoy story-telling, I enjoy doing things people don't like me doing. Just being bloody-minded really!" This episode is constantly cited as one of the best *Jackanory* episodes ever and it launched Mayall into doing voice over work.

Elsewhere at the BBC Rowan Atkinson and Richard Curtis had been waiting for over two years to hear if *The Black Adder* TV show would be renewed. Word came back that a second series was to be granted but, on the provision, that there were improvements made to the scripts (the beefing-up of Atkinson's Black Adder into the cunning, witty and downright sarcastic character that was briefly touched upon towards the end of the first series was one of the key factors). The BBC also insisted on a drastic deduction of external shots. Atkinson dropped out of writing the second series and Curtis brought in Ben Elton to help. The series was a huge triumph for all involved especially Atkinson who had found the beating heart of who Black Adder was and ran gleefully with it to create a now legendary character. The second series was also notable for its cameo appearances including Hugh Laurie, Tom Baker, Simon Jones and Miriam Margolyes. However, by far and away the biggest cameo appearance came from a man who was now making it his business to steal every single scene he was in no matter the TV show or who he was acting against.

When talking about Rik Mayall many will cite his brief appearance in *The Black Adder* series as some of his finest work, yet he has less than five minutes screen-time. Dropping in like an atom bomb on the episode *Bells*, Mayall's Lord Flashheart is a whirlwind of aggression, naughtiness, sarcasm and double-entrees. Mayall thrusts his lines out with extra emphasis on the last word in each sentence. This is such a strong-willed character that it is difficult to think of any other actor being able to pull off Flashheart with such vigour and guile. The bravado of the character is matched by the bravado of the actor. There is simply no stopping Mayall when he arrives. Every line he utters is an instant classic and "Woof!" is in somewhat common usage today. Even when Flashheart decides to swap clothes with Bob ("Weird. I feel better in a dress") it doesn't look or feel out of place for a character that seems open to anything – sexually. It is an outstanding cameo performance from Mayall, and once again he steals the entire series from under the nose of Atkinson. But that is what he set out to do. He told the writers that he was only going to play Flashheart if he could be funnier than Atkinson during his brief appearance. Director Mandie Fletcher told J.F. Roberts in his book *The True History of Blackadder* what happened when the cameras started to roll on Mayall: "Throughout rehearsals Rik would nod sagely as I said, "Perhaps you should do it this way…" "Yeah, fine!" And do it perfectly. But the instant he got in front of those cameras he went berserk! And if you look at the scene, you will see that everyone's standing around on that set, looking completely amazed at the force of nature that's just arrived."

If Mayall wasn't outlandish enough in his *Black Adder* cameo then his weekly TV appearance, alongside his comedic partner Ade Edmondson, on the variety show *Saturday Live* would showcase how zany & dangerous he truly could be.

"Good evening Ladies & Gentlemen, we are The Dangerous Brothers"

When transferred to television or film, live acts can lose a certain edge. The energy the room is feeding off when watching the live act doesn't always come across when viewed through a square box. The immediate danger that something could go wrong at any time while playing live in front of an audience isn't as palpable when the viewer is watching something they know has been edited and/or pre-recorded. However, one live act that never lost its edge was *The Dangerous Brothers*. In fact, if anything their move to television allowed Richard Dangerous and Sir Adrian Dangerous to be even more daring.

The seeds of *The Dangerous Brothers* can be traced back to Mayall and Edmondson's work in *20th Century Coyote* during their Manchester University days. The duo had naturally gravitated towards each other more so than anyone else in the comedy troupe. Soon they found themselves maniacally beating each other up on stage when one of them told a joke wrong or forgot what to say next. A very early sketch involved Mayall reciting a poem about Vanessa Redgrave and towards the end of the reading Edmondson would walk on stage and punch him in the balls.

As their performances started to gather notices, especially when they moved south and started performing at London's Comedy Store, they began refining the act. Each performance would begin with a light-hearted Knock Knock joke and then take a very swift nose-dive into violence and swearing. It was a rude awakening for some audience members who had never seen that type of violence, albeit comedy violence, in a club for comedy acts. One man who found it highly entertaining was BBC TV producer Paul Jackson, who had been charged with creating a TV show that showcased the emerging alternative comedy scene in the UK.

Boom Boom Out Go The Lights didn't find its audience in terms of viewing figures however it did give *The Dangerous Brothers* their first ever TV slot. Using the same routine as they had at The Comic Strip while toning down the swearing, Mayall and Edmondson launched into their Knock Knock joke and Gooseberry in a Lift sketch. In less than five minutes' worth of air-time the world was introduced to Mayall and Edmondson aka *The Dangerous Brothers*. While some audience members might not have enjoyed their chaotic brand of humour or the long drawn out explanation of the

Gooseberry Joke, some saw it as one of the turning points in comedy as it wasn't about delivering the punchline but more about the process of how to make an unfunny joke extremely funny by dragging out the delivery of said punchline.

In a January 2013 article for *The Financial Times* comedian Stewart Lee named *The Dangerous Brothers* appearance on *Boom Boom Out Go The Lights* as a defining moment in alternate comedy: "All I know is that, after seeing Rik Mayall and Adrian Edmondson's double act, *The Dangerous Brothers*, struggle in a Beckettian vortex with the basic mechanics of telling a joke about a gooseberry in a lift, while dressed like dishevelled members of the R&B mod band Nine Below Zero, I was never the same again. It was the opposite of comedy as we knew it."

This routine is what eventually saw them return to late-night comedy TV as they appeared on the Channel 4 variety show *Saturday Live*. But this was not your everyday Saturday teatime variety show. This was edgy, informative and political. Hosted by Ben Elton and featuring a vast array of alternate comedy talents including Harry Enfield, Morwenna Banks, Tracey Ullman, Craig Charles and many more. Individual and group skits were filmed live in front of a studio audience. This was true of all except one segment – *The Dangerous Brothers*. So dangerous were *The Dangerous Brothers* segments that they had to be pre-recorded and inserted (oo err) into the live show.

The first appearance of *The Dangerous Brothers* on *Saturday Live* nearly didn't happen. Their pre-filmed segment was to introduce the characters and show how dangerous they truly were by setting Sir Adrian Dangerous on fire… real fire… in a segment called *The Towering Inferno*. Richard Dangerous danced around while dousing Sir Adrian's legs in petrol. At one-point he turns to the camera and says: "I advise not to try this trick at home as it invariably ends in death." When Mayall strikes the match and touches it onto Edmondson's trousers the fire rises up his legs at double quick pace and looks to be heading towards the torso very quickly. Suddenly, we hear Sir Adrian shout "STOP!" and the video stops. Sir Adrian walks in front of the paused video and tries to explain what went wrong. Then Richard appears and tells him to stop speaking to the people at home. The scene inevitably ends in a fight.

However, despite the comical insert at the end of segment, Edmondson was in real danger during the scene, as he explained to *FHM* years later: "They put this special gel on my legs, which was only supposed to go up to my knees, but I must have been feeling particularly confident that day because I told them to go all the way to my groin. I said, "If the flames come too high, I'll shout out the emergency code word." The trouble was I forgot the word, so they let me burn like kindling." Edmondson's legs were badly burnt and his eyebrows were singed as well. Dangerous by name, dangerous by nature. That antic-gone-wrong set the tone for the rest of *The Dangerous Brothers* segments on *Saturday Live*. Sadly, it took a whole year from the *Saturday Live* pilot airing to seeing a full series on the channel. *The Dangerous Brothers* announced their return to television by shooting themselves out of a cannon, well actually it was just Sir Adrian who got fired.

Having learned nothing from their previous mishap, they continued to use fire in their act. This time Sir Adrian was fired through a flaming hoop and into a bucket of burning petrol. After the long, and hilarious, set up the cannon was lit and fired. But Sir Adrian didn't pop out. Instead he got stuck in the barrel and was forced out by Richard, who tipped the cannon downwards. That didn't stop Richard forcing Sir Adrian to smash through the windows then through the flaming hoop (he walked underneath it) then run through a brick wall and eventually end up with the burning bucket of petrol stuck on his head. Further sketches included them (not) snogging a real crocodile, consuming toilet cleaner, giving a crash course in how to snog women, firing submachine guns and showcasing their own unique brand of torture. One sketch fell foul of the Channel 4 censors and was banned from being shown. The segment, titled *Kinky Sex*, sees Sir Adrian return home early and, on believing himself alone, deciding to masturbate. The problem is Richard is at home, in his bedroom dressed in a PVC nurse outfit because he has been indulging in some naughty business with a dominatrix prostitute. Then some dwarfs arrive at the house (Not real dwarfs, actually three very sexy and scantily clad ladies) for an afternoon of romance and bondage. When one of the "dwarfs" notices a television camera in the house they think Richard and Sir Adrian are making a movie. This leads to the duo having to break the fourth wall to explain the context of the set piece, which ultimately descends into mindless violence while trying to hide the "dwarfs".

The skit ends when Richard encourages viewers to call in with ideas about how to end the sketch. The phone rings and a "Mrs Henderson from Strathclyde" suggests something which we don't hear but seconds later see as the entire set is tipped to the right almost like an earthquake. Mrs Henderson's prize is a night with *The Dangerous Brothers* and their chainsaw. The segment is tame by today's standards but in 1986 it is possible to see how it might have ruffled a few feathers of even those who enjoyed alternative comedy. It is a sketch that shows men enjoying the company of prostitutes, dressing in women's outfits and privately masturbating. It looks and feels like Mayall and Edmondson's response to the "No sex please, we're British" ideology that suggests Brits are afraid to talk openly about sex. Once again, they are ripping up the comedy rule book.

Looking back, *The Dangerous Brothers* was the first incarnation of Mayall and Edmondson's anarchic double act that they would continue to refine over the next decade or two. The U.K.'s equivalent of *Saturday Night Live*'s Festrunk Brothers (played by Steve Martin and Dan Aykroyd – "We're two wild and crazy guys!") but with more energy, vigour and danger. *The Dangerous Brothers* didn't care if you got the joke because it wasn't about the punchline, it was about the physical punch and the line that followed it. Mayall and Edmondson made an entire routine out of exposing how jokes are told. It was the equivalent to a magician showing how he made the rabbit disappear during the trick. It's doubtful anybody else could have got away with performing a series of behind-the-scenes exposés in a comedy manner and not get vilified by the comedy fraternity. Yet the brilliance of Mayall and Edmondson's work together not only had fellow comedians laughing at them it also had them scratching their heads as to how. From the outside, it was a double act that did little more than shout and punch each other. Beyond their violent exterior however lay raw comedic genius and they showcased that every time they went on stage and told the same

Gooseberry in a Lift joke. It didn't matter if it was your first time seeing it or your fiftieth it was still side-splittingly hilarious because Mayall and Edmondson made it so. It was the anticipation of waiting for the punchline that never came and the hopelessly hilarious build-up that made it addictive.

Who else could make you watch an empty studio in the anticipation that something, anything might happen? Mayall and Edmondson. One small sketch sees Sir Adrian dance around the empty studio as he believes Richard has left. There are long periods of an empty floor with a white backdrop as Edmondson races around the back to get into another position. But it matters not that we are watching an empty, downtrodden LWT studio. It is a waiting game to see how Sir Adrian will return in-front of the camera. There is laughter in even the most basic of Dangerous Brothers sketches.

The Dangerous Brothers is also unique in the sense that it flipped who was the dominant in the duo compared to their other output. Whereas previously and subsequently Edmondson would be the one dishing out the violence, in *The Dangerous Brothers* it was he who was on the receiving end of the jokes and pratfalls. Edmondson looking like a mad professor with his crazy sprouting blonde hair and purple suit that was slightly too short sells every punch, kick and swear word like an eccentric car salesman trying to sell a Ferrari. Sir Adrian is a softer, albeit slightly dumber, side of an Edmondson character. Mayall's over-the-top confident Richard Dangerous shows that he could play the dominate performer in the relationship and play it very well. His snivelling, weasel-y better-than-you attitude is what makes him so hilarious. His energy and aggression are so over-the-top that if he were a real person then he would have been sectioned long ago. But in the world of television, and the hands of Mayall, he is like a bouncing ball of energy constantly firing hilarious dialogue at the viewers.

Yet it is Richard's pompous nature towards his Sir Adrian that is so on the nose in terms of commentary on class and society. He looks down on his friend, he feels he is smarter than his friend and as such refuses to do the childish, and dangerous, stunts. He instead leaves those to the dunderheaded Sir Adrian. Occasionally the mask slips and we see the real

Richard (Rik?) as he gallivants around the studio with gleeful abandonment, shrieking and hollering. It is only then that we see Richard and Sir Adrian are cut from the same cloth. They are both lower class scum but one is pretending to be upper class toff. It is Richard's strange yet curious haircut: the top of his head shaved apart from a small island of long hair right at the front and long flowing locks down the side and back that give the impression he might have been a teenage punk before being dazzled by the new Yuppie movement. The whole act is a scathing look at class divide during Thatcher's reign told through the means of slapstick comedy.

The Dangerous Brothers is not top-rung Mayall and Edmondson. However, it was an important stepping stone in them establishing a routine that would eventually define them as one of the greatest comedy duos of all time.

Paul Jackson (producer/director): I set up *Saturday Live* for Channel 4 and I wanted them. I said did they want to come and do a regular thing, and even thought about them being in the cast every week. They said "No" but could they pre-record a series of sketches. I think we did two live and eight pre-recorded.

Helen Lederer (actress): It felt very much as though they were in their own knowing bubble of successful work. They not only knew it worked at the time but had huge enjoyment inventing and messing about but with purpose and intelligence.

Jackson: It was genuinely dangerous because by this time we were all slightly falling for our own myth. To be honest, nowadays you could not do it. Health & Safety would not pass a lot of those things that we did.

Michael Redfern (actor): Everything they did was dangerous.

Lederer: They liked physicality. The more edgy and near the knuckles the better. It was a requirement.

Carla Mendonça (actress): It was incredibly dangerous. I don't recall them doing it live though.

Jackson: The famous Towering Inferno came within a whisker of setting Ade's face alight. But that is not what we thought at the time. At the time we thought how could we re-write the end? He [Edmondson] came within a couple of seconds of burning his face really quite badly.

Mendonça: They always had a fire officer and had risk assessment. Even though they were brilliant clowns, they were also very technical.

Lederer: There's me in a skimpy Basque, which was most unusual. But in those days, you just got on with it.

Norman Lovett (actor): I was corpsing [unintentional laughing during filming of a scene] because they made me laugh, but they kept it in [the show].

Lederer: I was very aware there was an energy and synergy between them.

Jackson: There was almost a chicken run element to it all, and an element of macho about it.

Naked Video was BBC Scotland's answer to *A Kick Up The Eighties*. Originally a radio series, it was ported over to TV in May 1986 and ran until 1991. It retained the radio cast including Gregor Fisher, Tony Roper and Jonathan Watson alongside bringing in talent such as Helen Lederer and John Sparkes. Through this show, viewers would be introduced to characters such as Rab C. Nesbitt, Siadwell and Drunk Sloane. While Mayall didn't appear in-front of the camera he was behind it occasionally writing sketches for the first couple of series. It wasn't until mid-1986 that Mayall appeared on-screen again. This time in a feature film spinoff of the ITV comedy series *Whoops Apocalypse* having already performed, albeit briefly, in the TV series. Mayall appeared in the film as an inept commanding officer of a bumbling SAS Squad. His official title according to the credits was Specialist Catering Commander due to the squad disguising themselves as caterers. Mayall's performance looks and feels more like that of his best mate Ade Edmondson– barking orders, swearing and headbutting people. It is an energetic scene of chaotic shouting and non-stop gunfire but sadly lacks any genuine humour. His screen time lasts little over five minutes in a film that didn't make much noise either in the UK or in the US where it was released two years later.

Mayall may not have struck gold in the movies quite yet but the pop charts were a different matter entirely. Pop singer Cliff Richard had already received a boost to his profile thanks to the use of his song *The Young Ones* in the main theme for the TV show (it was re-sung by those involved in the show). Richard received another shot in the arm when *The Young Ones* reformed in 1986 to feature on a re-release of his 1959 hit *Living Doll*. While Richard sang lead vocals he was assisted and ultimately overwhelmed by the backing vocals of Vyvyan (Edmondson), Rick (Mayall), Neil (Planer) and Mike (Ryan). The single ended up spending three week's at Number one on the singles chart with all proceeds going to Comic Relief. An official video was also produced that climaxed with scenes of Vyvyan knocking everyone out with a wooden mallet. Richard and The Young Ones also sung it live at the Comic Relief stage shows towards the end of 1986. Richard only appeared at one of the three nights. The other nights saw Bob Geldof take Richard's place.

Once pop music had hold of Mayall, it didn't let go as he further appeared in a video for avant-garde, synth-pop band Art Of Noise. The song was titled *Peter Gunn* and singer Duane Eddy provided vocals. The video was a spoof of the classic film noir private detective films. Mayall played the lead character, a private detective who sets about cracking the case of a bank heist. He continually breaks the fourth wall by nodding, winking and generally mugging up to the camera. He doesn't utter any words, it is all about the action. The video conjures up images of Michael Jackson's video for *Smooth Criminal* as the central character dances and fights his way out of bars. Even by today's million-pound music videos this is quite the lavish piece with dance numbers, moody sets and a clear nod to PVC fetishists, not to mention the appearance of Mayall who was still riding the wave of success afforded by *The Young Ones*. His appearance would not have come cheap, as he explained to performer Anna Chen when she and her friend Kirstin (who also featured in the video) asked if he was being paid the same as them: "He look appalled and said he wouldn't get out of bed for that little."

Mayall appeared in yet another music video, this time for Circus Circus Circus who featured not one, not two but three Richards in their band (Ric Clark, Rich Spicer and Richard Bentley. The other band members were Mark Shaw and Doug Hart). This Richard/Rich/Ric grouping was the reason Mayall appeared in the video for their single *Butcher Bitches*. He had met the band in a club and they had joked that they were all called Rik. He found that hilarious and agreed to be in the video playing a geeky fan of the band.

Mayall went back on tour during 1986. Having enjoyed a successful Australian tour with his cohorts from The Comic Strip, Mayall set out for another tour on the other side of the world. This time he took Ben Elton as his support. They had been touring the UK together on and off for three years. Elton told *The Australian* newspaper about how they built their stand-up careers together: "We toured throughout the 80s and drank a lot of beer and, you know, sort of tumbled out of motorway service stations; we had fun. We wanted to do something half as good as Python or the Goons or Dad's Army." Australian union rules demanded that they have a support act and the promoter booked the all-girl rock band The Jam Tarts. One of the members was Sophie Gare who Elton later married. Mayall also had an extra helping of love come into his life during the year as he became a father for the first time when Barbara gave birth to their daughter Rosie.

Mayall celebrated the end of the year by appearing on *Come Dancing with Jools Holland*. A comedy & music New Year's Eve spectacular for Channel 4 that featured diverse acts such as The Outer Limits, Ruby Wax, Raw Sex, Go West, Jimmy Ruffin and the WHO DARES WINS team.

Everything was coming up roses for Mayall by the end of 1986. The following year would seem him bloom into one of the biggest comedians on television with two shows in which he played the lead roles. Both of them scathingly satirical.

"Hi. God bless. Drive safely. Look after mum. Hi. Richie Rich here. Some dates are still available"

Few comedians enjoyed the luxury of a blank cheque from the BBC so they could write whatever they wanted. Especially comedians who had only appeared on the network for the first time a few short years beforehand. Yet that is exactly what happened with Mayall. This blank cheque was also extended to Ben Elton and the two began developing ideas about what they could lampoon this time. It quickly became obvious. With *The Young Ones* they had used their experience of being students to write the sitcom. Now, having become the darlings of the alternative comedy scene and having lived in London long enough to have first-hand experience of the clique that was mainstream showbusiness, the next evolution for Elton and Mayall was to satirise TV's light entertainers. Targets included people such as Bruce Forsyth, Jimmy Tarbuck and Little and Large. Elton and Mayall felt establishment entertainers who appeared week-in, week-out on either the BBC or ITV had become boring and weren't showcasing what was really happening at that time in Britain. Thus, Elton set about writing *Filthy, Rich & Catflap*, a comedy show about a talentless TV personality, the drunken bodyguard assigned to look after him and the TV personality's inebriated agent.

As Elton wrote the episodes they were sent to Mayall, who had gone to Australia for a stand-up tour. He then sent the drafts back with little notes scribbled on the pages. As the show began to take shape a decision was made to bring in a couple of Mayall's comrades from *The Young Ones* – Adrian Edmondson and Nigel Planer. Producer/director Paul Jackson returned too. As did Ed Bye, who had previously directed one episode of *The Young Ones* and helmed four of the six episodes of *Filthy, Rich & Catflap*. Reports in the press at the time suggested that *Filthy, Rich & Catflap* was a sort-of sequel or natural successor to *The Young Ones* but actually Elton wanted to write a more contemporary piece designed to move on not just the characters (who have a vague link back to *The Young Ones'* counterparts) but also the actors as he included extended scenes of anarchistic violence that even *The Young Ones* wouldn't have gotten away with.

Remember: They had a blank cheque and could do just about anything they wanted. Including bringing in a random assortment of guests including pop group The Nolans, Breakfast TV presenter Anne Diamond and Carry On starlet Barbara Windsor. There was also room to bring in some famous faces from the alternate comedy scene with the likes of Stephen Fry, Hugh Laurie, Harry Enfield and Mel Smith turning up. Filmed in 1986 at BBC Manchester's New Broadcasting House studios on Oxford Road, most of the actors and director Paul Jackson had to travel from London every week to film in front of a live studio audience.

Premiering on BBC Two on 7th January 1987, the six-episode series was met with baffled reactions from critics and the public alike. It seemed that most were expecting a new version of *The Young Ones* anarchy but what they got was satirical comedy that broke the fourth wall and was littered with graphic slapstick violence. It did not strike a chord with most viewers and by the time the last episode aired on 11th February it looked like it wouldn't return even though the voice-over announcer said that a second series would be forthcoming. While in Australia on a promotional tour for the Bottom movie *Guest House Paradiso*, Mayall was asked about *Filthy, Rich & Catflap* and responded: "I miss Catflap and so do many fans in England. It got so hammered, because it wasn't *The Young Ones* – which was hypercritical… *The Young Ones* got hammered when it came out as well." *Filthy, Rich & Catflap* was a flop for the BBC and it affected Mayall, as he told *The Sun* years later, to the point that he didn't leave his house for three weeks for fear of being pointed at by people saying, "That's the bloke who isn't funny anymore."

Filthy, Rich & Catflap is a curious beast of a TV show. What starts out as an unofficial follow-on from *The Young Ones*, from two immature men living together through to the anarchic violence and the inclusion of a pop group, it very much seemed business as usual. The first couple of episodes stick to the same formula, only moving the setting to London and slightly twisting the characters to reflect the establishment that Elton and Mayall wanted to poke fun at. While occasionally funny, it does look and feel like all involved were trying everything possible to find a formula that suited both them as anti-establishment comedians and the audience who wanted something fresh to enjoy.

In those first couple of episodes some jokes work while others are way off the mark. However, by the third episode it appears that the show's aesthetic, and the characters, had finally clicked. These three individuals fitted into each other like adjoining jigsaw pieces even though they are poles apart. Edmondson's performance as bodyguard Eddie Catflap finally moves on from the chaotic shouting and swearing of Vyvyan in *The Young Ones* as he shapeshifts into an alcoholic, sarcastic lay-about who only takes part in small snatches of violence. He is much more interested in getting sloshed than hitting someone, that is unless someone has nicked his pint. Ninety percent of Edmondson's performance in the later episodes embodies the style of acting that would become his signature for over a decade. His rambunctious attitude coupled with his inebriated state proved popular in *Bottom*. Catflap is still a rough-around-the-edges character and at times   the role must have required great restraint from Edmondson to avoid descending into Vyvyan all over again (the credits sequence of the last episode shows a reversal back to Vyvyan). In *Filthy, Rich & Catflap* it is possible to literally see Edmondson as an actor and the character he portrays morph into an entirely new and updated creation. Edmondson is not given enough praise for his work in this show. It is the series that allowed him to grow up as an actor.

The same can be said about Nigel Planer's character too. The dunderheaded Neil from *The Young Ones* becomes a distant memory when Planer's Ralph Filthy, a sleazy celebrity agent, walks through the door. His comb-over and slightly twisted goatee grant him a mature look beyond his years. This is perfect for a character who has lived through all the showbiz luvvie stuff the industry can throw at him. A character who is slowly on the wane but is clinging to his last few ounces of self-respect, and the only real client he has left.

His constant catcalls of "daughter" towards Richie Rich suggests a desperate need to make his dominance known. To make sure his client still knows that Ralph Filthy is the boss: "I am the boss of you. You work for me." It is a complete 180 degree change of acting for Planer when compared to his Young Ones persona. This is a towering and powerful performance, laced with the wretched stink of alcohol. Much like

Edmondson, Planer's performance in *Filthy, Rich & Catflap* allowed him to grow as an actor and show the world that he was so much more than just Neil from *The Young Ones*.

But Planer had competition for who would be the stand-out of the show. Mayall's dominance on-screen is quite contradictory in nature. He is bolder than brass yet can be seen cowering like a scared cat. Rich's obsession with the towering powers of 1980s light entertainment – Jimmy Tarbuck, Bruce Forsyth, Bobby Davro – borders on stalker-like behaviour. His desire to be the next Tarby is so overplayed in a brilliantly surreal manner that watching the show now you believe that Richie Rich could have been a contender for a light entertainer on prime-time television were it not for the fact that he is so pathetic in his ability to perform.

Mayall initially struggles to find his character in the first few episodes. However, by the fourth episode he well and truly knows what makes Rich tick. He gleefully galivants around the flat as if on display to millions worldwide (and in a nice, meta twist, he is). His belief in himself is out of this world. His hunger for fame and glory knows no bounds whilst he is in the safe confines of the flat. Outside the flat is a completely different matter. Outside, with his contemporaries, he becomes either the scared cat clawing anyone within reach because he feels he must, or he goes so crazily over-the-top that he gets pulled off (oo err) before the show has finished. Mayall felt his character Richie Rich was about "acting out my obsession with myself and showbusiness." Much like his two co-stars, Mayall's character allowed him to be wilder and crazier than ever before in a scripted comedy. He, eventually, flourishes in the role. Episode five contains the early seeds Edmondson and Mayall's soon-to-be-made *Bottom* as their characters sit around the flat antagonising each other and generally being Richard and Edward in all but name.

During a game of Trivial Pursuit, the very bored Catflap asks Rich a question that doesn't appear on the cards. The answer is Jimmy Tarbuck, Rich's favourite light entertainer. However, he cannot think of the answer and we see Mayall pull a series of ridiculously hilarious faces. He contorts his lips upwards and opens his eyes as wide as possible. He up-turns his nose and then begins to speak in almost snorting dialogue. This is Mayall not just stealing the scene but also stealing the show. His ability to know when to "go big" is exceptional. He comes alive in a split second and tears off like a hurricane destroying everything in its path. Mayall's unrelenting energy is the beating heart of the entire show. The final scene of the final episode showcases this brilliantly as Rich is, by this point, the top light entertainer on TV. As he enters the room with all the gusto of a man possessed he sits down to watch himself on TV. He crouches on his chair waiting for the programme to start but once he appears on-screen he bounces on the chair like a small, excited child. Occasionally turning to camera to sing along with the programme or point out that it is he on TV. This scene no longer seems to feature a character called Richie Rich. It feels as though we are now watching Rik Mayall watch himself on primetime television and get excited by it. The too-crazy-for-TV comedian has finally made it to the top of the TV landscape.

Any second of the show when he is not on-screen is arguably less funny than the moments he is on-screen. However, the cheeky bugger finds a way to make sure he is in even the most non-Mayall scenes. Witness his grandstanding in the episode where The Nolans sing "I'm In The Mood For Dancing" he pops in and out of the shot with a wide grin and some outlandish dancing. It is ironic that one of the biggest British pop groups of the 80s are singing their biggest hit but are being upstaged by an alternative comedian who has found fame on the most reserved TV network in the UK. Even Auntie Beeb couldn't stop the juggernaut that was Mayall at that time and he fully exploits the free reign he was offered for *Filthy, Rich & Catflap*.

The comedic brilliance of *Filthy, Rich & Catflap*, beyond the performances, stems from Elton and Mayall being given free reign to poke fun at those they hated. The gatekeepers of television's light entertainment genre took not just a ribbing but an absolute beating from Elton and Mayall's writing. Coming from an anti-establishment comedy background they hated the safe, formulaic comedians that ruled the airwaves and told the same mother-in-law jokes every week. They had decided it was time to shake up things. They took all the tropes of standard entertainment presenters and dialled it up to eleven. The bitchy back-biting of the TV industry, the constant one-man upmanship, the belittling of certain contemporaries, all this was hidden behind the publicised smoke screen, the accepted lie that "we are all one big happy family in light entertainment."

Not only did it pull back the curtain to show the inner workings of the business, it also pulled in some celebrities to appear in certain episodes. Normally these famous faces would have been appearing on Tarbuck's or Forsyth's shows and were very much mainstream celebrities, yet the brilliance of Elton and Mayall's work had these pop stars and actors lampooning not just themselves but also the shows they regularly appeared on. Did these celebrities/pop stars get the joke? Did they understand why they were on the show? It is difficult to know.

Filthy, Rich & Catflap was a great big "FUCK YOU" to all those Saturday/Sunday night television presenters who had been dominant for far too long and it was all done on a television network (The BBC) that was a pioneer in establishing that safe brand of television. It was a brilliantly subversive move by Elton and Mayall, but audiences were not ready for it. *The Young Ones* fans who tuned in didn't understand why their anarchic, anti-establishment heroes were now part of the glitterati brigade they had previously poked fun at. Those older viewers who sat down to find out what the fuss was about didn't like that these rough, ready and violent characters were poking fun at their television favourites – Tarbuck, O'Connor, Forsyth etc. It was too fresh for some audiences and too fuddy for others. However, in the present comedic culture in which alternative comedy is prevalent in most TV sitcoms (mainly thanks to Elton and Mayall paving the way) *Filthy, Rich & Catflap* has matured into a stinging yet hilarious indictment about the light entertainment industry.

Paul Jackson (producer/director): The BBC were desperate for a young audience. Rik & Ade were still working together and they got together with Nigel [Planer]. The BBC was asking what else they wanted to do and that they could do anything. Rik and Ben [Elton] basically said: "we wrote *The Young Ones* about our student life and we've been in London for a few years now, on the fringes of showbusiness, so we will write a series about the Z-list end of showbiz." We didn't even have the show them [The BBC] scripts. We made *Filthy, Rich & Catflap* through the variety department for various technical reasons for getting more money. We went to Manchester to record because there were no studios in London that we needed.

Rupert Bates (actor - Milkman): I had a part with Arthur Smith. We played milkmen in one of the early episodes. I got a hatchet in the head. I had to come in and say whatever the line was because Ade says: "Ahh, it's the stork bringing another baby" and he comes to the front door and buries a hatchet in my head [*laughs*].

Jackson: I think we made a mistake in the running order. There was an episode where all the milkmen get killed, which was the most *Young Ones* like episode, and for various reasons that got put out first. Whereas I wanted to put The Nolans/*Blankety Blank* episode out first because that, very clearly, took it into the realms of showbiz. Whereas the milkman one was kind of *The Young Ones* but Rik was an actor instead of a student.

Michael Redfern (actor - Policeman): All I remember is that it was so out there. It was exciting because you never knew what you were going to be doing or what the scene was going to be.

Jackson: I thought Filthy was a really nice and new creation. He wasn't based on anything anyone was doing at the time.

Nigel Planer (actor – Ralph Filthy): I'd've been quite happy doing more *Young Ones* or *Filthy, Rich & Catflap*, but things moved quite fast.

Redfern: I was amazed how professional they were and how everything was worked out meticulously.

Jackson: I do remember the Oo Er Missus episode very well. I thought that was a very funny episode at the time. Chris Barrie doing an impression of me in the gallery [*laughs*] and them creeping around The Nolans dressing room [*laughs*].

Andy de la Tour (actor – Club Boss): I haven't watched an episode of it since it was made. I thought then it didn't wholly work. I thought the conceit was slightly odd. The comedy was modern at times, contemporary, but the setting was almost 1950s… the feeling of 1950s. The sleazy West End. The sleazy Soho of the 1950s. I thought it was a slightly odd match and I'm not sure it worked that well.

Bates: It is a good piece of work and it is interesting. It is funny. There are great moments in it. I've watched it a couple of times since and it is a great piece. Perhaps it is more smiles television than outrageous television.

Jackson: I think the BBC would have taken another series. Although I don't think they loved the show and I don't think it has ever been repeated [on the BBC], which I always thought was very strange.

Bates: The expectations of your target audience are so high, the bar is set so high, and because they are expecting something big that when it doesn't meet their expectations they automatically switch off.

Planer: I loved doing *Filthy, Rich & Catflap*, but it wasn't meant to be. Rik and Ade went ahead and did Bottom without Ben Elton and Me. I think that worked out pretty well.

Lloyd Peters (founder of 20th Century Coyote): I met Ben Elton, by accident, in a train station and *Filthy, Rich & Catflap* had just bombed. I think it got seriously criticised for being sexist. I saw Ben and he asked me what I thought to it and I said: "This is the problem with satire, you cross a line and you are lambasted as the very thing that you think you are satirising. I think *Filthy, Rich & Catflap* is not clever enough or careful enough to tread the line and goes over the line. You don't actually know it is a parody or a satire as it is being as disgracefully rude as the thing it is pretending to satirise." He wasn't very pleased with my reaction [*laughs*].

De la Tour: The airwaves are filled with people who don't really do anything except try to be famous. They haven't got any actual skills. They buff up nicely and try and make a living being famous by being on each other's shows. The world may be much more appropriate for *Filthy, Rich & Catflap* now.

"I've got the largest majority in the House of Commons"

What kind of person gets away with naming their character "Bastard" (It's B'Stard actually) on primetime television? Rik fucking Mayall, that's who. While *Filthy, Rich & Catflap* didn't set the world on fire, Mayall and his comrades were still riding the crest of *The Young Ones* wave and many tuned in to see what the anti-establishment, comedic actors would do next. Still, nobody expected Mayall to take on a character like Alan B'Stard. It was so establishment that it was against everything he had done and said previously… or was it?

This role was written specifically for Mayall by TV writing duo Laurence Marks and Maurice Gran at the request of the actor. Marks & Gran started their TV writing career by producing sketches and monologues for *The Frankie Howard Variety Show*. By the 1980s the duo had written hit TV shows such as *Holding the Fort*, *Shine On Harvey Moon* and *Relative Strangers* (a spin-off of *Holding the Fort*). Marks & Gran were invited to speak at a conference all about the future of TV comedy in the UK. One of the people in that audience was Mayall who approached Marks & Gran about writing something for just him. But they dismissed his suggestions as simply an actor trying to find any old writer(s) to create a new vehicle for their talents. They also weren't too fond of Mayall's stylings: he was dressed in a homburg hat and a huge astrakhan coat indoors (it was a tribute to one of his comedy heroes – Tony Hancock).

Months later when Marks & Gran met with Mayall again on Terry Wogan's chat show however, something started to sparkle between them. They arranged to have dinner and throw a few ideas around. Mayall said he wanted something that showcased his worst excesses – cowardice, cruelty, depravity and greed. Marks & Gran instantly recognised those as words to describe backbenchers for the Conservative Party under Margaret Thatcher's rule. The show was pitched to the head of comedy at Yorkshire Television, Vernon Lawrence, who just also happened to be a huge fan of Mayall's. As a result, he was sold on it immediately. Marks & Gran set about writing and had a cunning plan on how to discover what it was like inside the Houses of Parliament. They exercised their constitutional right of requesting to be taken around the government building by their local MP, none other than Michael Portillo. Making mental notes of the environment and the way MP's acted, Marks & Gran set about writing *The New Statesman*. They did stay in touch, and became friends, with Portillo however some other MP's took against them writing a satirical show about politics starring an anti-establishment actor such as Mayall.

Hired to play B'Stard's wife Sarah was Marsha Fitzalan, a regular on TV serials. She had previously appeared in the BBC's 1980 adaptation of *Pride and Prejudice* along with single episode appearances in *Brush Strokes*, *The Professionals* and *Three Up, Two Down*. The role of B'Stard's right-hand man and all-round decent chap Piers Fletcher-Dervish was to be played by Michael Troughton, an actor who had, much like Fitzalan, appeared in many TV shows as one-off or occasional characters. Troughton had appeared in *Boon*, *Minder* and on both ITV's and BBC's *Playhouse* TV series. As *The New Statesman* had been commissioned by Yorkshire Television it was to be filmed at their studio in Leeds. Production found it cheaper to fly Mayall and Fitzalan up to Leeds than pay for train tickets or a private car. Each episode was filmed twice, firstly without an audience and then later in the day with an audience. However, problems occurred when it turned out that what they were saying in the first recorded segment could have been libellous. So, at the last-minute Marks & Gran altered lines of dialogue before cameras were due to roll. "I would freak out but Rik, you could give him a script and he would know it instantly. It was amazing how quick his brain was" recalled Fitzalan to the *Henley Standard*. It also didn't help filming time-wise when, much like shooting *The Young Ones* in front of a studio audience, the laughter would be so loud it would drown out the actors and meant that some filming inevitably went on longer than expected.

The first series of *The New Statesman* debuted on 13th September 1987 across the ITV network. It was met with critical and commercial acclaim. Even those that the show was satirising – The Conservative MPs - loved it and reports started to come out of the House of Commons that those inside were starting to act and dress like B'Stard.

The second series of *The New Statesman* began in January 1989 and when the last episode aired on 26th February it left viewers with a cliff-hanger – who gunned down Alan B'Stard? The answer to the question was discovered when a one-off, hour-long special called *Who Shot Alan B'stard* was aired eleven months later on the 14th January 1990. That piece of television won Marks & Gran the award for Best British comedy at the 1990 BAFTA Awards. A huge political spanner was thrown into the works for the writing of series three. As Marks & Gran arrived back from a jaunt to America they were told that the Prime Minister Margaret Thatcher has resigned. All of their early drafts for series three had to be scrapped and completely re-written. Fortunately, Mayall came to their aid as shortly before filming was due to begin (and scripts still being finalised) he fell down a flight of stairs and broke his arm. Which meant that production had to be postponed until their star actor was completely healed, which in turn gave Marks & Gran some breathing space during their writing period. Series three finally hit TV screens almost a year to the day since the last time B'Stard was on television – 6th January 1991. This one episode and the series that followed proved to be a hit. Consequently, one last series was commissioned for broadcast during November and December 1992. The show finished with Mayall's odious character sneering that if The Queen wanted to meet him then she must come to him.

While that seemed like the end for *The New Statesman*, Alan B'Stard lived on in a one-off special – *A B'Stard Exposed* – made and aired by the BBC on 30th December 1994. There were regular guest columns by B'Stard in *The Sunday Telegraph*, *The Daily Mail* and *The New Statesman*. These were in fact written by Marks & Gran but professed to be by B'Stard. In 2006 B'Stard returned but in a slightly different guise. Marks & Gran had written a stage show called *The Blair B'Stard Project*. Mayall was unsure of returning to the character, especially in the newer climate of Rock N' Roll politics that prime minister Tony Blair had been a part of. However, Marks & Gran explained how B'Stard had moved on and how it was him who invented New Labour and not the Prime Minister. *The Blair B'Stard Project* played a select number of regional theatres to sold-out crowds. Marks & Gran decided it was time to bring B'Stard home to London's Whitehall, so tweaked the original play into something fresher for 2007 and renamed it *Alan B'Stard's Extremely Secret Weapon*. It played to sold out audiences and rave reviews right on the doorstep on Downing Street and Mayall could not have been happier "Twice in my lifetime so far, this character has presented itself to me to change the establishment of the British kingdom. I brought down Thatch for my people. And now I'm bringing down 'Bleurgh', for my people who I love and love me." There was one last hurrah for B'Stard as Mayall stepped into his shoes again for an advertising campaign against the AV system in UK parliamentary elections. The advert finished with B'Stard as prime minister. A real-life warning that if the general public didn't back the NO to AV vote then a scheming, lecherous Machiavellian like B'Stard could easily waltz into power.

When did Rik Mayall play a Rik Mayall character that wasn't strictly a Rik Mayall character? When he played Alan B'Stard. In another comedian's hands B'Stard could have been a lightweight caricature of any/all politicians yet in Mayall's hands he became a weaselly, odious cretin that everybody loved to hate, especially the politicians of the day. The first series sees Mayall finding his feet as B'Stard and while he is nasty and slightly perverted, it is nowhere near the B'Stard of the second series and beyond. That's when Mayall takes the character to lower than low lows while still managing to make the audience laugh and enjoy what a true bastard B'Stard has become.

Marks & Gran's satirical writings flow almost poetically out of Mayall's mouth as he tongue lashes all those that enter his arena. Even romancing his wife is akin to going to war as he battles with her not just to take her clothes off but also over who will be the dominate one, inside and outside the bedroom. The brilliance of Fitzalan's performance as Sarah B'Stard cannot be understated either as she gives Mayall a run for his money in the sheer nastiness stakes. Even though she takes B'Stard for everything he's got there is still the sense of a shy and retiring woman in amongst the wicked witch of the West persona she develops.

Troughton's Sir Piers Fletcher-Dervish is the perfect folly for B'Stard as he bends, breaks and fawns over his esteemed boss. This trio of characters deliver very little hope of making the right political decisions throughout the entire series yet there is something lurking underneath the surface of each character that offers a small glimmer of hope that they will eventually do the right thing at the right time. Inevitably they don't though.

If ever Mayall was born to play one comedic role then Alan B'Stard is it. He has slightly anarchistic tendencies along with a slapstick element that only Mayall could ever deliver in such a unique style. Underneath the Savile row suits and the curly hair, lurks the beating heart of Rik from *The Young Ones* only this time with more bravado (see: Lord Flashheart) and slimyness (see: Richard Richard). By the time his character reaches series four it doesn't look and feel like watching Mayall play a character, instead it is an almost political documentary where the lead MP just happens to wear Rik Mayall's skin. Mayall disappears into the role like a method actor who has been studying the character for months on end before even uttering one line of dialogue. This is the brilliance of Mayall as B'Stard in that he is so believable as a sneering, snivelling member of parliament that if it wasn't so funny and outlandish then it would be tragic and slightly scary to imagine MP's like B'Stard exist.

Marks & Gran (and Mayall)'s creation was a huge shot in the arm for mainstream satirical comedy and without a doubt paved the way for Scottish writer/director Armando Iannucci's work such as *The Thick Of It*, *Veep* and *The Death Of Stalin*. Nobody could have expected that the people who *The New Statesman* was ridiculing would find it appealing, and then try to become an Alan B'Stard. The members of Parliament may have changed over the intervening years but the satire that *The New Statesman* delivers is still as relevant today, if not more so, than ever before.

Maurice Gran (co-creator/writer): We [Marks & Gran] got talking to Rik and he didn't want to talk to us because we were producers and he thought they were to be despised, and then when he found out who we were he got really excited because The Young Ones had finished and he had seen Shine On Harvey Moon. So, he said he wanted to do a comedy where he played a grown-up part. We said: "What do you want to do?" and he said: "I want to play someone who encompasses all my worst attributes. I want to play someone who lies and kills and fornicates and cheats and is a coward." So, we said: "You want to play a Conservative MP then?" and so thus was born the character that was to become Alan B'Stard.

Geoffrey Sax (director): I was very keen to do it. I thought it could be more than just a normal sitcom, we could expand it out more. It could be more visual than the comedies that were being made at that time.

Gran: We approached Vernon Lawrence [Head of Light Entertainment at Yorkshire Television] about doing a show with Rik and he said he would love to do a show with Rik but didn't have any slots. We met up with Rik and wrote up a proposal, and the proposal was like a who's who entry. We sent it to Vernon and he phoned up very quickly and said he had found a studio. I don't know what poor bastard he had to disappoint or what show he had to cancel but we got one of those slots.

Sax: I think at the time it was going to be called The Bastard Files.

Gran: ITV said you can't have a character called Bastard. So, we asked if we could have a character called B'Stard, which seemed to be alright.

Laurence Marks (co-creator/writer): What used to happen was when we had a script or storyline it would go to the lawyers of Yorkshire Television because it was quite unlike anything else on television and it had to be run by the Yorkshire Television lawyers and they would write notes back like "It would be better if you took out Margaret Thatcher's vagina and replaced it with her underwear."

Gran: We spent a long time collaborating with Rik. He was never the writer on the show but we always discussed stories with him and he had input. He always used to say: "More jokes, more jokes, more jokes" and we would say there needed to be more story.

Sax: We did a read through of the script and then he [Mayall] and I and a couple of other characters workshopped it because he wasn't sure at the time as to how to pitch the character, how far he should go with it. It was about three days in and we were rehearsing a scene where he had to say to his accountant that there is nuclear waste being dumped under a primary school and his character just sort of carries on. I remember we talked about it and decided that that was the sort of thing that he [B'Stard] would not understand why it was a problem. Why would you not do it? It is a state school [*laughs*]. And with that he found the character. He played it quite charming but was unable to emphasize with poor people. Anyone who wasn't like him he probably thought they should be lined up and shot [*laughs*].

Marks: I once told Vernon Lawrence that there was no point in doing the show if we can't go way beyond the boundaries of British television.

Sax: The way Rik would work was he would come in and when we were rehearsing the scenes he hadn't learnt his lines, but by the end of the first rehearsal he knew his lines perfectly. He never forgot a line.

Gran: We would write during rehearsals and we would write up to five minutes before the studio started. It was a continuing process. It was made under extraordinary speed and Rik worked very very hard. He was very creative and he was very kind to the other actors.

Sax: He often said to Michael Troughton "Look, if you do this and then turn on that line, you'll get a bigger laugh. Trust me." He was all about it being as funny as possible and it didn't matter who had the bigger laughs, whether it was him or another character.

Marks: We had written the first two episodes [of series three], which largely featured Thatcher, and Rik rang us up asking if we had heard the news, we were in Los Angeles at the time, and we said: "What's the matter?" and he replied: "It looks like Mrs Thatcher is going to be kicked out and that will bugger up our first two episodes." Maurice and I came back to London and we were collected by a driver at Heathrow and we asked him what the news was and he said: "Haven't you heard? She's gone." Which meant we would completely have to re-write the two episodes we had written. What Rik did, not at our instigation I must tell you, is threw himself down a flight of stairs and broke his arm. Which gave us the delay to write the two new episodes. I think they now call that 'Taking one for the team' [*laughs*].

Sax: Rik and I never had a cross word at all. It was always just about the work. We used to laugh all the way through. It is always quite dangerous if you laugh in a rehearsal because it means that the audience aren't going to laugh. But they always did.

Serena Gordon (actress - Victoria): It was the first time I had ever done TV in-front of a studio audience. It was a hotel bedroom of some party conference and I was playing a secretary who he [B'Stard] ends up jumping into bed with. We had to tear our clothes off and jump into bed and then they shouted "Cut!" We had to do it about nine times and it was continually embarrassing have to get dressed again, especially as Rik kept tearing all the buttons off my shirt. He was fantastic. He made it very fun otherwise it could have been a very excruciating experience.

Christopher Ryan (actor – Ioannis Douvalopoulos): It was a different character for me. I think I was supposed to have halitosis or something and I was in the room and he was edging away from me. That made me laugh. We were almost doing a circle. Me chasing him and him peering over his shoulder and running away [*laughs*].

Sax: There is a line where Piers says there was a debate on pornography and he had to look at all the dirty books. I said to Rik: "Look, if you are facing the window when he says that line and then you turn, I think you'll get a better laugh" and he said: "Actually, I think I can get three laughs on that" I said: "How are you going to do that?" He replied "The first thing I'll do is as soon as he says 'dirty books', if I'm facing the window, I won't move and that will get a laugh. Then I'll twitch my shoulders and that will get another laugh, and then I'll turn and say the line." On the day he got three laughs off one line. He just knew where the laugh was. I thought I knew comedy until I worked with him. He was a master at it.

Gran: We did three series over four years and then we had a break. Then we did another where he was a member of the European Parliament. We revived *The New Statesman* as a stage play. Rik was fantastic in that. The quad bike accident did affect his line reading but he used it to his advantage. One time he came on-stage and couldn't remember what he was supposed to do next so he said to the man playing his sidekick: "If, for arguments sake, this was a play, what do you think I would do next?" and he replied "Well, you'd probably cross the stage, drink that glass of Brandy and say 'Fuck me, I'm bored'" and Rik said "OK, let's do that then" and the audience went mad with laughter.

Marks: My favourite moment in *The New Statesman* never took place in the studio. It was when Alan was assassinated outside the houses of Parliament. He was gunned down by an automatic rifle. I thought that was a good piece of television visual comedy. It was worthy of a film sequence. Also, it meant Maurice and I were free because he was dead. Then Yorkshire Television asked if we can work out a way of bringing him back from the dead. It's not often a character from a television show gets an obituary in a national newspaper.

Gran: I'm very fond of his party-political broadcast about the health service when he said: "In the good old days you were poor, you got sick and you died."

Sax: I did wonder if we would ever get any politicians copying B'Stard. But I was surprised at to how much it did resonant through Parliament. It was great [*laughs*].

Mayall's two big appearances on TV in 1987 were *Filthy, Rich, & Catflap* and *The New Statesman*, so it didn't really matter that his third outing was scrapped before it aired. ITV spent a considerable amount of money and energy shouting from the rooftops about their new sitcom airing in February called *Hardwicke House*. The show was set in a British comprehensive school where the kids were naughty but the teachers were even naughtier, and cruder. The first episode came with fanfares and all sorts of write-ups in magazines such as the *TV Times*. However, after the first episode aired (a feature-length edition) on 24th February, it was so widely panned by critics and viewers as grossly offensive rather than funny that ITV were left in a state of panic. Episode two aired the following night but that received even more hatred, so ITV took the decision to pull the plug on the remaining five episodes. Episode five would have seen Mayall and Adrian Edmondson appear as two ex-pupils freshly released from Borstal Prison and ready to cause trouble. Those performances were never to be seen. It has never been released on VHS or DVD in the intervening years.

Actor Roger Sloman reasons why it wasn't well received upon transmission: "Somebody in scheduling made a mistake and put it out before nine o'clock. It went out at eight o'clock and so when it went out the phones were buzzing. Poor Roy Kinnear was on holiday but when he came back there were all these reporters waiting for him at the airport asking for his opinion but he had no idea what had happened. It wasn't something that was meant to go out [at eight o'clock]. So, someone made a boo-boo there. It got buried." *Hardwicke House*'s co-writer Simon Wright also got caught up in the fury over the show: "It was sort of *The Young Ones* meets *Grange Hill*. It was about a secondary school and it was really wild and completely inappropriate for the eight o'clock slot. What happened to the series was it was transmitted on a Tuesday night at eight o'clock and it was before there was a TV watershed. Thatcher actually raised it in Parliament. It did lead to the nine o'clock threshold. It was really anarchic. They transmitted the hour-long episode and the BBC switch board was jammed for four hours even though it had played on ITV. Then they played the second episode the next night and, again, there was the same chaos. The next morning me and Richard Hall, who co-wrote it, went on

TV to talk about what we had done and when we came off-air we were told that ITV had pulled it. Apparently, they destroyed the tapes."

The pop charts didn't reject Mayall though, and this time wasn't with Cliff Richard. This musical adventure involved being part of a four-piece band known as Bad News. After the huge praise for *The Comic Strip Presents...* episode that focussed on the band and their road to glory(?), EMI Records decided it was high time to release an album of the band's music. The original members Vin Fuego (Edmondson), Den Dennis (Planer), Spider Webb (Richardson) and Colin Grigson (Mayall) all came together to record an album that included tracks such as *Masterbike*, *Bad News* and *Hey Hey Bad News*. It also featured a rousing rendition of Queen's *Bohemian Rhapsody*, which was released as a single and peaked at number 44. The self-titled album was produced by Fuego and some guy called Brian May. It only spent a week in the charts where it came in at number 69. A follow-up single called *Cashing In On Christmas* was released at the start of December but failed to reach the Top 40. Sticking in the music world, 1987 saw the release of the debut single *What A Girl Wants* from UK pop band The Company She Keeps. An infectious upbeat slice of pop music that benefitted by having Mayall play different roles in the video. Firstly as a dodgy newspaper seller, then an upper-class slimy womanizer, a policeman and finally a dastardly villain. Mayall continued his assault on pop music videos when he appeared in Motorhead's *Eat The Rich* accompanying video. The track was the accompaniment to *The Comic Strip Presents...* second feature film *Eat The Rich*. A cannibal comedy that would be a genuine horror film if it didn't feature humour throughout. The original Comic Strip gang only put in cameo appearances and Mayall's performance as Micky the Union Boss is one that we've seen from him before – an upper-class pervert. He dances with Jennifer Saunders's Lady Caroline using one-word answers as she asks him questions. At one point he tries to lift up a woman's skirt and gets a slap. The film flopped badly at the box office and Channel 4 cancelled the next schedule feature film *Five Go To Hell*. ITV produced a sketch show called *First AIDS* that was specifically aimed at young people to inform of the dangers of AIDS. This one-off broadcast included musicians and comedians. Mayall's sketch saw him and a young lady sitting on his bed about to engage in sex before realising that they need a condom otherwise they will catch AIDS. Mayall's performance is an extension of Rik from *The Young Ones* as he tries to woo the young lady but is unsuccessful so spouts ridiculous lines in the hope of impressing her. It is a highly informative piece underneath all the crazy Mayall-ness.

Mayall appeared in a corporate training video called *Managing Problem People: Behavioural Skills for Leaders*. Only this was no basic corporate training video. This was a six-parter written by Stephen Fry and starring the likes of John Cleese, Dawn French, Emma Thompson, Geoffrey Palmer and Nigel Hawthorne. Mayall appeared in the second vignette called *Big Mouth Billy*, where he played the title character. The video analyses how Billy promises everyone everything but very rarely delivers on his promise. That is until his boss, played by John Cleese, helps him plan efficiently, set effective schedules and realistic deadlines. The seventeen-minute video has never been released to the public but is available to hire from some local libraries and is in the British Film Institute's archive.

Mayall got to work with another *Monty Python* cast member in early 1988. Post-Monty Python Graham Chapman was gaining interest from American TV networks who wanted him to create his own work. One idea of Chapman's was a TV series called *Jake's Journey*. It was to be a story of a young boy who meets a knight (no word on if he said "Nee" or not) and embarks on a time-travelling quest. CBS Studios loved it even before the pilot was shot with the head of comedy at the network reportedly laughing heavily even at the script stage. A pilot episode was commissioned with Chapman playing Sir George the Knight (he also was due to play The Queen as well). Chapman pulled in Peter Cook to play a King, Liz Smith as a witch and Mayall as a Troll. It was rumoured that when the pilot aired it didn't receive a positive reaction from the American viewers as it was too *Monty Python*-esque. The truth is that it never went further than the pilot due to a writers' strike that year in Hollywood, director Hal Ashby's ailing health and Chapman's own health problems. The episode did air on CBS and a copy is held in the Library of Congress, and, if rumours are to be believed, a few VHS tapes of the episode survive in the vaults of private collectors. From what little footage there is online it appears that Mayall's

Troll had a farting problem and was a character very much in the vein of the bridge keeper from *Monty Python and the Holy Grail* - bonkers and slightly stupid.

Sadly, *Jake's Journey* was never meant to be as Chapman died of cancer on 4th October 1989. The script for *Jake's Journey* was finally published in 2004 by Chapman's writing partner Jim Yoakum in his book *OJRIL: The Completely Incomplete Graham Chapman*.

Mayall returned to his TV comedy roots for Series 3 of *The Comic Strips Presents...* when it arrived on Channel 4 during February and March 1988. The first episode titled *The Strike* had Peter Richardson (also the writer and director for the episode) playing Al Pacino playing Arthur Scargill in a film about a Welsh mining strike. Jennifer Saunders played Meryl Streep in the film within a film. Mayall took on two roles: firstly, as a hideous hunchback who drinks in the local village pub. Covered in prosthetics he snivelled and sneered his way through a short scene. Secondly as Speaker of the House of Commons who approves Scargill's plan to not shut down the mine. Mayall's Speaker had a chin strip of grey hair and sat on a sack of wool. Crazy but all in a day's work for *The Comic Strip Presents....* Seven days later and it was *More Bad News* (the title of the episode and possibly a warning to the British public who were tuning in). A follow on from the first episode about the band Bad News and how they had been faring since the episode was broadcast. It turns out that Mayall's character Colin Grigson worked in a bank during the day and wasn't very Rock 'n' Roll at all. In fact, he wore a wig when performing. This episode was much more *Anarchy in the UK* meets *This Is Spinal Tap* and Mayall is front and centre throughout. He struts his stuff with gusto while wearing a leopard print jacket and tight leggings finished off with bright white heeled boots. He also gets to mug up to the camera and the viewer gets another glimpse of that introvert/extrovert persona that Mayall crafted so well in later years. It is a thoroughly funny episode. However, it wasn't that funny for those setting up the sequence to be filmed at the Monsters of Rock concert at Donnington Park. Producer Simon Wright still has nightmares about it: "We shot that in Donnington at the heavy metal festival. They don't fuck around up there. They had bottles of piss and milk cartons full of piss chucked at the stage. The roadies from the other bands fucked up all their equipment, changed all the levels so they sounded awful. It was just ridiculous. But we survived it."

Mr Jolly Lives Next Door was broadcast on 5th March. Written by Mayall, Edmondson and Rowland Rivron with Mayall and Edmondson as proprietors of an escort agency who are equal parts stupid and devious. It was a chaotic blend of *The Dangerous Brothers*, *The Young Ones* and (future show) *Bottom*. Mayall schemed his way into people's lives (and underpants) while Edmondson punched people or put grenades in his pockets. It was classic Mayall and Edmondson and, even to this day, is seen as one of the best ever episodes of *The Comic Strip Presents...* Simon Wright, the producer for the episode, remembers everyone being very excited to work with Peter Cook: "The admiration was so intense. He was utterly charming. It worked really nice. It is such a dark piece. Strange but fun."

The Comic Strip comedy club was right in the very heart of London's West End. However, the club's stage was a world away from the stages on Shaftesbury Avenue that saw performances of legendary plays and musicals down the years. Mayall finally went from basement club stage to West End stage between April – July 1988 at The Phoenix Theatre when he and other actors such as John Sessions, John Gordon Sinclair and Stephen Fry appeared in a production of Simon Gray's *The Common Pursuit*, a play about Cambridge University undergraduates setting up a literary magazine. Mayall's narcissistic performance of Nick was the perfect folly to Fry's gentle Humphrey, and resulted in a successful run. Off stage Mayall became a father for the second time as he and Barbara welcomed a son, Sidney, into the world.

Mayall had been off television screens for over a year before he returned in April 1989, and after his scandalous appearance on *Jackanory* many would have thought he wouldn't be allowed on children's television for quite a while. However Central Independent Television had other ideas and signed him up to front *Grim Tales*, a weekly kiddies TV programme where he would read fairytales by the Brothers Grimm. The production was created by his friends Bob Baldwin and Rikki Finegold who tailored the show around Mayall's eccentric nature. It essentially required Mayall to tell stories to camera while sitting in an armchair that literally had moving arms and legs. He would run through the gamut of voices for each story: "My humour is mostly to do with performance. I've never been naturally funny," Mayall commented to *GQ Magazine* years later. Each episode was interspersed with abstract animation created by different animators. Twelve episodes were broadcast during the spring of 1989 and included classic stories such as Rapunzel, Rumpelstiltskin and Hansel and Gretel. The show was a hit with the kids, and some adults although it pained them to admit it.

It would however be Mayall's next TV appearance that would live long in the memory. One word describes better than any other his cameo on BBC screens on the evening of 19th October 1989 in the TV series *Blackadder Goes Forth*. That word is: legendary. Mayall swaggers onto the screen as Wing commander Lord Flashheart with all the gusto of a sexual tidelwave, and he proceeds to joke at Captain Blackadder's every expense. Mayall dials Flashheart up to eleven once again and this time the character becomes bigger and more self-absorbed than anyone would have thought humanly possible. Somehow, through this, Mayall makes him completely loveable.

There are only a handful of actors that will ever be remembered, outside of their own work, for outstanding cameo appearances yet Mayall will always be one of those actors. He took a one-line joke of a character and created a larger-than-life performance with lines such as "Just because I can give multiple orgasms to the furniture just by sitting on it", "I'd let them stew in their own juice. But let me tell you, if I ever tried that I'd drown" and "Leeeeeeeeetsssssss Dooooooooooo Ittttt". Even Atkinson, once again, had to just stand back and let Mayall's daring fire into every corner of the scene like a sexual spitfire – WOOF! Flashheart was a small yet important character in Mayall's illustrious career.

The same cannot be said for his cameo in episode seven of the TV show *Snakes and Ladders*. Broadcast at the tail end of 1989, the show was written by Laurence Marks & Maurice Gran (*The New Statesman* co-creators) as a vehicle for Adrian Edmondson. Set ten years in the future (1999), Giles (played by Edmondson) is an upper-class toff who, due to an admin error, swaps places with a down-on-his-luck Scottish guy called Gavin (John Gordon-Sinclair) and gets to experience how the lower classes live and suffer. Edmondson seems miscast in the role. He lacks the crazy energy that he usually exuded. Mayall's appearance see's the two of them sit down and have a chat about alternative comedy while in a mental institution. On the surface it's a dull conversation between two lifeless characters. However, underneath lies a huge tongue-in-cheek gag as Mayall describes the rise of alternative comedy in the 1980s, clearly using his own rise to fame as the basis for the whole conversation. It is a cleverly written segment. The show lasted only one series of seven episodes. It failed to ignite like *The New Statesman* did.

Another cameo beckoned for Mayall. This time as Death in the forty-minute comedy drama *Maurice Dobbs Makes A Movie*. A strange curio of a piece about a young man, Maurice Dobbs, who inherits a fortune and sets out to make his own version of *2001: A Space Odyssey*. The film-within-a-film narrative is used throughout as Dobbs becomes more and more obsessed with making the film and in-turn alienates the cast & crew along with his girlfriend. Mayall pops up at the end commanding Dobbs to follow him. When Dobbs offers to play Death at Chess (a reference to Ingmar Bergman's *The Seventh Seal*), Death replies that he doesn't play Chess but can play darts. Sadly, Dobbs forgot to include a set of darts on the prop list. The featurette ends with Dobbs following Death while muttering about how he wanted the film to be "a confirmation of one's existence as a human being."

The road was calling Mayall and once again Andy de la Tour became his comedic wingman, so to speak, for a sixty-seven-date tour around the UK during 1989: "In 1989 Phil McIntyre called me up and said: "Rik wants to go out on the road. He hasn't got much of an act. He wants new stuff. Would you like to work with Rik to help him write a new act for himself?" So, I said: "Yes, that would be great." Phil rented a rehearsal room in Soho and Rik and I spent two weeks, just the two of us, in this huge rehearsal room doing stuff, making stuff up and writing a routine. It was two of the most creative weeks I've ever had in my life." They were still touring in the lead up to Christmas as December saw them start in Scotland and end in

Devon. Such was the demand for tickets that the tour was revived for two weeks in March 1990. In the end Mayall and de la Tour had played over one hundred dates around the UK.

By the end of the decade Mayall was virtually a household name thanks to his anarchic performances in *The Young Ones*, *Filthy Rich, and Catflap* and *The New Statesman*. He also continued to blaze a trail across the comedy world as he further pushed the boundaries of alternative stand-up comedy. The 1980s had been very good to Rik Mayall.

Filming on *The Young Ones*

Edmondson and Mayall try to blow up the *Saturday Live* studio

This is my House

Phoebe Cates and Mayall in a promotional photo for *Drop Dead Fred*.

The Hammersmith hardmen.

Chris Wade and Mayall during the recording of *Cutey & the Sofaguard*.

Mayall with writer Mike Bennett (left) and One Media iP CEO & Chairman Michael Infante (right) signing the contract for *Bedtime Stories*.

A promotional shot for *The Last Hurrah*.

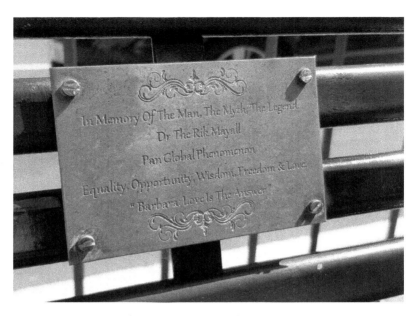

Words to live by. The plaque on the Rik Mayall memorial bench in Hammersmith.

A 20ft mural on the side of Harlow Playhouse. Created by street artist Gnasher.

1990s

(*The New Statesman* changed his name to *Drop Dead Fred* and bared his *Bottom*)

A new decade started with Mayall working with old friends. His return to *The Comic Strip Presents...* TV show wasn't until 15ᵗʰ February 1990. Almost two years since he last appeared. This time he had a small part in the episode *GLC: The Carnage Continues* as the slippery, perverted Lord Mayor of London who is ousted in a coup d'état led by Robbie Coltrane's Charles Bronson as Ken Livingston. The episode was set up as a vague sequel to *The Strike*. A further year passed before Mayall appeared on-screen again. This time he had headed to Hollywood. Appearing in *Little Noises* opposite Crispin Glover, Tatum O'Neal, John C. McGinley and Tate Donovan. However, this project wasn't caught in the bright lights of the Hollywood movie industry. Instead it was more the ugly step-sister to mainstream cinema.

This low budget (almost no budget) feature film told the story of a struggling writer trying to achieve fame by stealing poems from his mute friend. Director Jane Spencer told *Hound Dawg magazine* how Mayall became involved: "I had seen Rik in reruns of *The Young Ones*, and I asked my casting director, Deborah Aquila, if we could approach Rik for a role in the film. He loved the script and wanted to play 'Mathias' so that was that! I remember during the shoot he was always very sensitive regarding making sure his character was not 'too big' because of all the TV comedy he had done."

The film tells a story centred around the idea of greed and how far some people will go to be famous. Glover's struggling writer is the very definition of a bohemian. He wanders through the film with his head constantly down; rarely looking people in the eye. He is more interested in sitting on the swings trying to understand the words on the page or twirling around in the rain than interacting with other people. While the film is set in L.A. where people need big voices to be heard, the major characters are all introverts, except one character – Matthias Lichtenstein.

Mayall's portrayal of Matthias, a British literary agent, is completely at odds to the rest of the film. It is almost as if he has wandered into the wrong film set and the director simply left him in the final cut to give the piece a bit of energy. Sadly, not enough energy though as he is restrained from his usual chaotic antics. Dressed impeccably in a suit with a short bobbed haircut, he struts around with flair but it's not the typical Mayall whirlwind performance we are used to seeing. The film itself sits somewhere between low budget arthouse and no budget High School project. No wonder it made little noise at the box office. However, there is another reason why it didn't find its audience: "I had an original Director's cut that I was very happy with, and this cut (in rough cut) got into Sundance." Explained Spencer to *Hound Dawg magazine* "Unfortunately, when I was then going to polish it into the final cut, one of the producers got involved and was constantly attempting to change my cut to make the film more 'commercial' for screenings at the festival. I was upset to find out that this producer actually recut a lot of my film for Sundance, without my permission, and screened the cut there. I was in shock and just did the best I could under the circumstances in promoting the film at the festival. Sundance ultimately found out that this producer had recut the rough cut and they backed me as an artist with a letter re: what happened, which was lovely of them."

Back in Blighty *Grim Tales* series two continued to draw a large TV audience. Mayall returned with glee and continued to tell more Grimm Brothers fairy tales from his weirdly moving armchair, occasionally rising and prancing around the small yet vivid set. The second series consisted of ten episodes and included classics such as *The Frog Prince*, *The Little Peasant* and *The Wolf and the Seven Little Kids*. Only four episodes included the abstract animation this time, instead director Bob Baldwin chose to focus more on Mayall's lively performances. Sadly, this series was the end of the road for *Grim Tales* as another was never commissioned. However, an audio cassette of eleven stories was released in 1992.

Mayall did get back to feature films, well his voice did at least, when he worked on the animated movie *The Princess and the Goblin*. An adaptation of George MacDonald's 1872 novel, this British/Hungarian/American co-production featured a heap of classic British actors with Mollie Sugden, Joss Ackland, Claire Bloom and Roy Kinnear lending their voices. Mayall voiced Prince Froglip, a deceptively sadistic frog who wants to rule over everybody and will stop at nothing to see that it happens. Mayall's delivery of Prince Froglip's lines were splatteringly hilarious as he short tongued his pronunciations and added extra rasps on certain words.

At a time when Disney animation was starting to find its second wind, other animated studios were still trying to out-Disney Disney. *The Princess and the Goblin* is a far too lightweight animated movie to ever seriously trouble Disney. It is no surprise that it failed critically and commercially. However, by the time of release Mayall was back to treading the boards and it was only a matter of time before best mates Mayall and Edmondson took to the stage together. However, nobody would have predicted it would have been in a West End production of Samuel Beckett's *Waiting For Godot*. The duo had used Beckett's work as a jumping off point for some of their early comedy routines, so this was a natural fit for them. The new production, and the first in the West End for thirty-six years, was rubbished by the critics. *The Daily Mail* lambasted them, saying: "This is not acting, this is showing off." However, fans of the duo ensured full houses for its run from late September 1991 into early 1992.

Fans who enjoyed *Waiting for Godot* were in for a treat with Mayall and Edmondson's next collaboration. But before exposing their bottoms on British TV, Mayall headed back to Hollywood and took another crack at a comedy feature film.

"HELLO SNOTFACE!"

Hollywood is haunted by the thousands, if not millions, of British comedians who went there to try their luck in the movies but bombed out. Only a handful have ever made it: Dudley Moore, John Cleese and more recently Ricky Gervais. Others have had one or two bites at the US comedy cake but failed to make it last. Rik Mayall had already ventured across the pond to shoot the small independent movie *Little Noises* alongside Tatum O'Neal and Crispin Glover. But that wasn't a full-on comedy and thus didn't fully utilise his talents. Mayall needed a comedy vehicle that showcased his anarchic energy, the same energy that had made him famous in the UK. Rik no doubt hoped that playing an imaginary friend who bounces off the walls and flicks snot at people could have been the performance to make him a global superstar.

But let's rewind first. How did *Drop Dead Fred* come to be? It all started in the offices of *Reader's Digest*. The book editor for the family magazine was Elizabeth Livingston and years earlier she had been having trouble with her young daughter and her supposed imaginary friend Drop Dead Fred, who would be wonderful during the day but a devil at night. Drop Dead Fred would be blamed for everything. But as the daughter grew up Drop Dead Fred faded away. Then, a few years later when her daughter was in high school and being bullied, Livingston said to her friend Carlos Davis, a film producer/screenwriter and best-selling novelist, that she wished Drop Dead Fred would come back to cheer her daughter up. In a bizarre twist of coincidence, Davis and his writing partner Anthony Fingleton were, at that time, working on a script about a girl in high school who had an imaginary female friend. But they were struggling to make it work as either a TV show or a film.

On his way home from the restaurant Davis suddenly realised that switching the female imaginary friend to a male is how they could make his and Fingleton's unfinished project finally work. Fortuitously, Davis had been made aware of Mayall several months prior to the events of the Drop Dead Fred project as he had been trying to generate interest in another project he was working on: an imitation of *Beverly Hills Cop*. It was to star John Cleese as a British Policeman who is sent to New York to solve a crime in a very comedic, almost Fawlty Towers style, way. But then Cleese dropped out because the financing came through to finally make his passion project - *A Fish Called Wanda*. When Davis was told Cleese was out he started looking for a British comedian as big as Cleese to fill the role. At that time, in the late 80s, there was no-one with the same crossover potential as John Cleese.

However, word came back to Davis for him to check out a younger comedian called Rik Mayall who had been making waves on the alternative comedy scene. Davis flew to London to meet Mayall and discuss the *Beverly Hills Cop* imitation he had written. The first thing Mayall told Davis was that he wasn't going to do his project. He liked the script but didn't like the idea that originally it was written for John Cleese. Mayall only wanted to do a project that was specifically written for him "They were great guys and understood my reservations about playing a role like that" he told *Fantazia* magazine. Davis had nothing at that time so bid Mayall a fond farewell.

Four months later, Livingston's article about an imaginary friend appeared in Reader's Digest and suddenly everything fell into place for Davis and Fingleton as they combined their imaginary friend project with Livingston's and wrote a treatment for Mayall under the title of *Drop Dead Fred*. Within three days of the treatment landing on Mayall's desk he had agreed to do it. He also requested to work closely with Davis and Fingleton on tailoring the script to his abilities. During pre-production Mayall would pace around the room suggesting lines and jokes, then Davis and Fingleton would work the story around them.

A problem arose when it came time to find financing for the film. Mayall was adamant that it should not be a British film, it should be an American film that had worldwide appeal. However, trying to secure finance from American movie studios for a film about an imaginary friend that was to star an unknown British comedian proved very tricky. Eventually the money came from Polygram Filmproduktion in the Netherlands via British production company Working Title Films, who managed to secure a budget of just under £7 million. Things moved swiftly from there forward.

To sell the film to American audiences the producers looked to cast an American woman in the role of Elizabeth Cronin. Big names such as Molly

Ringwald, Julia Roberts and Winona Ryder were mentioned. Yet it went to 80s teen star Phoebe Cates. Originally, Carrie Fisher had auditioned for the role of Elizabeth but it was felt she was too old (She was thirty-five at the time), instead she was offered the role of Elizabeth's friend Janie. The part of Charles, Elizabeth's boyfriend, had names such as Josh Brolin, Michael J. Fox and Keanu Reeves attached to it. The role ultimately went to *Animal House* actor Tim Matheson. Marsha Mason was cast as Elizabeth's mother Polly aka the mega-bitch: "I took the part because I loved the scene when Rik is looking up my skirt and says 'Cobwebs' [*laughs*]".

The budget was acquired in April 1990 and filming started at the beginning of August. As it was to be an American movie it needed to be filmed in an American city and Minneapolis was chosen because producer Paul Webster felt it had an all-round American look to it and not many movies were made there. Filming also stretched across to the smaller Twin City of St. Paul. Once exterior filming was finished it was on to Paisley Park Studios in Chanhassen, Minneapolis to shoot the remainder of the film. Originally a recording studio built by the pop star Prince, it also had a soundstage which was designed for tour rehearsals. However, when Prince was filming his *Sign O' The Times* movie in 1987 he used the soundstage for re-shoots. *Drop Dead Fred* was the first feature film shot at Paisley Park that did not feature the musician. Several sets were built at the studio including Drop Dead Fred Land that is bathed in neon lights and features skewered art work. Mayall joked that the set was actually the inside of Phoebe Cates's head: "She must have a problem. She'll be checking into the Betty Ford Clinic very soon." It was rumoured that Prince would wander the sets at night entertaining himself with all the toys and playsets on display.

When filming wrapped at the end of September, the production team moved in to the editing suite and put together a cut that could be shown to test audiences. When that time came audiences had one big problem with the film – the death of Drop Dead Fred. The end of the film saw Mayall's character die, but test audiences felt that it was too upsetting an ending, even though he is imaginary. Cast and crew scrambled to film a funnier, more upbeat ending that didn't involve Drop Dead Fred dying. Instead he simply moved on to another child who needed his help. This new ending was received very positively by test screen audiences.

If only those reactions transferred to the critics and mainstream movie goers when *Drop Dead Fred* was released in the US on 24th May 1991. Esteemed movie critic Leonard Maltin could only recommend *Drop Dead Fred* "for people who think nose-picking is funny." *The L.A. Times* said it was "an erratic stab at making madness sensible." Worse was to come when Gene Siskel named it his worst film of the year. *Drop Dead Fred* slunk out of U.S. theatres within four weeks, having made only $13 million. By the time the film was released in the U.K. on 11th October it had already been classified as a bomb, driving away any interested film-goers before it had even had a chance. It was labelled a financial and critical failure, and it was the end of the road for Mayall as a Hollywood star.

They say time heals all wounds. Nothing could be truer than in the case of *Drop Dead Fred*. Over the intervening years the film has gone from being a stinker to a cult classic and then onto infiltrating the mainstream comedy genre. *Drop Dead Fred* lives again! It is the slapstick antics that make an immediate impression when watching the film. While the more aggressive slapstick moments are few and far between – getting his head trapped in the fridge and being kicked in the balls – *Drop Dead Fred* still has energy to burn. Much like a wrestler "selling" a move to the crowd, Mayall over-articulates and over-plays his movements to make them larger than life. His over-the-top anarchic style is in full flow and he uses it to create a character that should be hated yet is almost instantly loved. This zany, madcap performance is nothing out of the ordinary for Mayall. In fact, it appears slightly toned down compared to his work on *The Young Ones* and *Bottom*.

While UK audiences had become accustomed to, and loved, Mayall's crazy style, it was American audiences who simply were not ready for Rik Fucking Mayall and found his performance so outlandish that most couldn't handle it. As such, *Drop Dead Fred* flopped badly in North America. It is always the boundary pushers that are initially vilified for trying to bring something new to the masses. Yet, when mainstream Hollywood finally caught up to what was happening in the alternate comedy world those that came through the Rik Mayall shaped hole were held up as flagbearers for the new style of comedy. Mayall's performance as Drop Dead Fred should be mentioned in the same sentence as Peter Sellers as Inspector Clouseau, Leslie Nielsen as Lt. Frank Drebin and Jim Carrey's performance in *The Mask*. Those actors created characters that are still, to this day, rated as some of the best comedic performances on film. Tragically, Mayall's dynamite and, at times, tender performance was only spoken about by those who grew up with the film. Thankfully, with *Drop Dead Fred* finding a new audience all these years later it means people of all ages and sexes are revaluating it and discovering a hilarious, if rowdy, fantasy comedy.

With this new-found love for *Drop Dead Fred* has come a discovery that the film has some very important things to say about mental health. Scholars, critics and fans now discuss how the film is a deep dive into the mental state of a woman who has been ditched by her husband, is constantly put-down by her over-bearing mother and her deep-seated longing for her father to come back. These are not topics you would expect to feature in a slapstick comedy. Yet they are possibly the most important parts of the film. The interpretation that Drop Dead Fred is Lizzie's repressed rebellious side acting out after all the emotional distress she has been put through is a profound one. Blaming everything on Drop Dead Fred is her get out clause. A way to fend off the anger, even as an adult, that she is receiving from her supposed loved ones.

When Lizzie's mother takes her to a psychiatrist in a bid to coax her out of her depression, we are shown how ill-perceived mental health issues can be from those who do not suffer from them. Essentially, her mother is saying: "Talk to this guy and get these pills down you and everything will be fine." Of course, it's not. Lizzie's problems are much more deep-rooted than that. She needs/wants to express herself but is afraid for fear of what her mother and/or husband will say to her. Lizzie is told to "Rip it up and start again" by Drop Dead Fred and, eventually, that is exactly what she does. She finally takes back control of her life. We see the protagonist come out of her shell, find herself and become comfortable with herself.

Carrie Fisher's Janie asks Lizzie to repeat: "I don't need a man to complete my life. I'm perfect the way I am." This links to one of the central messages in the film of not letting anyone rule your life, alive or pretend. This message is so significant and yet it is arguably only when watching the film in later life that you find yourself agreeing with the statement entirely.

Drop Dead Fred may have been literally living in the box for years, but it was Lizzie who was figuratively locked in that box, and it took her imaginary friend and huge mental strength to break free.

Carlos Davis (writer): Rik was nervous as hell in meeting me. I first met him in London. He wanted to know what John Cleese thought about him and I said: "In all sincerity he thinks the world of you." First thing he said to me was: "I'm not going to do your script [the *Beverly Hills Cop* imitation]. Think of something we can do together." I had flown all the way over just to hear those words [*laughs*]. About four months later I was having lunch with a friend of mine who was the editor of Readers Digest and had just written a non-fiction piece about her daughter when she was little having an imaginary friend called Drop Dead Fred. Liz said to me: "Sometimes I wish Drop Dead Fred would come back and cheer her up." At the same time Tony and I were working on a script that we couldn't get a handle on about a girl at school with an imaginary friend. We could never figure out how to make it work. I was walking home and it hit me – Rik Mayall as Drop Dead Fred. I wrote out something sent it to Aude [Powell – Mayall's agent] and she wrote back to say Rik is interested.

Anthony Fingleton (writer): Carlos, my writing partner, knew Rik through *The Young Ones*. I had never heard of him. We met with Aude Powell, his agent, and she said that Rik would love it and one thing lead to another and we sat down with him and it just started pouring out of him.

Davis: Tony & I wrote the initial draft, which was just the set up. Rik had read it and there were notes everywhere on his copy. At one point he said: "OK, the best friend. Tell me about her" and I explained that she was a lawyer and that she lived on a houseboat just because we hadn't seen that before, usually they live in an apartment. He said: "I get it, I get it" and he literally leaped up on a piano, clapped his hands so loud I swear it was a thunderclap and said "Right, we sink the houseboat!"

Fingleton: We sat, almost in awe of him bouncing around Aude Powell's office. Just ideas tumbling out of him. It was hard to keep up.

Davis: I would transcribe everything and then three days later give it to him and he would sit with his pencil, always a pencil, deep in conversation trying to figure out how exactly to make it work and get the beats right.

Fingleton: There was a woman named Sarah Radclyffe who was one of the partners at Working Title at that time. She knew him because he had done a couple of movies and said he would be perfect for *Drop Dead Fred*. That's how we got Ate [de Jong – the director].

Ate de Jong (director): I had gone to Hollywood and I always gave my videos to whomever was about. I was always networking. I gave Carlos Davis and Tony Fingleton a few of my films and I had completely forgotten about it. They called about seven or eight months later and asked if I wanted to do *Drop Dead Fred*. I had to fly back to London. Working Title were producing the film and they arranged everything. I had to meet with Rik at the office of his agent. He was very polite. He had seen a few of my films. There was an openness to my Dutch films that I think he liked.

Davis: Rik was the one who insisted we shoot it in the states. I thought for sure we would shoot it in England. Rik wanted it to be an American movie with him in it.

Fingleton: Rik was insistent that it be shot in America and be an American film. The fact he had an English accent was neither here nor there, and it is funny that not much was ever made of the fact that he had an English accent.

de Jong: We said if it has a non-L.A. look then that is better because people all over America would identify with it better.

Davis: Phoebe [Cates] had made *Fast Times At Ridgemont High* and *Gremlins*, so I called her and asked if she knew of Rik Mayall and she did. So, I sent her a script and I got a phone call saying that she would do it. That's how we got Phoebe.

de Jong: Marsha Mason was somebody who was not an easy person [to deal with] but I respected her very much. Everything she ever said was about quality and not about ego.

Fingleton: It was the manic craziness with Rik. Things like "Let's poo her out on the table" had not been heard in a non-porn movie [*laughs*]. The entire crew had never met anybody like him. The crew loved him and they loved to laugh with him. He was very sweet with the little girl who was playing the child, and she loved him. That was the way of him, he was a very sweet person.

Davis: Rik once told me that [Laurence] Olivier found his character through the nose. The nose was very important to Olivier in terms of finding the character. For Rik it was always the hair. Once he found the hair the rest of it would come both internally and externally. It was also very important what boots he was going to wear. He tried every possible thing and finally we were walking past a store for women's boots and he saw exactly what he wanted. So, he asked for the biggest pair, which didn't fit him, but he showed the costume designer and said: "I want these in red."

de Jong: We talked about border of what he could and what he couldn't do as a character, and the writers were very important in that also. Once we set those borderlines he said: "Well, now I can do anything because as long as I know the borders it is fine." He was extremely positive and always energetic.

Fingleton: Someone like Rik you just give him an idea or a suggestion and then you fasten your seatbelt and sit back because it is very difficult to describe the energy and the mind of Rik, how it could go from one thing to another in a nanosecond. It was quite extraordinary to watch.

de Jong: The one person who ad-libbed was Carrie Fisher. She added dialogue.

Davis: Kevin Kline wanted to be in the film as he was flying out every weekend [to see Phoebe] and we put him in something that didn't work. It just didn't work because he was in it.

de Jong: The executives at New Line wanted several bits cut out as they felt it went a bit too far. There were a few things that they cut which I thought were very funny. We did test screenings and people did like the ending. That ending was Rik had disappeared and Phoebe went to Mikey Bunce, who already had a child, who then said that she saw Drop Dead Fred but we never saw him. It was a cut away and that was it. People had a feeling that Fred had died and they didn't like it. So, we re-shot another ending which is now in the film. In that sense the test audience was right. It worked for the audience a lot better.

Davis: We went to Minneapolis with the world premiere and the governor declared it *Drop Dead Fred* day and it was an invited audience. It was huge, maybe two thousand people. Completely sold out. I think Paul Webster [producer] spoke first and then I spoke and then Rik got up. I had never seen him live up until that moment and for ten minutes he had them rolling in the aisles. The lights were so blinding so I couldn't look at the audience. I could only hear this wall of laughter. It was a unique experience.

de Jong: The film grossed well for a small independent film. It was the best independent film of the year [in North America]. In Britain it was not seen as an independent movie, it was seen as a Hollywood movie. Because of the press it wasn't seen as a special movie and that disappointed me a bit.

Fingleton: What was disappointing was that he [Mayall] didn't get wonderful reviews in England, and I don't know why. I think that scared him a bit. It was number one in Australia for eight weeks. It beat out Kevin Costner's Robin Hood, which was a big Hollywood movie. It ruled the box office in Australia.

Davis: My favourite review of the bad ones was the critic that said in the last sentence something like: "Watching this movie has made me lose the will to live" [*laughs*] We hadn't had one like that before.

Fingleton: It became a cult film because it was word of mouth on it. It was a revelation to me that it would have that kind of impact. I was once in California with a friend of mine and I was trying to explain to him that it was a cult film and he wasn't quite sure what that meant, he wasn't in the movie business, so I said that it was a movie that had another life. He still didn't quite understand. We had a nice waiter waiting on us and I called him over and said: "Have you ever heard of a movie called *Drop Dead Fred*?" and the guy said: "Are you Kidding? YES!" and then started to quote lines from the movie. My friend sat their open-mouthed and said: "Oh, I see what you mean."

Davis: We tried to make a sequel but Rik said: "I don't repeat myself." He claimed he didn't want to do it again but there came a point when the idea, not a remake or sequel, but *Drop Dead Fred* twenty years later. By then Universal owned the rights so they decided to take a stab at it first as a sequel. This was our attempt at number three in the sequel department and it never really happened. We got Mark Platt, the man who would go on to do *Wicked: The Musical* and quite a few other things, interested in *Drop Dead Fred*. He watched it and we told him how we would remake it. He wanted to find an American comedian and nothing ever happened until one day I got a phone call from Tim Bevan and he said: "Congratulations! You've got Russell Brand" and I said: "Who the hell is Russell Brand?" Then he dropped out and then he was interested and in the end we wrote a version of it and then they hired someone from *Saturday Night Live* to re-write it and then, as we say in the business, it blew up on the launching pad.

Fingleton: The funny thing was that when the remake was announced Carlos has Google Alerts set for whenever *Drop Dead Fred* is mentioned and he gets a ding on his computer. What happened was there was over half a million websites, blogs etc saying things like "Russell Brand is no Rik Mayall", "Leave the movie alone", "Best movie ever made" and my personal favourite was: "*Drop Dead Fred* is the worst film ever made. I've seen it three hundred times so I know what I'm talking about" [*laughs*].

de Jong: At some point the California Society of Psychiatrists used the film as therapy for people with attachment disorders. I am delighted because I lucked out. I tend not to take credit for the film because I think Rik is the film.

"GAS MAN! GAS MAN! GAS MAN!"

Mayall and Edmondson's working relationship had always been strong and they made each other laugh constantly. Thus, it only seemed right that they would eventually want to do their own show without Ben Elton or their *Young Ones* co-stars.

They had honed their crazy on-stage work over the years and saw an opening to tweak The Dangerous Brothers/Rik and Vyvyan characters into older versions of themselves who had left Bristol, moved to London and become losers at life. Mayall and Edmondson pitched this new show called *Bottom* to Paul Jackson who, by the late 1980s, had become an independent TV producer. The BBC had been desperate for more episodes of *The Young Ones* but the team had stood fast in their opinion that twelve episodes over two series was enough.

The BBC was so hungry for more *Young Ones*-esque material that even the failure of *Filthy, Rich & Catflap* didn't dissuade the BBC from giving Mayall and Edmondson's latest project the green light. Jackson took *Bottom* to Alan Yentob, head of BBC Two, who virtually commissioned it on the spot but with one caveat – the title had to be changed to something less rude. When Jackson relayed this message to Mayall and Edmondson they unequivocally insisted on keeping the title. They knew that if it ruffled feathers at the BBC, specifically Yentob's, then it was the perfect title for the show.

With a greenlight from the BBC it was all systems go and Mayall and Edmondson began to write their new series. Jackson and Alex Armitage had co-founded Noel Gay Television, an off-shoot of the Noel Gay Organisation which represented actors, producers and writers, as an independent television company with an office based in central London. Mayall and Edmondson felt they needed an actual office to write in so Jackson set them up with their own room at Noel Gay Television. They kept strict hours of 10am to 6pm and churned out pages upon pages of material for the show. Mayall offered a rare insight into their writing style when he was interviewed by Michael Aspel: "I think it was Mel Brooks who said 'in any writing relationship you get a pacer and a typer' and Ade is the typer and I'm the pacer. I'm sort of behind him a lot."

By 1989 Mayall and Edmondson were ready to film an episode of *Bottom* to show Yentob and the bigwigs at the BBC what their new anarchic sitcom was all about. Shot entirely on a BBC soundstage, except for the opening credits, which was shot on location in Hammersmith, the episode called *Contest* establishes Mayall and Edmondson's characters: Richard Richard and Eddie Hitler respectively, as two unemployed survivors struggling to make ends meet in London. Edmondson told *Time Out* magazine that *Bottom* is written from the perspective of life "after university and before regular income when there was no student hand-out, no student buddies and you were forced to walk miles to the butchers to save twenty pence or buy the supermarket brand of baked beans." Some might have seen it as an updated version of *The Young Ones* minus a couple of characters but Mayall was keen to squash that idea: "I don't think we are stepping back with this; *Bottom* is the first thing we've written together for some time, and I think it's the best thing we've done; it marks a new chapter in a relationship that will hopefully last as long as we live."

But before Mayall and Edmondson filmed the remaining five episodes of the first series they took on another challenge. They took to the stage in a revival of Samuel Beckett's play *Waiting for Godot*. A two-act play involving two characters who are waiting on the arrival of someone called Godot (who never shows). The discussions of Vladimir and Estragon (the central characters) are simple yet cover ground such as religion, philosophy, psychoanalytical, alongside many self-referential issues. Beckett's two characters were based on those from the French entertainment genre of vaudeville – a comedic situation without a moral. The play was, amongst other things, an early form of slapstick comedy, first performed in Paris on 5th January 1953. Two years later the English language version received its premiere. From that moment on it became what audiences of the British Royal National Theatre voted: "the most significant English language play of the 20th Century."

Mayall and Edmondson had already appeared in the play (Mayall aged eight and Edmondson during his University days). Their revival of the play premiered on 23rd September 1991 at the Queen's Theatre, London. The critics hammered it but the crowds loved it. Mayall and Edmondson enjoyed staging the play. Those months rehearsing and then eventually staging *Waiting for Godot* gave Mayall and Edmondson additional ammunition for their own creations. Richard Richard and Eddie Hitler were essentially Mayall and Edmondson's own take on Beckett's Vladimir and Estragon – incompetent and ineffective vagabonds. They were the same characters underneath it all, just Mayall and Edmondson's were strongly rooted in the modern societal structure: "It's about two guys at the bottom of the heap. But obviously we called it *Bottom* to make people think we were doing bottom jokes. I think *Bottom* is what could have happened to us if everything had gone wrong," Mayall told *Arena* magazine.

The first episode broadcast was not the pilot that had been shot in 1989, it was an episode called *Smells*. Airing on BBC Two on the 17th September 1991. The remaining five episodes that made up series one were broadcast on subsequent weeks (*Contest*, the original pilot, was broadcast as the third episode). The entire first series was produced and directed by Ed Bye, who had previously worked on *The Young Ones* and *Filthy, Rich & Catflap*. The short-lived jazz ensemble The Bum Notes provided the opening and closing pieces of music for the show. Their cover of B.B. King's Bb's Blues accompanied the opening and their version of Last Night by The Mar-Keys was used during the closing credits. The Bum Notes, who were secretly comprised of Adrian Edmondson, Charlie Higson, Rowland Rivron and Simon Brint, put a slightly funkier edge to both tracks. The show wasn't a hit out of the gate, more a steady grower that continued to attract an increasing number of viewers. It gained a cult following just off the back of the first series, much like *The Young Ones* did nine years previously. *Bottom* picked up Best New Comedy show at the 1992 Comedy Awards, beating out *Terry and Julian* and *2point4 Children*. Mayall and Edmondson were not there to accept the award so that was left to director/producer Bye.

Mayall and Edmondson were never ones to rest on their laurels, and within weeks of series one finishing on BBC Two they were back in their tiny office at Noel Gay Television writing a second series. A slight increase in budget meant they could afford to set a couple of episodes outside of the flat and/or with additional characters. Bye returned as director and told *Time Out* magazine: "*Bottom* is all about pointing out people's inadequacies... well, men's inadequacies. *Bottom* is a critique of 90s male mores. The metre for *Bottom* is a combination of Hancock and slapstick. No one is actually going to use Richie and Eddie as role models." The first episode of series two was called *Digger* and premiered on 1st October 1992. Four further episodes beamed into living rooms around the UK on a weekly basis. The sixth episode, entitled *'S Out,* had been written and shot but was pulled from broadcast before the scheduled transmission. The episode saw Richie and Eddie go camping on Wimbledon Common encountering all manner of foul things and humans. The episode was filmed and completed before the murder of Rachel Nickell on Wimbledon Common in the summer of 1992. The BBC and everyone associated with *Bottom* felt it was entirely inappropriate to show the episode in the UK at that time (the episode eventually aired on the BBC three years later in 1995).

The show continued to gain fans and it came as no shock to hear that when the BBC conducted a survey into who was watching *Bottom* the bulk of viewers were males between 15 and 30 years of age. "Boys, and adults with boys' minds" Bye jokingly told *Time Out.*

After series two Mayall and Edmondson took a break from *Bottom* on TV, instead they decided to take the show on a UK tour during the Spring of 1993. The fanbase had grown exponentially and the duo wanted to go ruder and cruder than the BBC would allow them to. The only place they could do that was on stage. "They are in for a very long episode of *Bottom.* It is a bigger show and slightly ruder," Edmondson suggested. With Mayall adding: "If they like what they saw on the tele then they'll come along and get more of the same." *Bottom: The Live Show*, with its claustrophobic Hammersmith flat stage set, was the TV show at its finest as the audience watched the duo struggle to even be in the same room together even though it was evident they couldn't live without each other. The show was performed across sixty dates at different venues around the country including Rhyl's New Pavilion, Lincoln Ritz and Leicester's De Montfort Hall. Every single night was sold out, with audiences lapping up Richie and

Eddie killing themselves on an electric lavatory (an Eddie Hitler version of the electric chair). Mayall eloquently told the *Daily Express* why they took *Bottom* on tour: "Our reward is to hear people laughing – that's why we keep doing it. What better way is there to spend your life?"

After the success of *Bottom: The Live Show*, Mayall and Edmondson locked themselves away again and began to write series three. Premiering on the 6th January 1995, *Bottom* series three was a slightly different venture. It had more sets, more locations and more actors. It also saw a change in producer and director. Ed Bye, who had been the producer/director on series one and two, was replaced with Bob Spiers, a veteran director of the comedy genre and had previously worked with Edmondson and Mayall on a couple of episodes of *The Comic Strip Presents...* Producer Jon Plowman was also brought in to oversee the new series. Plowman had previously been a producer on *Alias Smith and Jones*, *Shooting Stars* and *The Imaginatively Titled Punt & Dennis Show*. He had also been instrumental in creating the talk show *Wogan*. Series three of *Bottom* really came out swinging both in-front and behind the camera in terms of talent. It went out with a bang as well when, in the final episode, the "Hammersmith hardmen" are gunned down by the SAS after they attempt to blackmail the Prime Minister about a sex tape they have uncovered. "It's sordid and domestic," Mayall explained to the *Radio Times:* "We're pairing it down all the time so you get nearer the bone of the joke. It's a question of how much we can do in that kitchen and living room."

Bottom's only mis-step was the feature film *Guest House Paradiso*, mainly because it took the hapless couple out of the flat and transplanted them miles away from Hammersmith. The films saw them take proper jobs and interact with other human beings, something they very rarely did in the TV series. Changing the surnames didn't help either because then it gave the impression that it wasn't a Bottom film at all, just another one of Mayall and Edmondson's crazy partnerships. Later promotional materials for *Guest House Paradiso* used the tagline *The Bottom Movie* so fans understood that it was part of the TV show. The film flopped critically and commercially in the UK. But this mis-step mattered not to the legions of *Bottom* fans who poured into theatres around the country to watch Mayall and Edmondson beat the shit out of each other during the *Bottom Live* tours. Subsequent tours got wilder and cruder as they went on because they were not restricted to what they could and could not get away with on the TV show. "We dug our own grave with them [the live shows] really," Edmondson told Australia's *Triple J* radio station: "because in the first one we had this bit where we got a roadie to shout out 'Have a wank!' because it led to a sequence that was quite funny. On subsequent tours people come just to shout 'HAVE A WANK!' So, by the end of the last tour we were going into theatres with two thousand people shouting 'HAVE A WANK!'." The live tours took the *Bottom* franchise to the next level of anarchy, and Mayall and Edmondson revelled in it.

A fourth series of *Bottom* was pitched to the BBC. It was to be a spin-off from their third live show which saw Richie and Eddie marooned on the tropical and fictional Hooligan's Island. In August 2012 it was greenlit but by October it has been scrapped. Edmondson told *Radio Essex*: "There isn't a *Bottom* series four. There isn't anything. [Rik and I] started working on something and then we realised why we stopped working together. It wasn't working." Mayall offered another take on the scrapped series when he spoke to *Den of Geek*: "In simple terms, I phoned Ade and said 'Hey why don't we do *Bottom* but have it as older blokes?' It got called *Hooligan's Island* which I wasn't so keen on because we had used that title, I think it was just a working title at the time, but the BBC snapped it up. They said alright, write a couple of episodes and see if you get anything. Ade said we're not old enough and that we should do it in ten years. I said that in ten fucking years I won't be able to think, the two brain cells I have left will not work! There is a fucking thing called acting and something called make-up but he said 'No I don't think we're old enough!'" The BBC also confirmed that the show would not be going ahead. It had been nine years since Richie and Eddie last appeared on-stage and seventeen years since series three premiered. It appeared that Mayall and Edmondson had finally reached their bottom.

Most fans came to *Bottom* for the anarchic violence. It was Rik and Vyvyan meets The Dangerous Brothers dialled up to eleven. It was violent, hurtful and, at times, sadistic. Yet it was done it such a way that it never felt nasty or despicable. The show drew a clear defining line about which way it swung when portraying violence and it was very much towards the cartoon end of the sadism scale. Mayall, especially, was extremely knowledgeable when it came to slapstick violence (he loved Laurel and Hardy) and when he joined with Edmondson way back in their Manchester University days they began to study and re-enact chaotic violence first as 20th Century Coyote, then The Dangerous Brothers followed by *The Young Ones*. They could be accused of playing the same characters time and again, but *Bottom* was different. The violence was more profound, more anarchic and more extreme than any of their previous work. There was more blood too. It was, at times, like watching a horror movie as crimson stained the flat walls and floor. When Richie cut his finger off the blood gushed so much that it seemed never ending. When Richie fell off the step-ladder, his leg bent completely the wrong way. The time Richie got a dart in his head during their camping trip to Wimbledon Common wasn't pretty either. Eddie got his fair share of violent beatings as well – an umbrella rammed into his penis or being punched off the flat's roof - but he usually came out the other side as the victor of the duo's violent struggles. In reality neither of them won as they had to face up to the fact they were still stuck with each other and that the violence would continue into the next day and the day after that ad infinitum.

There was no stopping Richie and Eddie's violent tendencies and that is what viewers loved. At any moment violence could break out over the smallest of things and escalate quickly into a full-blown fight where they would roll around the flat using any and all objects available to them. A TV over the head was funny. A chair to the rib-cage was funny. A pencil rammed up the noise was funny. But nothing beat watching one of them get whacked with a frying pan. If the Acme Corporation created two real-life characters then they would be Richie and Eddie and they would use the same weapons as were used in *Bottom*, just toned down slightly for the kiddies. A kick in the balls was always funny to watch though. Yet it wasn't just the slapstick comedy that made *Bottom* so great. It was also the relentless comedic dialogue that kept the show barrelling along and the laugh-per-minute count very high. The show, and Mayall in particular, used the rule of three principle. A main staple of the comedy genre, the rule of three is a process by which the comedian says three quick jokes, in succession, about events or characters. Each punchline needs to be bigger than the last, eventually landing on a huge belly laugh for the audience. Mayall and Edmondson however didn't stick to the three punchlines if they knew they could take the rule further. They created their own Rule of Three. The perfect example of *Bottom*'s version of the Rule of Three is this exchange in the episode *Culture* that gets wilder and more elaborate the further the argument goes:

Richard: "Hey, that's it. What about pin the tail on the donkey?"

Eddie: "We haven't got a donkey"

Richard: "Well… pin the tail on the chicken"

Eddie: "We haven't got a tail"

Richard: "Oh… pin the sausage on the chicken?"

Eddie: "We haven't got a chicken"

Richard: "Pin the sausage on the fridge"

Eddie: "Or a pin"

Richard: "Sellotape a sausage to the fridge"

Eddie: "WE HAVEN'T GOT A SAUSAGE"

Richard: "PUT A BIT OF SELLOTAPE ON THE FRIDGE"

The rule of three was used sporadically in *The Young Ones* and *Filthy, Rich & Catflap* predominantly when Mayall and Edmondson's characters are interacting. It is in *Bottom* where they pushed this comedy rule to new limits and created their own style.

The *Bottom* rule of three involved starting the joke on a sensible yet funny object/idea and by the end of the dialogue ending up on an object/idea that bore little to no resemblance to what had initially been talked about. The rule of three only became more elaborate with Mayall and Edmondson at the helm. They took it to places that it had never gone before. Writers who have worked with Mayall constantly cite that he was always looking to go bigger and better with the final punchline, regardless of what was written in the script. He always felt there was a better laugh to be had with a sharper word or action, and he was always right.

The majority of comedians would never dare venture as far as Mayall and Edmondson did with their workings of the rule of three. But Mayall and Edmondson were never any ordinary comedians at any stage of their career. They were boundary pushers. They pushed the sitcom out of the safe habitat it had sunk into during the 1980s and 90s and created, in *Bottom*, a sitcom that upped the game for all future sitcom writers and actors. Mayall and Edmondson were never going to make a safe sitcom. Their forte was in anarchic comedy and on this score Bottom delivers. What other sitcom would offer the opportunity to almost die from laughing while watching two idiots bicker about watching Miss World?! Or trying to have it off with 'birds' while dousing themselves in pheromone sex spray?! Or constantly hitting each other with a frying pan because they don't have a TV?!

Yet *Bottom* wasn't all punches in the face and kicks to the groin. It spoke intelligently about real life issues including the Falklands War ("For what? A few farmers and a flock of penguins"), unemployment benefit ("He said I had too many savings." "How much have you got?" "Eleven pounds eighty. He said that should keeping me going for at least two months.") and loneliness ("That was a nice chat… shame I haven't got someone real to talk to"). Upon broadcast the show was never given credit for talking about real world problems, mainly because they were disguised behind slapstick humour. Underneath this, was a commentary on how tragic the world is for the working class especially two middle-aged men with no jobs and no prospects, they truly felt like they were at the bottom of the barrel.

Existentialism also featured prominently in the show. Richie would describe how lonely he was without "a bird" and, at times, how he felt great anxiety if he ever was to have sex and wouldn't be able to last the duration. This toxic masculinity made Richie struggled with made him the most complex of the two characters and one that psychiatrists would have had a field day with. But Eddie also suffered. Mainly his was despair at being lumbered with sad loser, Richie. Eddie never saw himself as a failure because he always had alcohol to numb the pain. It is pretty clear that Eddie is a functioning alcoholic. His first thought each morning is 'where and when can I get my first drink?' He stoops to hiding alcohol in the flat, but also forgets where he hid it, illustrating just how addicted he is. When the alcohol ran out he would drink bleach just to get his fix. The bottle was his best friend. Thus, both of them, in their own depressing way, struggle to find any meaning in the universe, in Hammersmith and even in their own flat. Bottom explored existentialism via a microcosm of human behaviour through the eyes of two sad losers living in Hammersmith.

If slapstick comedy, real-life issues and existentialism wasn't enough, Mayall and Edmondson also brought surrealism into the show. The episode *Hole* see's the two loveable dossers (tossers?) stranded on a Ferris wheel only to be saved by the hand of God. But, they realise, they don't believe in God so His hand vanishes and they plummet (to their death?). *Bottom* didn't care who it lampooned, the show operated in a very real and forthright manner. It shone a light on society rejecting two individuals because they have nothing of value to offer the wider world. Instead, they figuratively, and occasionally literally, boarded them into a flat together and offered nothing in the way of help. They were cast adrift by society and left to fend for themselves. No friends. No family. No hope.

Yet Richie and Eddie found hope and solace in each other. They knew they were stuck together until their dying breath so they tried to make the best of a bad situation. If that meant hitting each other with a frying pan then so be it. However, it also meant debating issues that affected their standing in society. It was brilliantly clever writing and it was something that 99% of other TV comedies have never even got close to.

It's Laurel and Hardy. It's Tom & Jerry. It's Steptoe & Son (Galton and Simpson's writing was wholly influential on Mayall and Edmondson's work). It's nihilistic comedy at it's very best. *Bottom* will, deservedly so, be forever seen as Mayall and Edmondson's finest collaborative work.

Roger Sloman (actor - Mr. Harrison): When they [Mayall and Edmondson] did *Bottom* they got a chance to really shine and do their own thing.

Christopher Ryan (actor - Dave Hedgehog): I was doing a play somewhere and they sent a script and said 'this is the character [Dave Hedgehog] and would you be interested?' I read it and thought 'This is very good, terrific in fact'.

Bob Warans (properties buyer): Paul Jackson called me up and said 'We are doing a show called *Bottom*' and I just laughed.

Lynda Wood (costume designer): They gave me scripts to read. All these weird characters came out of their brains.

Jon Plowman (producer - series 3): They wrote together and they arrived in the rehearsal room with something quite complete. With stunts and things, some of which had to be worked out and some of which they knew they could do. Rehearsing partly became about working out which bits would be pre-recorded and which bits would be live.

Warans: We used to go to the rehearsal rooms at North Acton. I'd go in for a meeting with them [Mayall and Edmondson] and they would go through various elements of the scripts. I would take notes and they would describe exactly what they wanted. They were very professional.

Wood: Rik wanted an old raincoat, like a flasher's mac. I found the shirts and the horrible ties and the trousers. It was his [Mayall's] idea for the horrendous pants. I found some Y-fronts but they were not that big or droopy. So, I took them to a dressmaker and had them made into that stretchy style. I always used to jokingly ask him if he wanted braces to hold them up [*laughs*]. There wasn't any worry about willy bulge because they were so big [*laughs*]. I think Ade came with his own suit but I got the raincoat and hat.

Plowman: My memory of it is how nervous Rik would get and he would say to me 'If you are going to give me notes then give them to Ade because I'll be in my dressing room throwing up.' He was one of those performers who was intensely nervous beforehand but once he was "on" the comic energy was entirely there and you were amazed that he had been anything less than up for it.

Warans: The crew would go in about ten o'clock in the evening on the Thursday to start putting the set up. We would be in by eight o'clock the next morning doing the fine dressing. They would do a technical run through in the afternoon and then at five o'clock they would go into make-up. The audience would arrive at six o'clock and then recording would start about seven/seven thirty.

Ryan: Steven O'Donnell I had never met before and he was a terrific actor. We had our own little double act in a way. We popped in for a couple of episodes each series.

Sloman: Having done *The Young Ones* and then to be asked to do *Bottom* was great. I wasn't a running character. I was only in two episodes. I loved working with them.

Carla Mendonça (actress - Jenny): I remember at the time being frustrated that I didn't have more lines but Cindy [Shelley], who played my friend, had more and she was in *Howard's Way*, which was a huge hit at the time, and I think the boys [Mayall and Edmondson] had a bit of a crush on her [*laughs*].

Michael Redfern (actor - Mr. Cooper): I remember there was one episode where I had to smash Rik's head on the counter [*laughs*]. I got to do a bit of violent action for once. It was a really good acting job.

Mark Lambert (actor – gas man): I didn't audition. They very kindly directly offered me that part. I read it and immediately thought it was funny.

Andy de la Tour (actor - Chief Inspector Grobbelaar): It was obvious [to me] how to play Chief Inspector Grobbelaar. I had to pitch it at a certain level, a certain high level energy & performance because that's what Rik and Ade were doing.

Rupert Bates (actor - Mr. Tent): I was very lucky to play the flasher. It is one of those bits where you just really enjoy doing it. I was sort of happy, at the time, to go naked but they said you can't go completely naked [*laughs*]. They had some fake rain and I had to come and thrust myself into the tent. It is beautifully directed. Their faces and screams when it happens [*laughs*].

Helen Lederer (actress - Lady Natasha Letitia Sarah Jane Wellesley Obstromsky Ponsonsky Smythe Smythe Smythe Smythe Oblomov Boblomov Dob, 3rd Viscomptress of Moldavia): I didn't quite believe it [her character's name]. But I knew it was funny, so not entirely surprised. I just laughed. They [Mayall and Edmondson] take an idea and play with it either to simplify it or exaggerate it – this was the latter.

Lambert: What I loved about them was I was able to suggest some ideas like sticking the fork in my balls. They immediately embraced that. They put polystyrene in my crotch so it wouldn't hurt.

Mendonça: My now husband [Clive Mantle] was in the same scene as me because he was at the bar with Harriet Thorpe. It is where we met for the first time. We went off and married different people and then came back and found each other. It is funny when we watch it 'Let's watch our first experience together' [*laughs*].

Ryan: We Spudgun and Hedgehog we normally visit the flat and sit there and eat and talk. There was the funny Christmas one with Gold, Frankincense and Grrr [*laughs*].

Lederer: I was trying very hard not to crash his [Mayall's] laughs. But it was also a very hysterical sort of atmosphere. The studio audience hung off their every word, facial expression and mistake. It felt safe but edgy.

Plowman: My other memory of it, apart from enjoying it, was doing my favourite episode which was the one on the big wheel because it was so bizarre to be doing it in-front of an audience when we were no more than four feet off the studio floor and yet had to imagine us being many feet over Hammersmith.

Warans: We had to design a Ferris wheel in the studio. So, we [Prop team] naughtily planned a little daytrip to Blackpool. We sat on the Ferris wheel for three hours while we drew it and took various pictures and then took ourselves off to Harry Ramsden's for a Fish & Chip lunch and then got on the train and came back [*laughs*].

Wood: I had to dress all the extras on [the show]. Who were pretty sad characters [*laughs*] I would line up the costumes and they [Mayall and Edmondson] would come in and say things like 'That's not grotesque enough' or 'that's not seedy enough.'

Warans: I just remember lots of things blowing up and people being hit over the head. It was a mad show [*laughs*]. We had to make quite a few frying pans because they would go hammer & tongue at each other. We would go through three frying pans an episode.

Lambert: The famous scene of me being beaten up with a frying pan [laughs] the reason it went on for so long was because Rik decided he was going to catch the soundman out. So the soundman was making the sound as he bangs me on the head with the frying pan. In rehearsal we did about four bangs. But if you watch [the episode] I think he does about twenty. He went on and on and on. But at the same time it got funnier and funnier and funnier. The studio audience went absolutely hysterical. It was fantastic.

Simon Pegg (actor – Mr. Nice): Working with Rik? It was amazing. He was incredibly sensitive.

Ryan: To me they [Mayall and Edmondson] were always very very relaxed. Mainly because they had this confidence.

Bates: Ade always seemed to be incredibly chilled and relaxed about everything. Rik was concerned that everything was going to be alright. He wanted it to be right and he got it right.

Lambert: They were forever having to retake shots because they were making each other laugh. Sometimes, in-between takes, Rik would be quite serious because he would have to be talking about the technical side of things. Then he would just switch on the Rik persona. The audience adored it.

Mendonça: The show was done in-front of an audience and when something went wrong Rik always looked a bit cross with himself. Ade was always joking with the audience. Rik was very technical and instinctive.

Pegg: What amazed me about working with Rik was that he still cared about the camera crew laughing at him, like it meant something to him after a take that people found him funny. That was a sweet, kind of vulnerability that I appreciated.

Plowman: Ade was always the more practical one. Rik would sometimes go off on flights of fantasy about how they might do something. Ade was the slightly pulling back force. It was how they bounced ideas between themselves.

Ryan: They [Mayall and Edmondson] would find fun in everything. Not in a nasty way. It was in a witty and clever way.

Lederer: Rik committed to everything he did.

Mendonça: I had no idea what a cult it would be. Years later when I did *My Parents Are Aliens* there were young kids who came up to me and said 'Oh my God! You were in *Bottom*.' I am very grateful to have been included in that.

de la Tour: I've had people come up to me and quote my lines who weren't even born at the time [the show aired]. It's marvellous. A guy said to me 'I wasn't allowed to watch it [Bottom] because I was too young. Then I watched it with my mates on DVD.' I think that's great.

Redfern: My son, who was at school during that time, never said anything about my work or what I did and then he came home one day and said 'Dad, I'm so pleased you're an actor.' I asked why he said that because he had never said it before and he replied 'You were in *Bottom* last night' and because of that his street cred had gone through the roof at school [*laughs*]. Even his teachers came up to him and said 'I saw your dad in *Bottom* last night' [*laughs*].

134

Sloman: In terms of fandom, *The Young Ones* and *Bottom* are up there with *Star Wars*. You get huge kudos for having been in *The Young Ones* and/or *Bottom*.

Mayall continued his voice work into 1992 when the BBC commissioned a series based on the works of Beatrix Potter. This animated anthology series followed the adventures of *Peter Rabbit and Friends*. It had a bizarre release schedule with three episodes broadcasted in 1992 followed by three more in 1993. Two more episodes appeared in 1994 and the final episode was shown in the summer of 1995. There were a total of nine episodes spread over three years.

The series used the voices of many other famous British actors including Hugh Laurie as Johnny Town-Mouse, Alan Bennett as Timmy Willie and June Whitfield as Josephine Rabbit. Mayall's appearance was saved until the penultimate episode *The Tale of Two Bad Mice and Johnny Town-Mouse*. He voiced Tom Thumb and on this rare occasion his voice work doesn't stand out. If you listen really close you can tell it is Mayall with his snively, weasely voice work, but it is a quieter, less energetic performance.

Mayall ventured into the studio with Mike Batt, singer-songwriter known for creating The Wombles pop act. It was while Batt was working on the musical Men Who March Away that he started to write a story about a slug called Ergo who wished he could play the piano and could marry a fairy. He becomes a General and goes to war against the Pigfrogs who only come out at Christmas to try and squash other creatures. Mayall recorded all of the narrator's dialogue for an intended eleven episode podcast. Sadly, they never got made due to a last-minute drop out of a famous singer who was due to record vocals. A movie adaptation has been teased for several years and a small teaser can be found online.

One of the stranger appearances from Mayall during this era is when he popped up Marks & Gran's (*The New Statesman* co-creators) new TV series as himself. The successful sitcom writing duo also called on him for a brief cameo (well, why wouldn't you?) in the romantic drama *Love Hurts* starring Adam Faith and Zoe Wannamaker as new couple Tessa and Frank who try to navigate the choppy waters of their relationship. Mayall appeared in series one episode five as himself (a rarity). Where he was seen playing on a bouncing castle before being hounded by the press for a statement. Upon which he talks about the charity he is supporting as a favour to his friend Tessa and then grabs her and throws her onto the bouncy castle for a quick snog. While it was a comedic appearance from Mayall there was a reserved nature to his performance. The opposite can be said about his brief appearance on The Full Wax, a sketch comedy show hosted by American comedian Ruby Wax and featuring an assortment of British and international comedy talent. Appearing in a segment called *Where Are They Now?*, Wax visits Mayall in an insane asylum where he has been locked up for going comedy crazy. It is full of the usual gung-ho attitude that Mayall brought to these brief cameos. Dressed in pyjamas that look very similar to the ones used in Bottom, he tries to convince Wax he isn't crazy only to end up singing "Bring Me Sunshine" while wrapped in a straitjacket.

Mayall and Ben Elton set out on a UK tour during the summer of 1992, seven years after their last one. The tour wasn't a grand affair as they stopped at smaller venues such as Wrexham Plas Madoc Leisure Centre, Gloucester Leisure Centre and the Brentwood Centre. Tickets cost a modest £10-12. This short stand-up tour signified the end of Mayall as a solo stage performer. Mayall and Edmondson were riding high with the success of Bottom, yet they were not too busy to return to their TV comedy roots in a new episode from *The Comic Strip Presents...* called *Red Nose of Courage*.

Edmondson took centre stage as Coco the clown who is unhappy and so decides to venture into politics under the name John Major. Yet, under the identity of Coco he falls in love with Labour leader Glynis Kinnock (played by Dawn French). Trying to run the country while hiding his alter ego and falling in love causes clown shoe-sized problems for Coco. The episode saw the original Comic Strip team return. Alexei Sayle played Coco's father. Robbie Coltrane banged the gavel as the Speaker of the House of Commons. Nigel Planer got to play a drunken home secretary and Jennifer Saunders appeared as Margaret Thatcher. Mayall got a slightly larger part as Shadow Home Secretary James Huntingdon. He played it sleazy as he tries, unsuccessfully, to woo Glynis Kinnock. It is a dialled down Alan B'Stard yet there is still some enjoyment to see Mayall get away with playing a lewd political character again. The episode had all the hallmarks of a good *Comic Strip Presents...* production as it lampooned politics while also having a twistedly funny storyline.

Mayall returned to the big screen in a new addition to a much-loved British film franchise: The *Carry On* series of films. The feature films released throughout the 1960s and 1970s were, at times, single-handedly propping up the British film industry. However, by the end of the 1970s times were changing and the saucy comedy of the *Carry On* films were proving less and less popular. 1978's *Carry On Emmanuelle* was the final release until someone had the bright idea of producing a new *Carry On* film to tie-in with the 500th anniversary of Christopher Columbus discovering America, and so *Carry On Columbus* was made. The majority of the original *Carry On* cast declined to appear (some had already died) so the producers looked to bring in fresh comedy faces and turned their attentions to the alternative comedy scene. *The Comic Strip Presents...* was the place to find new blood and as such roles were given to Peter Richardson, Alexei Sayle and Nigel Planer.

Mayall appeared as The Sultan of Turkey giving a performance that, while typical Mayall, somehow didn't allow him full use of his talents. Scrunching his face up and then snivelling at those who appeared before him was all too an easy performance for him. Though the film featured new wave comedians from the 1980s, some of whom had risen the ranks because of their hatred towards the British comedies of the 1960s and 70s, the script was still stuck in the past. The result was like watching oil and water trying to mix. *Carry On Columbus* was a flop when released in October 1992. It proved to be the nail in the coffin for the series.

One beloved British series that was still going strong was the children's story time show *Jackanory*. After the uproar that Mayall caused when he appeared on the show in 1986 it is no surprise to find he wasn't asked back for several years. He returned for a three-part telling of *The Fwog Prince The Twuth!* by Kaye Umansky at the end of 1992. Dressed in a sharp suit and a pair of white gloves Mayall proceeded to tell the story in a calm manner. That is until he voiced the Prince when he suddenly let rip with a large, brash and slobbering voice. He snorts and honks with rich aplomb. Sadly, this appearance on *Jackanory* has been almost forgotten yet it is a typically hilarious performance from Mayall.

Throughout 1993 Mayall spent much of his time promoting the latest video games from Nintendo. His adverts for *Street Fight II, Tetris 2, Nigel Mansell's World Championship* and *Mario All Stars* all featured variations of Mayall's wacky acting. Yet it was the advert for *Zelda: Links' Awakening* that was Mayall at his best – smooth, charming and playful with a slapstick ending. Mike Hayes, a former Nintendo UK marketing director, told *Nintendolife.com* what it was like to work with Mayall: "He often sat down with John [Lloyd – the director] and I when he didn't have to. He really contributed to some of the scripts. This brilliant comical stupidity came from within him and that to me is what made the ads great." Mayall was so well paid for the adverts that he nicknamed his house Nintendo Towers. "Because it was so last minute, we didn't have much chance to negotiate. So even by today's standards he did get paid a big chuck of change" recalled Hayes.

Mayall was hot property on the BBC thanks to *Bottom* and the return of *The New Statesman*. How could a rival channel poach him? Simple, give him his own showcase. *Rik Mayall Presents:* was commissioned by Granada television and aimed to be similar to London Weekend Television's 1971 *Six Dates with Barker*. It would showcase the comedian in very different guises. The TV movies would not follow on from each other; they would be their own self-contained pieces of work. The first of three *Rik Mayall Presents:* aired on 20th May 1993. *Micky Love* was a dark and tragic tale of an aging light entertainer who suddenly believes he is being pushed out of his highly-rated quiz show. Written by Peter Morgan (who would go on to great acclaim with his work on *The Queen, Frost/Nixon* and *The Crown*) it starred Jennifer Ehle, Alan Cumming, Peter Capaldi, Anne Reid and Damian Lewis, amongst others. The storyline was familiar to Mayall as it was the other side of the fence to the one he explored ten years prior when he was poking fun at light entertainers of the day.

Mayall's performance is captivating throughout. He flashes that false smile for the cameras masking the true horror that behind-the-scenes he is viewed as 'past it.' He flip flops from energetic to lethargic and depressed in the blink of an eye. His portrayal charts the tragic downward spiral of a once-brilliant entertainer now reduced to spouting the same catchphrases time again. While he may hate Cumming's young, flashy Deane on the surface, secretly he admires him, and is jealous of someone who is now as edgy as he was thirty years ago. There is more than a touch of Ben Elton to Deane as he freely pokes fun at the establishment who are providing his platform. Nearly everything about the Deane vs Love storyline could have been seen as ripped directly from the real antics of Mayall/Elton tearing down the light entertainers during the early 80s. There is also a line of argument that this show could be interpreted as an unofficial sequel to *Filthy, Rich & Catflap*. One in which Richie Rich finally became a light entertainer and lost his edge. Now he is hosting a middle-of-the-road daytime quiz show under the name *Micky Love*. And he secretly hates it.

The episode drew in nearly two million viewers and while it showcased Mayall operating in the comedy genre the viewer also witnessed him going to a more serious and psychologically dark place in his performance. The following week's movie *Briefest Encounter* saw Mayall revert to slapstick comedy in a two-hander opposite Amanda Donohoe. Newly acquainted Greg and Siobhan are ready for a night of sex at her flat. However, things don't quite go according to plan. This gruesome comedy of errors gave the viewers 90% chaotic Mayall and 10% romantic Mayall. Possibly for the first time ever on screen Mayall gives a heartfelt romantic performance early on in this episode. From the moment he turns and smiles it is clear that under all the gurning Mayall still had a face that oozed sex appeal and the episode builds on that. Only later does it flip to a crazy, blood-thirsty game of cat and mouse between Greg and Siobhan as they each become weary of the other's intentions. Mayall and Donohoe are a delight to watch as they perform their mesmerizing dance. There are very few who could keep up with Mayall's energy yet Donohoe more than holds her own throughout. Though it's not the stand out movie of the three, watchers are treated to seduction and sabotage in equal measure in *Briefest Encounter*

The third movie was called *Dancing Queen* and featured Mayall as a bridegroom stranded in Scarborough on his wedding day when he should be in Maidstone. He strikes up a friendship with Pandora, the stripper from his bachelor party, in the hope she can pay for him to get back in time for his wedding. Without any doubt, *Dancing Queen* is the best of the first series of *Rik Mayall Presents:* as it offers up an entertaining mix of comedy, drama and adventure. Serena Gordon, who played the bride-to-be Sophie, remembers what it was like filming it: "I had to wear a wedding dress and be the bride who was jilted at the altar. The dilemma that he was in of trying to get back to his wedding was really palpable. You felt your adrenaline running because you wanted him to get back. Even though he had Helena Bonham Carter in a pair of fishnet stockings. Which, of course, would be appealing for anybody [*laughs*]."

The film is shot with a warming red hue that even makes Scarborough in late winter look warm. Yet the true heat comes from the interplay between the wannabe upper-class Neil (Mayall) and the working-class Pandora/Julie (Helena Bonham Carter). There is still the cheeky glint of mischievousness in Mayall's eye, yet it is reigned in in favour of a character who, at first, is a horrible human being who then transforms into an understanding and caring man capable of at last seeing the bigger picture. Pandora is more complex. There are skeletons in her closet and ghosts in her past that she doesn't want to revisit. Her issues are deep-rooted, but she never shows them. Instead she is all about having fun and living in the moment. This is a philosophy that she instils in Neil, eventually.

A core theme that runs through the movie is that of opposites attract. Neil and Pandora come from very different walks of life and, at first, struggle to talk to each other due to their disdain for each other. However, as night turns to day in Scarborough they soon begin to realise they are more alike than they first thought. They find that middle ground between their class differences and bond via ice cream. There are a couple of other fascinating themes playing out in *Dancing Queen*. One is class difference. Neil is about to marry into an upper-class rich family and, having already endured the interference from the in-laws on his and Sophie's special day, knows he has to adapt. The story plays out almost as a battle of wills as he tries to preserve his middle-class status. Neil makes a point of saying to Sophie: "I thought I was marrying you, not your mother." He is under immense pressure to bow to his in-law's as they have power and money. But everything on show in the film depicts them as snotty, horrible upper-class twats. It is no wonder Neil is reluctantly pushing back against it all, even at the expense of possibly upsetting his future wife.

Another theme on display is the treatment of the working class by the upper class. As Pandora is a stripper, Neil's so-called mates feel they can talk down to her. They also offer her extra money for additional favours and are, in short, a repugnant group of men who thankfully get put in their place. Female empowerment is another theme in the movie as Pandora, who has been given a rough ride in life, doesn't let it affect her. Instead she makes the best of every situation and ensures she never falls for the wrong man again. She is a liberal woman who thinks nothing of taking off her clothes if it means getting richly paid. She isn't ashamed of her body but will likely punch any man who tries to grope her. Pandora is a well written, well-rounded feminist character.

A deep dive into *Dancing Queen* would almost inevitably unearth more themes and ideologies to explore. It is a movie that has a lot more going on under the surface than most give it credit for. Above all, it is charming, funny and sweet. *Dancing Queen* is a heart-warming movie about the kindness of strangers, and it is one of Mayall's finest ever straight performances. "*Dancing Queen* was just the most beautiful story" comments Gordon "Nick Vivian, who wrote it, wrote such a touching story. We had fun in that. Nick Hamm, who directed *Dancing Queen*, he was a lot of fun. It was a really lovely company. I think Dorothy Tutin played my mother and I remember she was wonderful. I think we were all brilliantly cast."

The first series of *Rik Mayall Presents* garnered Mayall a British Comedy Award for TV Comedy Actor. While ITV were showing a different side to Mayall, he was off touring the country with his *Bottom* co-star Adrian Edmondson as they took the BBC show around the UK for a successful tour. *Bottom Live – The Stage Show* rolled around the country for ten weeks during 1993 playing to packed out theatres. The show was recorded at the Mayflower Theatre in Southampton for a later VHS release.

So the story goes: British TV station Channel 4 commissioned a series of contemporary Operas. One of those operas commissioned was *Horse Opera*, a twisted take on the classic Spaghetti Westerns. Originally it was a play called *Cowboys* by Anne Caulfield. It was brought to the attention of Stewart Copeland, the drummer in the pop band The Police, by his long-time friend Bob Baldwin, a British film and TV director. Copeland says "I didn't really like the text that much, not because it was badly written or anything, but just because I didn't go for its basic premise, which is that the United States is 100% evil and that 250 million people should pack their bags and re-emigrate back to Europe and give back the lands to the Indians." Copeland hired writer and Opera director Jonathan Moore to adapt the work into a more contemporary piece. Copeland stayed on the project to produce the score.

Horse Opera screened on Channel 4 on 13th February 1994 and told the story of George, a tax clerk by day and Chairman of the Nottingham Cowboy Society by night, whose mind wanders to the American West and his mythical journey there. Mayall plays legendary deputy sheriff/town marshal Wyatt Earp who talks his singing parts rather than singing in operatic style like the rest of the cast. It is a woefully bad stint from Mayall but he was never a singer and thus the casting here seems misguided. It's not just the singing that's an issue however, he also appears to struggle with deciding how to play Earp. Is he a comedic version of the classic legend or a completely new incarnation that bears little resemblance? Very little of the humour from Mayall lands well, his delivery struggles to hit the comedy high notes he was known for and you can see he is trying but *Horse Opera* was not the place for the unique Rik Mayall brand of madcap zaniness.

Horse Opera is madcap and zany for all the wrong reasons. Bar Mayall, the cast is filled with those who can actually hit a note, but in no other opera or entertainment output will you ever see a baritone singer enunciate the line "Do you have the correct permit for that?" to an undertaker with a dead body. Sadly the zaniness comes across as unequivocally bizarre and downright WTF. Even Mayall's exit is surreal as he sits atop a giant sofa that resembles a hamburger which itself is positioned on top of a Cadillac car bedecked in the colours of the American flag. It is no surprise to learn that the contemporary operas didn't get recommissioned by Channel 4.

Mayall returned to voice work for a story about a young social outcast who defeats not just the school bully but also a mysterious beast. Author Philip Ridley had won several awards for his children's novel *Krindlekrax,* which featured weird and wonderful characters, and who better to voice it all than someone who can easily conjure up multiple voices on a whim? The audiobook featuring Mayall's voice work was subsequently released to all online stores. There was also a brief voice appearance as Young William Tell in the British children's animated TV series *Oscar's Orchestra*, a BBC production about a talking piano called Oscar who rebels against an evil dictator who has banned music around the world. Dudley Moore, one of Mayall's comedic heroes, voiced Oscar.

The beginning of 1995 saw *Rik Mayall Presents:* return for a second series on ITV. Three more TV movies showcased Mayall's ability to jump between genres and let him explore alternative methods of delivery than the usual slapstick violence. *The Big One* aired on 29th January. Mayall played Lewis Fox, an estate agent who steals the identity of a dead gangster unaware that there is a bounty on his head. It was a gentle start for the new series that had Mayall lightly playing Fox as a sort of down-on-his-luck guy who has the gift of the gab but always goes one step too far. Writer Piers Ashworth recalls how he became involved: "I think that Andy Harris, who was head of comedy at Granada Television, said 'we've got this thing that's not really working for us can you come up with an idea?' I was just working on films. I had never done anything on television. I said I would think about it and then kind of wrote the first page which was the opening where he [Lewis Fox] turns to camera and says: 'I'm a liar. True. I swear.' I sent him this thing not really expecting anything. He called me and said he loved it. I wrote the episode and then they said that Rik loved it and they were going to make it." Supported by a cast including Saffron Burrows, Phyllis Logan, Phil Daniels and Edward Tudor-Pole, the episode has its highs and lows in terms of entertainment. It is a dramedy that just about manages to pull off both the comedy and the drama, mainly thanks to Mayall's fourth-wall breaking performance. "It was an interesting configuration of characters" Ashworth says "Rik was fantastic in it. It was a fantastic thing for Rik as it showed that he could do all this different stuff."

The following week's movie was woefully unremarkable. *Dirty Old Town* saw Mayall playing a homeless man on the streets of London who, through an accidental mix-up, is believed to be a future hit screenwriter by a production company. Mayall barely says a word throughout the episode as he haphazardly stumbles up the ladder of success. It is an uneventful role and performance from Mayall and one that possibly read well on paper but doesn't transfer onto the screen. Additional support comes from Helen McCrory, Francis Barber and Michael Kitchen, but even their parts are little more than film biz people playing at being big time. The central message of the film – that you never know what might be around the corner – gets lost in a movie that is lifeless and lacks real emotion.

12th February saw the final *Rik Mayall Presents:* movie air on ITV. *Clair De Lune* is the story of a cab driver whose late-night pick-up turns out to be a mysterious femme fatale. *Clair De Lune* offered something that audiences hadn't seen from Mayall for a long time – an everyman performance. His cabbie, Toby, is a down-on-his-luck, run ragged single parent who will stop at nothing to ensure his daughter has an enjoyable birthday. There is no goofing off or zany face-pulling. Instead the portrayal is straight and heartfelt (something he should have done more of). This is a man already under pressure to deliver a great birthday for his daughter who then has to contend with an attractive brunette who has problems that soon become Toby's as well.

There is some delightful interplay between Mayall and Serena Scott Thomas (who plays femme fatale, Annie) as they are both unsure what to do next but have to be seen to be in command. The romance angle, while obvious it is coming, is never forced and becomes a delightfully heartfelt subplot. The single parent storyline shows the very real struggle for anyone who is raising a child on their own. Toby works as a cabbie while studying for his law degree (to get a better job) all the while ensuring that his daughter never goes without or even appears to be less of a child because she only has one parent. *Clair De Lune* is the best episode in the second series of *Rik Mayall Presents:* It is a sensitive and touching performance from Mayall in a movie that does everything to ensure this comedy-cum-thriller ends on a heart-warming note.

Mayall continued to appear on the BBC throughout 1995. In February he appeared in the kid's TV show *Wham! Bam! Strawberry Jam!* as a storyteller reading *The Highwayman* by Alfred Noyes. Dressed in the clothes of a highwayman on a dark set with only a small light and a flickering candle, it was one of Mayall's most lifeless performances ever. It lacks his usual storytelling energy. Instead it looks and sounds like he is struggling with the dialogue. Almost tripping over some of the rhymes. It is a world away from his magnificent *Jackanory* storytelling.

Following this less than successful screen outing, Mayall returned to tread the boards in London's West End. He had enjoyed his time working on Simon Gray's *The Common Pursuit* during 1988. So, when Gray announced a new play called *Cell Mates* about two convicts who break out of prison and escape to Moscow, Mayall leapt at the chance to appear in the play alongside Stephen Fry (a fellow *Blackadder* cast member). The play had warm-up shows in Guildford, Watford and Richmond before opening in London's West End mid-February (1995). But only three days into the run Fry left the show and disappeared from public view. It was later revealed that Fry was suffering from bipolar disorder. Gray called his actions "cowardly." Mayall kept quiet in public but behind the scenes he was distraught. Every night after the curtain came down he was in floods of tears because he was struggling to cope with the pressure. The play closed five weeks after it opened. Gray wrote a book called *Fat Chance* about the infamous production and dedicated it: "For Rik". That was a tough few weeks for Mayall personally and professionally, so a return to voice work was much-welcomed.

Author Simon Brett published *How To Be A Little Sod* in 1991. Told in diary form from the view of a baby who brings havoc and chaos to his parents' lives during the first year of his life. Its success quickly caught the attention of the BBC, who suggested turning it into ten minute, ten-part TV series in the same vein as the hit Hollywood film *Look Who's Talking*. The show was part-animation, part-live action with Mayall voicing the Little Sod in his own unique style. There are brief glimmers of the anarchic Mayall voice that accompanies the screaming Little Sod yet it's more the sarcastic attitude of the baby that makes him an instantly hilarious character. The flip reverse of the whole parent/baby teachings is made even funnier by Mayall's voice work with deeply satirical lines such as "The trouble is they are not very bright. And at first they may even have some wild notions that they control you. Even that it's still possible for them to have a life of their own after you are born – hahahahahaha." This is Mayall's Peter Pan moment (in animated form) and he does not disappoint. Mayall could roll this kind of larger-than-life voice work off his tongue without a second thought. The show aired once a week on Tuesday evenings on BBC One and it was a ratings success. No second series was commissioned however even though Brett had written further books.

Mayall continued to poke fun at the British government as he appeared in a one-off series called *Look At The State We Are In* on BBC Two. Mayall and his comedy partner Adrian Edmondson took a comedy swipe at citizen's rights in the first episode called *The Organisation*. The episode focusses on the head of a British mafia organisation and his underling as they try to go legit. That is until Mayall and Edmondson burst into the room with all the gusto of Richie and Eddie wearing sharp suits and even sharper haircuts. Without a laughter track this episode comes off more like an informational video about the perils of dodging taxes in Britain and at only ten minutes in length it feels twice as long. It has none of the energy and outrageous humour that Mayall and Edmondson would usually bring to something like this.

Strangely, for a man with considerable voice talents, Mayall's only flirtation with a well-known comic-book-turned-animated-movie franchise was his brief appearance in *Asterix In America* voicing Cacofonix, a singer/bard, for the English language dub released in 1995. Not one of the better Asterix stories or animated movies and Mayall's all-too-brief vocal appearance doesn't sit right with the character. Cacofonix was created by René Goscinny and Albert Uderzo as the comic relief in the Asterix books. He is a character who flits in and out of the storyline so when Mayall gave his vocal talents to this secondary character it was funny and entertaining but there was nowhere near enough of him to leave a lasting impression. Also, if there is any character who Mayall should have been voicing in the Asterix series then it should have been Getafix the village's slightly deranged yet very wise druid. A missed opportunity for the English language release.

Feature films in the cinema had proven to be a bad recipe for Mayall, but what about a direct-to-video film? Surely that could work? Possibly not with the odd choice of fronting a film called *Out Of My Head*. By the mid-90s the UK was in the midst of an explosion of dance music culture. This was born out of the illegal raves that operated towards the tail end of the 1980s and then went legal in the clubs and music festivals. With the rave culture explosion there was also a boom in youngsters taking illegal drugs. The highs might have been great while immersed in music under neon lights, but the lows were very low. None more so than when teenager Leah Betts took one ecstasy pill and hours later fell into a coma and died. Drug culture was sweeping the nation at an alarming rate. With that in mind, Initialand the production company behind *Channel 4 Goes To Glastonbury* decided to film a sixty-minute video that was to be sold in stores about the perils of drug taking.

Out Of My Head received a British Board of Film Classification of 18. It was firmly aimed at 18-25-year-olds and it featured Mayall in three different roles: Ricky - a teenage drug user, Tobi – an older gentleman who has experienced all the drugs and A Doctor – who speaks about what happens to the body when drugs have been taken. The video offers insight into each recreational drug and the perils that come with it. It also featured talking heads from real people who had had prolonged experiences of using drugs. Mayall's triple performance is hit and miss. His doctor is a safe, middle-of-the-road figure, mainly because he has to talk about the science and biology of the body with relation to drugs so it needed to be straight down the line, informative and understandable. Whereas his performance as Tobi, a slightly older user who has been there and done that, comes across as annoying and pretty pointless as he washes dishes and speaks in a sneering upper-class manner about how his experiences were so much better than the ones now. Thankfully, his performance as Ricki – a teenager ready for a good time - is over-the-top in a way that only Mayall could make entertaining and informative. He jumps and jives around the screen like his old character Richie from *The Young Ones*. This is the stand-out performance on the video. And one to savour.

Out Of My Head was meant to be a video discouraging drug use, yet it is difficult not to imagine it being played on a loop on a huge screen in-front of a packed nightclub dancefloor. It has all the hallmarks of a rave music video with its jump cuts, flashing imagery and iconic 90s dance tunes. It is difficult to know whether it would encourage or discourage drug use for 18-25 year olds. One thing is for sure, Mayall is clearly having an absolute blast.

He had almost as much fun with that as he did with what was to become one of his crowning achievements. Kenneth Grahame's novel *The Wind in the Willows* has become a classic in children's literature. Its first adaptation for television was in 1946 when it was transmitted live on the BBC. The first animated movie was produced by Walt Disney Productions in 1949. However, arguably, the most famous television or film adaptation came in 1995 from TVC. This version was bookended with live action segments starring Vanessa Redgrave (she also narrates the film). Yet it was the main animated section of the film that viewers young and old alike would come to adore. Beautifully rendered, almost like a moving painting, the film boasts genuine British acting royalty including Michael Palin (Rat), Michael Gambon (Badger) and Alan Bennett (Mole). However, it's Mayall who stole the show (yet again) and will forever be the first name associated with this film.

His version of Toad was a heady mix of Rick from *The Young Ones*, Alan B'Stard from *The New Statesman* and Richard Richard from *Bottom* but without the naughty words and double entendres. Toad is a blusteringly upper-class character who may, initially come across as annoying, but soon becomes the most entertaining character. Mayall loved voicing the frog: "Toad is an enormous git," he told *The Daily Mirror*. "He's posh, selfish, a windbag but has this huge lust for life. I like him very, very much." It was a performance that jumped off the screen. You could feel the energy emanating in both the character and the voice artist. Not only did Mayall give Toad a slight splutter, ala Donald Duck, he also got to do a lot of noises including pretending to be a motor car. His rasping brrrr's gave

Toad a larger than life persona that endeared viewers to the character even more. The animated film was broadcast on Christmas Day 1995 on ITV. "Most of the stuff I do on TV is too rude or violent to let children see," Mayall commented "But *Wind in the Willows* is perfect." The film was a hit with audiences on Christmas Day. Over time it has become known as one of the finest adaptations of Kenneth Grahame's novel and Mayall's work is now seen as the definitive performance of Toad.

One of Mayall's lesser-known voice works was released at the same time. Hans Christian Anderson's *The Snow Queen* had been turned into an animated movie by British director Martin Gates and featured a predominately well-known British cast including Dame Helen Mirren, Hugh Laurie and David Jason. There was also room to squeeze in Mayall as a rat called The Robber King. His delivery is snivelingly sinister and is most notable for the scene where Mayall sings. The song "I'm Down and Dirty" is a little ditty about how despicably evil the character is and how he will happily rob from the rich and give to himself. Mayall tries his best to sing but it sounds far too much like he is reading the lines rather than focusing on the tune. But to be fair, the song is pretty awful. None of it rhymes or even links together, which is normally a main staple of a song featuring in a kid's animated movie. This is one of the few times where Mayall's voice doesn't fit the part. The film itself is a slightly more adult-orientated version of the classic fairy-tale with much more hard-lined animation and a darker than usual tone to the story.

Mayall went for a hattrick of Christmas appearances in 1995 as, on Christmas Eve, he read the classic English fairy tale *Jack and The Beanstalk* for children's BBC show *Jackanory*. Dressed in high waisted trousers held up by suspenders, a stripy jumper and outlandish hair, Mayall gleefully rips through the rhyming story while over-indulging in all the actions as well. Half way through the story Mayall undergoes a costume change into a bright pink ball gown with feather boa sleeves, a sparkly necklace and a long curly blond wig. He hams it up wonderfully and in one moment he makes a point of slowly emphasizing the giant licking his gold. A further costume change towards the end of the episode sees Mayall don a long black cowl with a twisted hat and a crooked nose. The entire episode plays out as if Richard Richard was in charge of reading a bedtime story yet had to dial back the double entrée slightly. It is Mayall at his energetic best.

Another *Bottom Live* tour started at the end of 1995, imaginatively titled: *The Big Number Two Tour*, it ran into 1996 and sold over 500,000 tickets. The show was filmed at Oxford's New Theatre for home entertainment release later in the year. 1995 saw Mayall appear in nearly every entertainment medium possible, it really was another great year for the alternative comedian who had infiltrated the mainstream. The year was capped off personally with he and Barbara welcoming their third child, Bonnie, into the world.

After the commercial and critical success of the BBC's *The Wind in the Willows*, it only stood to reason that they would want to commission a sequel. However, this time they chose to adapt William Horwood's book *The Willows in Winter*, an unofficial sequel to Kenneth Grahame's classic novel. The format follows the same as the previous film as it was bookended by live action segments featuring Vanessa Redgrave. It was the animated movie itself however that continued to captivate viewers. Alan Bennett, Michael Palin and Michael Gambon all reprised their voice roles as Mole, Rat and Badger respectively. After receiving widespread acclaim in the first film it was only logical to bring back Mayall to voice Toad and this time Toad would feature more heavily as he is asked by Badger to help him and Rat find Mole, who has gone missing. In the sequel, Toad is dialled up tenfold with Mayall going for broke. Toad is twice as bad, twice as pig-headed and twice as obnoxious yet Mayall still makes him hilarious and loveable. If hearing Mayall pretend to be a car wasn't enough in the first film then this time we get to hear him pretend to be a propeller-driven plane. With Toad now being a central character, he also gets his own story arch about redemption. It is only when Toad escapes being sentenced for reckless flying and is saved from his burning house that he realises what friends are for. Mayall's work in *The Willows in Winter* won him a Primetime Emmy Award (The Television equivalent of an Oscar) for Outstanding Achievement in Voice-Over Performance. Following on from this success in 1996 Mayall had his voice featured in a computer game. *Bud Tucker In Double Trouble* was a PC game developed by Merit Studios. It was an adventure game that saw Bud Tucker, a pizza boy and lab assistant, try to uncover clues to find a cloning device that had been stolen by the evil Dick Tate, voiced by Mayall. Tom Sharpe's dark comedy *Ancestral Vices* got the Mayall narration treatment. A story about a Professor who is hired to write a damning report on an upper-class family. Soon he discovers the family and the town they live in are not quite what he expected. Hilariously evil throughout, it is another example of Mayall finding his multitude of voices and using them to the best of his ability.

As part of MENCAP's Blue Sky Appeal, an anthology book of travellers' tales called *Guillible's Travails* was published. It featured writings from such talent as Jeffrey Archer, P.D. James, Ben Elton, Melvyn Bragg and many more. Mayall contributed a short story called *The Wesleyan Method* about an English lady who wants to rent a small furnished house in Germany. She writes a letter to ask if there is a toilet attached to the house. Unfortunately the German schoolmaster doesn't understand English very well and believes she is enquiring about the Wesleyan Church. His reply explains the church is 7 miles away and to get there early as it can get quite busy but there are lots of seats available as well as standing room. It is a brief yet entertaining scatological joke.

Bottom Live 3: Hooligan's Island proved to be another triumphant tour for Mayall and Edmondson. This time the premise involved the duo being stuck on a desert island with an unexploded bomb. The tour ran from January through to March 1997 and was recorded at the Hippodrome in Bristol for a later release on VHS.

A couple of years prior the British film industry had received a shot in the arm when, in 1994, *Four Weddings And A Funeral* became a global smash. UK producers scrambled like mad to find the next big transatlantic hit that would make a megastar of a British actor or two (a la Hugh Grant). The fruits of the producers' labours started to bear fruit from 1997 onwards with huge hits such as *The Full Monty* and *Bean*. A year later *Shakespeare in Love*, *Sliding Doors* and *Lock, Stock and Two Smoking Barrels* hit cinemas and made a huge impact. In the same year *Little Voice*, a musical, made a star out of lead actress Jane Horrocks. But not twelve months previous she was acting opposite Mayall and American actor Danny Aiello in the British comedy *Bring Me The Head of Mavis Davis*. The title was a pun on the classic Sam Peckinpah film *Bring Me The Head of Alfredo Garcia*. But that is where the similarities ended as Mavis Davis tells the story of record company owner Marty Starr (Mayall) who discovers that his most famous act Marla Dorland, aka Mavis Davis, is worth more to him dead than alive. Starr also has to contend with promoting the hideous music of mobster Rathbone's (Aiello) son. What could be seen as an expose of some of the shadier dealings within the music industry is instead a laugh-free comedy that offers a weak assassination plot and equally poor characters.

Horrocks' Dorland screeches and screams her way through the film and Aiello is playing a role that he has done a million times before - a cliched New York mafia boss. Even Mayall can't save the film as he has very few moments to act out with his chaotic, anarchic temperament. Mayall told *The Express* newspaper why he was attracted to the role: "I think the characters I play best are the ones that are alien to me, or have characteristics I possess but suppress because I'm trying to be decent." But Mavis Davis is a film about a shady and slimy record producer. Starr could have been portrayed as one step removed from Richard Richard and that would have created a much better character. Reigned in significantly throughout it showed that Mayall, for all the love he received as a comedic actor, simply couldn't go straight, at least not in this movie. To add insult to the film vastly underperforming at the box office (It took just £46,000 in its opening weekend) Mayall's surname was spelt incorrectly (as Mayal on the VHS and DVD front covers).

Fortunately, in the same year Mayall appeared opposite Robert Lindsay and Imelda Staunton in the British comedy *Remember Me?* A quirky film that shows what can happen to a very normal and loving family when an unexpected old flame arrives at their door to cause trouble. Mayall played Ian, the unemployed and depressed husband of Staunton's Lorna: "I got a feeling inside myself that I wanted to be Ian for a while; there was a piece of me that connected with him. You've got to laugh at someone as selfish and self-obsessed as Ian" Mayall commented to *The Telegraph*. The put-upon performance from Mayall is distinctly different to his comedic performances yet he proves again in *Remember Me?* that he can make a straight part work. With little dialogue and a performance reliant on body movements and facial changes Mayall's stint in this project is delightfully serene with brief touches of farcicalness. This comedy character piece is one of Mayall's most underrated performances. Sadly, this entertaining British comedy of errors has disappeared from view. It is never shown on TV and is currently unavailable on DVD. However, the entire film is available to view on YouTube, so all is not lost.

Mayall got to narrate two of Joseph Connolly's books. Firstly, *Poor Souls*, a story about two couples who, in one week, discover more about themselves than ever before. Mayall is at his breathless and perverse (in a good way) best as pounds his way through the tragi-comedy story. Secondly, he gets to grips with another dark comedy called *This Is It* about Eric, a man who leads two different lives suddenly finds himself struggling to keep them separate when he is knocked down by a bus one morning. This time Mayall narrates in such a way that you feel every bump, bruise and problem that Eric is dealing with. Around the same time, Mayall narrated the audiobook for Terrance Dicks' *Horror: True Stories*. A collection of thirty fiendishly scary stories, and it is easy to see why Mayall took on the project as it meant he could go full-on with his wide selection of voices to ensure listeners had sleepless nights.

Another year, another Christmas time with Mayall on more than one major TV channel. Firstly, with an appearance on *The Bill*, ITV's long running police procedural series. Mayall played a villain called Patrick Massie who is a compulsive gambler, selfish and a generally unpleasant person that gets caught up in a case of a boy falling off a roof. Mayall was a fan of *The Bill*: "I love the show and watch it whenever I can." He also enjoyed playing a serious character for a change: "I've spent month writing a comedy screenplay with my pal Ade Edmondson. So I was keen to get back into a proper acting role. When *The Bill* script landed on my doormat it was perfect." This character is a big change of pace for Mayall. It is a very serious and quite a gritty performance. One that he seems to deliver with great ease. It is a shame he was never offered more dramatic roles as, if this performance was anything to go by, he would have been able to handle them. He slows his speech down and is quite solemn. However, towards the end of the second episode Massie is locked in a cell. This gives Mayall just a slight moment to dispense a little sarcasm at one of the police officers, followed by a devilish smile. Of the three episodes relating to the main storyline Mayall appeared in two. They were broadcast on the 16th and 18th December.

His second Christmas TV appearance was on Boxing Day in ITV's glossy adaptation of Oscar Wilde's *The Canterville Ghost*. Playing Reverend Dampier, Mayall doesn't appear until well over an hour into the film, riding into the scene on a stallion. As he strides into the house he bombastically declares: "I've come to fight the unspeakable evil in this house." It is a performance that conjures up images of Lord Flashheart from *Blackadder*. Never has a clergy man led with his groin into a room, that is until Mayall played one here. It is a spellbinding performance and one that saves the entire film from being a bit of a dud adaptation. The majority of the film lacks Wilde's original humour, that is until Lord Flashheart… oops sorry… Reverend Augustus Dampier arrives to banish the ghost via an exorcism in a manner that looks more like he is having multiple orgasms. It is classic scene-stealing move from Mayall. The energy, wit, wisdom and swagger that Mayall possessed however was very nearly wiped out altogether four months later.

CRAP THURSDAY

The county of Devon in the southwest of England is known for its picturesque beauty. It boasts stunning beaches, quaint towns and vast national parks. It is a world away from the hustle and bustle of city life. The Mayalls purchased a sprawling farm in a small village within the county where they could retreat to and spend quality family time together. It was on that farm that a miracle occurred. A man survived death and lived to tell the tale.

Rain had just started falling late into the afternoon of 9th April 1998 in Devon. There was nothing unusual about that. April showers, as the saying goes. The Mayall family were enjoying family time on the farm. Rik had been zooming around the land on his quad bike. His daughter Bonnie and her friend asked if they could sit on the back of the bike and be taken for a ride around the farm. Declining her request as it was beginning to rain, Rik rode off on his own. Whether it was the wet conditions or the hilly terrain or some other factor, we will never know but the quad bike flipped with Rik on it. That was the last thing he remembered until waking up from a coma in Plymouth's Derriford Hospital five days later. News of the accident started to filter out into the press and a nation held its breath.

The intervening five days between the accident and Rik waking up had been a nightmare for his wife and kids. Barbara had been the one who discovered Rik laid out on the ground with the quad bike on top of him. It had happened on a large, slightly inclined stretch of concrete road on the farm. An insignificant piece of road up until that point. As Barbara pushed the bike off her husband, she noticed a large pool of blood behind his head. He was also bleeding profusely from the ears and nose. A call was put into the emergency services at 5:30pm and an ambulance was dispatched. While waiting Barbara held Rik's hand and repeated "It's all right Rik, the ambulance is coming. You're going to be all right."

When the ambulance crew arrived they very quickly realised the severity of the situation and radioed for the Devon Air Ambulance. Unfortunately, it was in Torquay and would have taken forty minutes to reach the farm. Without missing a beat the ambulance crew radioed for the county's Police helicopter for use. It was on the scene within a few minutes. Rik was airlifted to Derriford Hospital but there was no room in the helicopter for his wife: "I just stood there as he flew off" Barbara told Helen Weathers of *The Mirror* "I didn't know if I would ever see him alive again." Barbara was driven to the hospital by a family friend while the kids stayed at the farm being looked after by the rest of the family who had come for the Easter weekend.

It took over thirty minutes for Barbara and her friend to get through rush hour traffic to the hospital and by the time she arrived Rik had been taken for a brain scan to assess the damage to his head. It wasn't until 9pm that a doctor came and gave Barbara information on her husband's situation. The scans showed that Rik had two life-threatening haematomas and a fractured skull. One haematoma had created a large expanse of blood between his brain and the inside of the skull on his right side. The other haematoma was tucked deep in the recesses of the left-hand side of his brain. As Rik's life hung in the balance, the doctors told Barbara the next 48 hours would be vital in determining which way his life would swing. The doctors explained that even if Rik did survive there was a very real possibility that he would have severe brain damage. There was good news though: the fractured skull meant that as Rik's brain swelled the skull expanded due to the fracture which in turn caused an easing of the pressure around it. As Barbara stayed by her husband's side for the next 48 hours the doctors were amazed by the nature of Rik's progress. The scans were suggesting one thing while the monitors were telling a different story entirely. It appeared to the doctors and nurses looking after Rik that he was, albeit slowly, starting to heal. The decision was made to take Rik off sedation on Easter Monday and see how he responded to it. On Easter Sunday Barbara explained to Bonnie, Sid and Rosie about their dad coming out of sedation: "Tomorrow is the day of Rik's resurrection."

On Easter Monday at 10:30am Rik was brought out of his sedation. He came around very quickly. Was that a good sign? The doctors and Barbara believed it was. Rik did not. He didn't like all the tubes going into his body and proceeded to start ripping them out. Because he was out of sedation there was nothing the doctors or nurses could do to stop him trying to pull out the tubes except hold him down. Friends and family took turns physically restraining Rik throughout the day. But, as Barbara witnessed,

Rik was never aggressive with those who were trying to restrain him: "He'd say 'Take your hands off me please'." Even his comedy partner Adrian Edmondson, who had travelled down to Plymouth to see his best friend, had to help pin Rik down. Without the ability to speak due to a sore mouth & throat, Rik could only grunt. Edmondson made a joke by saying that the next series of *Bottom* they would make could be set in the Stone Age and they will both just grunt their way through the show.

Barbara tried to explain what had happened, but Rik couldn't understand. He couldn't remember anything. His short-term memory had gone and his attention span was now nearly non-existent. "I had absolutely no memory of the accident. I wasn't in any pain and there was nothing wrong with my body," Mayall recalled months later in an exclusive interview with *The Mirror* newspaper "As far as I was concerned I should go home. I thought all my family and friends were holding me against my wishes."

Days later when Rik was able to walk he started to formulate plans to escape the hospital. He thought of stealing a nurse's uniform. Then he tried to squeeze into some green wellies to escape but the nurses found him putting on the wellies in the toilet. He whispered to his son Sid that he should nick a car and come break him out of the hospital, so they could zoom away into the night. Rik was also struggling to remember certain words. They were coming out all wrong. When he said "Aspirilla" he meant "Asparagus" and when he wanted some pencils to write with he asked for "lesbians". Rik was also still struggling to comprehend the full scale of the actual accident: "The fact that I could not understand that I'd had a serious accident started to worry me." Thankfully, the doctors were not worried and only two days after being brought out of sedation he was moved out of intensive care. A further scan showed the haematoma deep in his brain had started to heal. However, the one sitting between his brain and his skull had not reduced. This meant that Rik might have to have surgery further down the line to remove the blood. The doctors told Barbara that the short-term memory loss and inability to use the correct words would slowly disappear and she could expect to see vast improvements over the next couple of years.

With the Easter holidays over, Rik's children had to return back to school in London. The doctors were pleased with his recovery and agreed that he could be transferred to a private hospital on Harley Street. Delight turned to hilarity for Rik as he was taken from Plymouth to London in an ambulance with Barbara following behind in their car. Rik started to pull faces at his wife through the back window of the ambulance. He then pulled down his trousers and tried to moon her: "I thought I was being incredibly funny, acting like some drunken football supporter in a coach on the motorway."

A concierge at the hospital helped Rik with his bags and took him up to his own private room. Sensing this was less a hospital and more a hotel Rik made a break for it once he was alone. He walked out the front door, hailed a cab and set off to his house in South London. The hospital called Barbara to explain that her husband had escaped. What to do in this situation? Barbara was frantic with worry. Minutes later the doorbell rang and it was Rik on the doorstep. Back home safe & sound but Rik was still struggling with his memory. He became convinced his kids were hungry and ordered them a pizza. Barbara took Rik to bed and then called their local GP, who arrived at the house in minutes. Dr Elliot assessed Rik, gave him a sedative and suggested they take Rik to Charing Cross Hospital under the watchful eye of Dr David Peterson, a specialist in neurosurgery. Charing Cross ran a tighter hospital, and there was no way Rik would be leaving their care so brazenly.

The following week Rik had another brain scan. This one showed that the haematoma on the right side of his brain had almost disappeared. Sadly, the one on the left side between the brain and the skull had not reduced at all. While Rik showed huge leaps & bounds in his recovery at Charing Cross Hospital, the doctors were still worried about the haematoma not reducing in size and started to discuss the possibility of an operation to remove it. It would be a big operation with even bigger risks. The operation would see them open up the top of the skull, push it carefully to one side so they could dig into the brain and scoop out the excess blood but being very careful not to remove too much blood from the area for fear of death. The doctors suggested there was a fifty percent chance that

Rik could die. It was something for Rik, Barbara and the children to think about before deciding. Rik pestered the doctors into allowing him to recuperate at home rather than be stuck in the hospital still. After being watched over by the doctors and nurses for a week Rik was allowed to go home.

Elation at being home soon turned to boredom and, occasionally, feeling down. Barbara sensed that Rik needed a more relaxed environment to recuperate in, away from the hustle and bustle of London. It was decided they would return to the farm in Devon, and the scene of the accident. There, Rik would confront the metal beast that had nearly killed him: "At first I wanted to throw it off a cliff" He told *The Mirror*'s Helen Weathers "But I realised it was only a machine and I was a little insulted at how small it seemed." Once Rik had exorcised the demon that was the quad bike he settled down and began the road to physical and mental recovery.

Initially Rik enjoyed the freedom he had at the farm. But soon dark thoughts started to creep in: "I felt a huge sense of loss that the old Rik had gone and I could not get to grips with the new one." He struggled to write and even to think of jokes. It became a very emotional time for him. He also worried that he would never be able to act again and that he would have to rely on his family to look after him for the rest of his life. One thing that did keep his spirits up was the amount of fan mail he had received since the accident. Over 6,000 letters and cards had been sent from fans and well-wishers. It was the first time in his life that he realised how universally loved he was: "I felt completely overwhelmed."

The melancholy he was experiencing soon started to ease after Rik took up running. He would jog over two miles a day and also work on the farm. He ensured he got enough rest each day as well. Rik was on the mend by the time he had to go back to Charing Cross Hospital to see if an operation was required to remove the blood still trapped between his brain and his skull. Miraculously the blood had disappeared all by itself. He wouldn't need an operation after all. Barbara had been told to expect improvements with her husband's health over the next two to three years: "But after a couple of months Rik was completely back to normal." So much so that Barbara sent Rik out to fulfil a promise he had previously made to the TV show Jonathan Creek that he would appear in one episode. "I was nervous about it because I was still suffering from a little word blindness. So Rosie went through all the lines with me making sure I didn't forget any," Rik told *The Mirror* newspaper in an exclusive interview. The entire Mayall family had been to hell and back in the space of a few months. Through it all Barbara stayed positive: "I never thought Rik was going to die. I wouldn't let myself think like that."

In typical Rik fashion he played off this very real and life-threatening accident with jokes. Plenty of jokes. In the months and years after he would say, to everyone who listened, how he beat The Lord Jesus Christ in the battle of who stayed dead longer. Giving a typical Rik interview to Nick Owen several months later, he said: "It happened on, what my kids call Crap Thursday because it was the day before Good Friday, and I died that Thursday and then I came back on the Monday. The day after Easter day. Lord knows I'm a modest man, but I beat Jesus by two days" and then he gave the camera a sideways tilt of the head and a big cheeky grin.

There was a sadness to the screening of a new episode of *The Comic Strip Presents…* on the 12th April 1998. As the broadcast went out across the nation, Mayall was lying in a hospital bed unconscious after his quad bike accident. The episode, titled *Four Men in a Car*, took The Comic Strip guys and gals back to basics. Set predominately in a car, with four salesmen all trying to get to a convention in Swindon to find out who will be promoted, it is a claustrophobic comedy of errors with a Comic Strip Presents… slant. Mayall, Edmondson, Richardson and Planer are all cooped up in the car, each with their own eccentricities and observations. Things start to spiral downwards for the Yuppie-esque salesmen when they stop to fill the car with petrol and are rammed off the road. This results in them hiking to a remote, unoccupied house (or is it?). Mayall plays his salesman, Alan, suave, smooth and sexual – in his typical fashion. His constant battles with the others are a thing of beauty as they bicker over even the smallest of things.

The Comic Strip Presents… output over the previous decade had been very hit and miss. However, when the old gang were brought back together with material that played to their comedic strengths, without the big budget frills and spills, it created one of the best episodes ever. The original group may have got older, but they certainly had not lost their comedy touches. *Four Men in a Car* is classic Comic Strip material. It is *The Comic Strip Presents…* version of *Glengarry Glen Ross*.

Shortly after, Mayall was back behind the microphone providing voices for the Granada stop-motion kid's animated show *Tom and Vicky*. These ten-minute shows received a run of twenty-six episodes in total with Mayall voicing the characters Bert the Frog and Squidge the Crayfish. His voice work on Bert is high-pitched and chaotic, recalling the early days of his stand-up career. Whereas Squidge has a rather pompous attitude that at times makes it difficult to believe it is Mayall providing the voice. The show was aimed at the two to five age range as a fun, entertaining and educational show.

The return to work was special for Mayall yet not quite as special as his first on-screen appearance. After his accident he was unsure if he would ever work again: "It was pretty dodgy for a few years as they had to work out which pills I needed to be on to get the blood to run through the brain" he told *The Daily Mail*. Thankfully the doctors found the right pills and Mayall slowly recovered in order to take on the role of Detective Inspector Gideon Pryke, a man who has been paralysed from the neck down apart from his left finger, which he uses to drive his wheelchair in an episode of *Jonathan Creek*. Even though his mobility is limited in this performance Mayall still manages to steal every scene he is in. At times it looks like Jonathan Creek himself (Alan Davies) steps aside to let Mayall do his thing because he knows he cannot compete. Suited and booted with his mane of hair swept back, Mayall looks like he is enjoying every single minute of being back in the limelight. He even manages to get in on the action in one scene as a woman pulls a gun on him and he retaliates by knocking into her with his wheelchair. Pryke comes out of the whole episode as the stand-out character.

Director Sandy Johnson recalls what is was like directing Mayall on his first return to on-screen acting: "It was about six months after the accident and he had recovered quite well. He just had a few memory issues. He was almost back on form for *Black Canary*. Occasionally he got the words the wrong way around. But compared to some actors he was fantastic. He was really good." *Jonathan Creek* is a comedy-drama programme and that is exactly what they got from Mayall's performance – a lot of drama and a little bit of classic comedy. That anarchic twinkle returned to Mayall's eye. It was exciting to see him back on television (it aired on 24th December 1998) and viewers thought so too as this episode of *Jonathan Creek* is constantly rated as one of the best ever. (Author's Note: Mayall did suggest that he was offered the title role of *Jonathan Creek* in 1997 "But I was tragically unavailable." Is this true? Or was it classic Mayall self-promotion?). It would be a slow road to recovery for Mayall, yet he proved even with his appearance in *Jonathan Creek* that there was plenty of energy (and chaos) in him still.

1999 saw Mayall appear in-front of the cameras only once as he slowly recuperated. He continued to be prolific behind the microphone however. Bassetts Jelly Baby sweets served as the inspiration for the UK TV show *Jellikins* (known as *Jellabies* in some countries). The show was developed by brothers Jonny and Mikel Lewis and became one of the first fully CGI TV shows in the world when it debuted on 18th May 1998. The first series consisted of an unprecedented eighty-four episodes, with the finale airing on 20th December 1999. It was seen as ITV's version of the *Teletubbies* as the wibbly wobbly *Jellikins* went on a series of adventures in the Jolly Jelly World, all narrated by Mayall. His voice over work here is slow and more painfully pronounced, but that is nothing to do with the after effects of the accident. Instead it's for added emphasis on certain words and phrases to ensure the target demographic of two to six-year-old child can understand the dialogue. Mayall's voice echoes through the show as he softly talks to the *Jellikins* and also explains what is happening on-screen. It is a playful show that sadly looks quite dated nowadays. Yet Mayall's voice work is so well-defined that it is enjoyable to hear him experimenting with a more serene manner.

In the same week that episode two of *Jellikins* was airing, Mayall appeared on the opposite channel (BBC One) in a three-part crime thriller called *In The Red*. Interweaving storylines centred around a series of bank managers being murdered and the killer calling into a BBC radio station before each kill. These murders can be traced all the way up to Parliament which is dealing with its own problems during the Parliamentary elections. A huge cast included Richard Wilson, Richard Griffith, Sally Phillips, Reece Sheersmith, Warren Clarke, Rebecca Front, John Bird, Stephen Fry, John Sessions and Mark Gatiss. Mayall had fleeting appearances in all three episodes as economist Dominic De'Ath, an upper-class snob who turns his nose up at the Police when they come calling. It is a role that required Mayall to summon as much snootiness as possible, even down to the sneering smile. Sadly, with limited screen time, there is very little to see in Mayall's performance apart from him being a nasty piece of work to everyone around him. Maybe with more plot development for the character we could have seen where Mayall would have taken this role, and to what depths. By its end, the show becomes a confusing mess as intersecting storylines become too confusing and the viewer is left trying to figure out which person belongs to which part of the narrative. Also, trying to add satirical comedy into the mix doesn't work either. One or two fewer storylines and *In The Red* could have been an enjoyable political thriller.

Virgin Trains pulled out all the stops to get Mayall to feature in their new run of adverts in which he played an over-the-top, self-important businessman who decides to drive to his meetings hundreds of miles away instead of taking the train with his work colleagues. A series of mishaps befall Mayall's businessman along the way whereas his colleagues all get to their meeting on time and without any problems. The adverts were directed by Mayall's buddy from *The Comic Strip* Peter Richardson.

Mayall went back to voice work for the rest of the year as he narrated *The Sound Of Trumpets* for novelist, playwright and former Barrister John Mortimer. It told the story of an MP who had been fired from the Conservative Party and was slowly forcing his way into the oppositional Labour Party. It was easy pickings for Mayall who simply reverted back to his Alan B'Stard style. The audiobook was split into ten fifteen-minute segments and broadcast on BBC Radio 4. More audiobook work followed with Mayall narrating Francesca Simon's *Horrid Henry's Haunted House: And Other Stories*.

Without having to do anything, Mayall's voice found its way onto US children's TV show *It's Itsy Bitsy Time* when the episodes of *Tom and Vicky* that he had voiced two years earlier for UK TV were inserted into *It's Itsy Bitsy Time* along with other stories. *It's Itsy Bitsy Time* ran on the Fox Family Channel for nearly two years and showcased animation from many different countries. The nineties had been both a success and a failure for Mayall when it came to feature films. Emmy Award winning work in *The Willows in Winter* and a respectable box office return for *Drop Dead Fred*, but a terrible flop with *Bring Me The Head of Mavis Davis* and a poor box office return for *Guest House Paradiso*.

Mayall's last feature film appearance of the decade came in animated form (yet again) as he lent his voice to the English language version of the French animated movie *Le Château des singes* aka *A Monkey's Tale*. Playing the brilliantly-named Gerard the Gormless, this role is business as usual for Mayall as he spits out dialogue with great glee and relish. But the film is too serious to have a character like Gerard, and in turn Mayall voicing him, for it to actually work. Gerard is the right-hand monkey to Lord Chancellor Sebastien (voiced by John Hurt). It's very obvious that the film was going for a bad guy with a dim-witted sidekick ala Disney's *Aladdin*. But this lacks the magic of that movie and many other films that have those types of characters. Mayall's performance stands out a mile in a film that is so strait-laced you wonder if anybody had fun making it. The animation is lifeless, the music is dull and the story is un-engaging from the start. Even at only seventy-three minutes watching *A Monkey's Tale* (if only for Mayall's voice work) feels like a slog.

Mayall's voice work in a new animated version of *Watership Down* was very much the opposite of his work in *A Monkey's Tale*. This film was a co-production between Alltime Entertainment in the UK and Decode Entertainment of Canada. It loosely followed the plot of Richard Adams book, however the filmmakers were quick to point out that it would not be as dark or harrowing as the 1978 animated film. This new version would be more upbeat as it was to air during children's television slots on YTV in Canada and CITV in the UK. The show had a stellar British voice cast including Stephen Fry, Phil Jupitus, Jane Horrocks, Dawn French, John Hurt and Richard Briers (the latter two also provided voices for the original animated movie). Mayall voiced Kehaar, a black-headed gull with a vague Eastern European accent who seeks refuge on the down when he injures his wing. While not the comedic character he was used to portraying, there was a slight stupidity to Kehaar. His story was one of a fish out of water; a heart-warming tale of how he was taken in by the rabbits. Mayall does not give a big, dominating performance this time but instead shows his softer side. He appeared in all thirteen episodes of the first series, which ran from September through to December.

Another Christmas and another Mayall vocal performance. This time he got to voice Santa Claus for a BBC animated film called *Santa's Special Delivery*. The story revolved around Santa discovering that children don't believe in him anymore. He sets out to prove them wrong but it doesn't help that he accidentally shaves off his beard. It was broadcast on BBC One on Christmas day at 9:35am during the CBBC In Lapland segment. In this, Mayall's voice work is more relaxed than usual. Gone is the zany energy that he usually revels in. It is replaced with a strong, powerful and commanding delivery that one might expect of Santa Claus. At only twenty-four minutes it is a jovial and light-hearted story that is aimed at very little children and has a sincere message about believing.

The 1990s was the decade when Mayall co-created a new comedy sitcom that would be adored by millions. He tried his acting hand in Hollywood again, to middling results, and even got to show a darker, edger side to his acting. His voice work went from strength to strength, resulting in an Emmy win. He and Ade Edmondson took *Bottom* on the road and played to hundreds of thousands of adoring fans, and there was still time to appear in a couple of West End plays. But all of those accomplishments were overshadowed by an accident that almost robbed a family of a doting father and a nation of one of its greatest comedians.

2000s

(Where *King Arthur's Disasters* created a *Violent Nation* and brought about the return of Alan B'Stard)

For Mayall, the new millennium started with playing an old character. A specially-commissioned episode of the classic BBC sitcom *Blackadder* was produced. To be screened exclusively at the Skyscape screen in London's Millennium Dome eight times a day throughout 2000. The show reunited the old Blackadder writing team of Ben Elton, Richard Curtis and Rowan Atkinson, with the latter reprising his role of the sarcastic Edmund Blackadder. The story saw Blackadder and his moronic side-kick Baldrick travel through time and encounter dinosaurs, Queen Elizabeth I, William Shakespeare, Romans and the Duke of Wellington (sort of). The duo also drops into Sherwood Forest where they meet a band of Merry Men led by Lord Flashheart… sorry… Robin Hood.

Mayall's performance as the rob-from-the-rich-to-give-to-the-poor outlaw is basically his Lord Flashheart character in a different costume. The over-the-top bravado along with a penchant for double entrees is what makes this character so beloved - he seems to always get the girl as well. Here, he enjoys a snog with Maid Marion (played by supermodel Kate Moss) but doesn't leave in a cloud of smoke like his appearances in the original TV series. Instead he is killed by his Merry Men after Blackadder turns them against him. Considering everything that Mayall's characters have been through in the Blackadder series it is a shame to see him killed off. You want to see him get the girl and leave in a flash ("WOOF!"). Even though the idea wouldn't be fresh, with Mayall it would never be the same twice and it would never not be funny. Killing off Lord Flashheart… sorry… Robin Hood feels like an anti-climax for such a legendary character.

The episode eventually aired on Sky One in 2001 and a year later on BBC One. It marked the end of the Blackadder character but this was not the only return to a classic role for Mayall. He and his Comic Strip buddies Adrian Edmondson, Nigel Planer and Peter Richardson tried to replicate the success they had with *Four Men in a Car* two years previous with a sequel called *Four Men in a Plane*. This time the same four characters, on their way to a sales conference in North Africa, get stranded in the desert without food or water. Tensions, once again, start to boil over and home truths are told. It is a middling affair from The Comic Strip team as most of the laughs occur during scenes onboard the main flight; each of them are located in different boarding classes yet each believe they deserve to be in business class.

The comedy soon dries up once they are on land and trying to figure out how to stay alive. Mayall plays Alan bombastically yet the script lets him and the others down when it comes to serving up a decent fish out of water situation. It aired on Channel 4 on the 4th January 2000 as a special one-off reunion.

Mayall was arguably the perfect candidate to narrate the ever-crazy world of Dr Seuss's books and at the turn of the century he had his opportunity. Seuss's tongue twisting rhyming was no problem for Mayall when he voiced the *Dr Seuss Collection* audiobook, which consisted of *The Lorax, Dr. Seuss's ABC, How the Grinch Stole Christmas* and *One Fish Two Fish Red Fish Blue Fish*. Mayall's delivery of *How the Grinch Stole Christmas* might just be as good as Boris Karloff's original. Strangely, for a man with a brilliant voice, Mayall entered into only his second, and final, video game voice work project for the PlayStation game *Hogs of War* in 2000. Behind the scenes footage shows Mayall in the voice booth wearing a *Bottom* t-shirt as he voiced General I.P. Grimly and recorded noises for the pigs. Other additional voice-over work included Mayall being the voice of the *Brother* printers' commercials and narrating the radio advert for Strepsils.

Mayall's first feature film of the new millennium was a departure from his usual comedy turns. In *Merlin: The Return* he strapped on some sandals, grew a goatee and wore a blonde wig to play the title character. This British take on the Arthurian legend was a somewhat different version of (supposed) events. A gateway between the modern world and the mystical realm of King Arthur is opened by a scientist. Merlin, Arthur and Launcelot are thrown through the time wrap to the present day and must do battle with foes new and old. Much like the synopsis, the film is a mess of different ideas and themes where none of them come together to make even the slightest bit of coherent sense. Tonally the film flits between fantasy, comedy, family drama, romance, action and adventure without actually managing to make any of these elements even remotely engaging. The wishy-washy CGI doesn't help matters either. *Total Film* magazine's review said: "It's a word that has some might. It starts with 'Sh'. And rhymes with kite…". They weren't far wrong. Even Mayall can't save this film. His performance is, much like the entire film, all over the place. At times we see the sarcastic and slightly devilish Mayall and other times he is trying to play the part dead straight. Watching Mayall try to deliver fantasy film style lines without a smirk or a curled lip or a sexual double entrée is really quite bizarre. It simply doesn't sit right and even Mayall looks to be struggling to hold back a volley of naughty words. Fair play to Mayall for taking on a role outside his comfort zone but when the script is this bad you do wonder what he saw in the project. Some films are so bad they are good, *Merlin: The Return* is so bad that it's bad.

BBC Radio 7 broadcast a comedy play written by Mayall's old school chum and long-time friend Lloyd Peters called *A Higher Education*. It's a story about a drama lecturer whose day very quickly falls apart. Additional voices are provided by Helen Lederer and Phillip Glenister. The comedy/drama is funny and poignant, highlighting the difficult working conditions under which lecturers operate. Mayall is his usual lively self and enjoys a renewed rapport with Lederer. Peters clearly mined his own lecturing background for the piece and it shows, as it is an insightful and entertaining play. Peters explains what it was like working with his oldest mate on *A Higher Education*: "I wrote a radio play where he was absolutely fantastic with it only because he didn't stick to the script. Which was quite unusual for radio, and for the other actors who didn't know when to come in. It was a bit like a jam session where you don't really know where it is going to go. Very late on in the radio show where he totally improvised the lines. I was in the control box with the director, Polly Summers, and we just looked at each other and scampered through the script to see where he got it from. I was looking at Helen Lederer, who he was working with, and her face was sort of asking 'where the fuck do I come in?' [*laughs*]. That epitomised everything good about him."

A further step outside his comedy comfort zone occurred when Mayall took on the role of King Herod in the filmed version of Andrew Lloyd Webber and Tim Rice's rock opera *Jesus Christ Superstar*. The musical began on Broadway in 1971. A filmed adaptation was released in 1973. This new version used ideas from the 1996-99 UK stage production and was filmed as if on stage rather than real locations. Mayall found this new version of King Herod "so strange and so spoilt. And jealous. He is my type of character." Dressed in a white tuxedo with black trousers and slicked back hair, Mayall cavorts around the stage tormenting Jesus. Initially, the performance is end-of-the-pier camp but very quickly it turns dark and his mannerisms become quite evil. Watching the performance, one might notice a similarity with Al Pacino's performance in *The Devil's Advocate*. There is fun and laughter to be had but behind that twinkling eye lies the nastiest persona just waiting to burst through. This happens at the end of the song as he goes face to face with Jesus and sings: "Hey. Aren't. You. Sssssssssscared?" with a demented look on his face. Mayall's singing talents might not be impressive but this performance needed someone to deliver rather than the sing the lines. And who better than a man who has more voices than a ventriloquist? Mayall clearly relished playing the character and getting to "sing", so one has to wonder what other musicals he could have appeared in and been a smash hit?

Back behind the microphone, Mayall continued his voice work as Kehaar in the second series of *Watership Down* when it aired on CITV between August and October 2000. As with the first series, Kehaar appeared in all thirteen episodes of the show. This new version of Kehaar was different to the book and film version as he stayed with the rabbits much longer and formed a bond with them. Strangely, for the third series Mayall was replaced by another actor and it never aired in the UK.

The first opportunity Mayall had to appear on stage after his accident was in a production of the musical *A Family Affair*. It was a light-hearted piece that also starred Steven Pacey, Anne Reid and Susan Wooldridge. The play toured regional theatres during the Autumn of 2000. Towards the tail end of 2000 Mayall was back on ITV appearing in their critically acclaimed custom and excise crime drama series *The Knock*. He played government minister Simon Reid (a vast departure from the B'Stard days), Mayall was trim and clean cut. He lacked his usual chaotic, riotous behaviour but was still drenched in sliminess. That raised nose and upturned corner of the mouth that Mayall seemed to use in his dramatic roles was in effect here. While not a huge part, it nevertheless suggested that he enjoyed the freedom of dropping into TV shows for bit parts and doing a fine job. The snivelling, underhand and dodgy character she played so well are very much epitomised with his role in *The Knock*.

After a couple of false starts in unsuccessful feature films on either side of the Atlantic, Mayall must have thought his window to appear in blockbuster movies was rapidly disappearing. So, when the call came in from the producers of *Harry Potter and the Philosopher's Stone* film he was delighted. Even before filming began Mayall was waxing lyrical about how pleased he was to feature in a film adaptation of such a well-known book: "My agent said 'Hey Rik, want to be in Harry Potter?' I said 'What is it?' 'It's a book.' 'Oh, it's my favourite book, of course I want to be in it.' Never read a word [of the book]. She said "alright, you're in it.'" Mayall was cast as the poltergeist Peeves but when it came to shooting his scenes there was one big problem – the kids kept laughing at his performance. "I did my lines as Peeves to Daniel Radcliffe, who plays Harry, plus about 30 other kids and they all started laughing." Mayall told *The Daily Mirror* "They just wouldn't stop and in the end I had to stand around the corner and do it."

But his brief appearance in the film soon became a no-show when the producers called him three weeks later to say his scenes were not going to be included in the movie because director Chris Columbus wasn't happy with the way the CG Peeves looked. Consequently the character was binned completely. Mayall, of course, had the last word though. With his dry sense of humour and a wry smile he said: "I wasn't in it and it was crap. It was crap because I wasn't in it." He was invited to the premiere but due to Bottom touring commitments couldn't attend. Instead his children attended but Mayall hadn't told them he wasn't in the finished film. When they next spoke to him they said what a great performance he gave and how you couldn't tell it was him: "They thought I was playing Hagrid." (Authors Note: Mayall's Peeves did appear on the deleted scenes of the Blu-ray released several years later.)

Next, Canada came calling for Mayall to star opposite Skeet Ulrich, Natasha Henstridge and Leslie Nielsen in *Kevin of the North* (it was retitled *Chilly Dogs* for its North American release). A film about a man who has to participate in the Iditarod Trail Sled Dog Race to prove he is worthy to receive his grandfather's estate. Directed by Bob Spiers, who had previously directed Mayall in series three of *Bottom*, it pitted an American comedy legend - Leslie Nielsen - against a British comedy legend – Rik Mayall. Yet the film didn't hit the mark as it failed to let these two comedy greats off the leash, instead opting for a family friendly approach. Mayall's character, Carter is a bumbling buffoon written by someone who thinks all English people walk, talk and act like Carter. It is a horribly cliched character that even Mayall can't save. He is the butt of all jokes and seems completely out of place throughout. His usual anarchic energy is missing. But he isn't alone as Nielsen also struggles to make any of the lines funny. If a film has two great comedy legends and fails to raise even a titter then it could be considered a complete mis-fire. In this "wacky races in the snow" even the dogs are lifeless.

Thankfully, a return to TV proved a triumph for Mayall. BBC Choice was a new digital-only channel from the British Broadcasting Company. However, many households in the UK could not access it as their local BBC receptions had not yet switched over to digital. Consequently, during the early days of the channel, which had very little money, programming consisted of sketches from up and coming writers, directors and actors. Comedic writing partners Alexander Kirk and Simon Messingham were two of the lucky few who got a whole thirteen-episode series commissioned of a show called *Tales of Uplift and Moral Improvement*. Their idea was summarised as "dark, twisted stories from the heart of Edwardian England." It was basically adult *Jackanory* meets Rudyard Kipling or M.R. James or James Joyce, any Edwardian writer whose work ventured into dark territory. Each episode would showcase actors acting out the story while also being accompanied by a storyteller, and who better than the man who generated the most complaints to *Jackanory* in the show's history? Dressed in female Edwardian clothes, Mayall dropped in and out of the episode as Mrs Ffine Carmody.

As with his stints on *Jackanory*, Mayall proves himself as a master enunciator - his version of an upper-class Edwardian woman is wonderful. Kirk spoke to Mayallonline.com about going to meet Mayall for the first time: "We all went over to his house and he had a huge amount of beer waiting for us and immediately sent out for lots of pizza." Mayall was a dab hand at this sort of on-screen storytelling and while it may not rival his work on *Jackanory*, there is still much to marvel at in his performance on the show.

Murder Rooms: The Dark Beginnings of Sherlock Holmes was a critical and commercial success for the BBC when they screened the two-part drama on BBC Two during January 2000. It came as no surprise then, when a further four 90-minute episodes were commissioned and transferred to its flagship channel BBC One. The drama told the story of a young Arthur Conan Doyle and his tutor Joseph Bell as they team up to solve murders. The final episode of the first series, called *The White Knight Stratagem*, was screened on 2nd October 2001. While Ian Richardson and Charles Edwards continued their great work as Bell and Doyle respectively, this episode was stolen from them by Mayall. This time, however, audience saw a different Mayall on-screen. It was a collected performance, stern and powerful, as he calmly downed drink after drink while going toe-to-toe with Conan Doyle and Bell.

Mayall couldn't play it straight behind the scenes though. When promoting the show with *What's On TV* he was asked what made him take on the role: "Money," he replied with a grin. "Also, I was intrigued by the script. I was trying to work out the ending all the way through but I couldn't, which makes it perfect." This wasn't the first time Mayall performed in the Sherlock Holmes universe. He had previously played the great detective while at Manchester University.

A fourth tour featuring the shenanigans of Richard Richard and Eddie Hitler occurred in 2001. Riffing on Arthur C. Clarke's *2001: A Space Odyssey*, Mayall and Edmondson called their show *Bottom Live 2001: An Arse Oddity*. It was a tour that celebrated the fact the duo had been working together for twenty-five years. The story followed directly on from *Hooligan's Island* and finished with Richie and Eddie trapped in a dome-like structure. The show played 76 sold-out shows in theatres around the UK concluding on the 3rd of December. The live show in Nottingham was filmed for VHS and DVD release.

A second series of the kids' TV show *Jellikins* was commissioned in 2000 but didn't air until 2002. Unlike the first series which received an eighty-four-episode commission, the second series consisted of only thirteen episodes. Mayall returned as the narrator, and stuck with the slow, tranquil voice over. While it wasn't a ratings winner (the juggernaut that was the *Teletubbies* simply steam-rolled over it), the show was sold to several other countries including Germany, The Netherlands and the USA. It didn't, however, return for a third series.

Mayall, no stranger to pushing boundaries and breaking rules, created controversary with his anti-euro campaign advert in which he dressed up as Adolf Hitler. It was an advert filled with celebrities who were campaigning against Britain joining the Euro currency in 2002. The "No Euro" campaign advert incurred the wrath of a range of people including the European Commission who said that Mayall's part was "crass and offensive." Mayall hit back calling his piece "satire" and commenting: "Look, I'm saying what I say because if Hitler tells people to support the Euro then surely they won't. That's the point of it [the advert]."

Mayall continued to appear on British television throughout the year, but in audio form only as he voiced the adverts for *Horrible Histories* kids magazine and the Bill and Ben toy giveaway at *McDonalds*. He also appeared on *Classic FM* radio station reading classic kids stories *George and the Dragon* and *Robinson Crusoe*.

Mayall, Laurence Marks and Maurice Gran were a hot team during their years working on *The New Statesman*. It would only be a matter of time before they teamed up again for a new show called *Believe Nothing*. Mayall played Quadruple Professor Adonis Cnut (A. Cnut to his friends), Britain's cleverest man and one of the thirteen people secretly ruling the world. He is ably assisted by his butler-cum-slave Albumen and his love-interest-cum-fellow-professor Dr. Hannah Awkward. Mayall explained to *Manchester Online* why he took on the role: "There's so much to the series. Global warming is explained away as a hoax, Tony Blair is in it, so is David Blunkett. We see President Nixon, too. Anything is possible and you can't be sure of what is real, hence the title – *Believe Nothing*." However, the show never really hit the highs of *The New Statesman* and it is easy to see why: it is simply not funny. Mayall is stuck in a vortex unsure of how to play the character. He comes off like a cross between Richard Richard and Alan B'Stard but without one major ingredient – heart. The other iconic characters Mayall created had a real human heart underneath their extravagant exteriors that made you love them for who they were. Cnut lacks empathy, instead coming across as an arrogant, pig-headed arsehole. There is nothing endearing about him at any point. His relationship with Albumen is reminiscent of Blackadder and Baldrick but without the respect both of them have for each other.

Here, Cnut forces Albumen to press a hot iron to his groin, to cut his toe nails with his teeth and to be electrocuted while moving Cnut around on his wheeled library steps. If that wasn't bad enough then Cnut's relationship with Dr. Awkward is all over the place. One minute he is desperately trying to woo her and the next he is repulsed by her. The tone of the show is all over the place as it never knows if it wants to be an edgy late-night satire or a playfully light Saturday teatime sitcom. However, the show's worst crime is that it makes Mayall seem unfunny. Dialogue is delivered without his usual vigour. His comedic putdowns drift away without so much as even a chuckle passing the viewers lips (thank goodness for that ITV laugh track). The show aired on 14th July 2002 on ITV for six episodes. It never returned for a second series. Maurice Gran suggests the show didn't work because: "It was too similar but not similar enough to *The New Statesman*. I think we were a bit over ambitious and there were things we could have sorted out in series two. I don't think it really landed with the audience."

In 2002 British horror writer/producer/director Ray Brady released *Day of the Sirens*. A film about a serial killer who decides to go out in a blaze of glory during one summer's day in London. This low-to-no budget movie is a hideous mess. From the lead actor who looks like a George Michael tribute act to non-touristy tourists and the jiggly helicopter shots of London this is a film that many will never have heard of. Mayall's role is almost a cameo performance as his Domo Childs, camp radio DJ, dips in and out of the film while covering the escalating violence. It's a performance the requires Mayall to sit in a chair and talk into a microphone, and with what appears to be his script directly in front of him. There is no energy or charisma to the character but that is more down to a hideously cliched script that is written to show action, action and more action without actually showing the action. Billed as "Britain's answer to 24" according to movies2die4, not even Jack Bauer on his best day of defusing a bomb while being injected with a deadly toxin while trying to save his daughter from a pack of vicious wolves while also romancing and then killing his female colleague while wearing a manbag and huffing into his phone "Dammit Chloe!" would be able to save this movie.

Mayall stayed in the horror genre for another feature film when British actor/writer/director Richard Driscoll started work on *Alone in the Dark* way back in 2002. The film had the most bizarre cast list including Norman Wisdom, Jason Donovan, Robin Askwith and Eileen Daly, who all shot their scenes during different years. Marianne Faithfull recorded the narration and Christopher Walken was the voice of the Raven. Yet because Driscoll spent so long putting the film together it went through several name changes starting with *Alone in the Dark* and then onto *The Legend of Harrow Woods* followed by *Evil Calls* and then finally *Evil Calls: The Raven*. Mayall shot his scenes in 2002, in which he played Winston Llamata Jr - the spirit of a former hotel manager who tricks the lead character George into killing his wife. Mayall and Wisdom play the same character, dead and alive respectively. Mayall tries to inject creepiness into the part but it comes across as scheming naughtiness a la Richard Richard. The film itself is a hodge podge of low budget elements that even with such a weird and wacky cast it is near unwatchable.

Mayall & Edmondson appeared on stage in the West End on the evening of 29th September as part of the comedy ensemble paying tribute to the late Peter Cook at a posthumous concert. Their sketch involved *Bottom*'s Richie and Eddie trying to re-enact one of Cook's sketches but they both get confused and start performing lines from different Cook sketches. Mayall and Edmondson were singled out for a small amount of prise in an otherwise poorly received event. 2002 was one of the least successful years Mayall ever had on a professional level.

2003 saw Mayall appear in a production of Noel Coward's *Present Laughter*. Playing the charmer Gary Essendine. The 1930s-set drawing room comedy followed the story of an actor who never broke the façade, even with his friends and family. It was a character Mayall felt he had been playing for many years in his work: "vanity, a big ego, lots of sex. He's very similar to Richie in *Filthy, Rich & Catflap*." The play ran through regional theatres during the first couple of months of the year. Before that Mayall nipped over to the Costa Del Sol to film *Oh Marbella!* alongside Tom Bell, Craig Kelly and Mike Reid. The film was a comedy about various visitors to the Spanish resort. Mayall plays a hitman/time-share salesman with a gift of the gab and an eye for the ladies. Suited and booted, and with a trim head of hair, Mayall steals every scene he is in from the initial smooth-talking a couple into buying a time share to sex on the beach over a set of loungers. He describes his character Greg Dubois as "a duplicitous, utter bastard." The film premiered at the Cannes Film Festival on 15th May 2003. Upon release *Oh Marbella!* never really found its audience in the UK or in Spain however it is a surprisingly pleasing comedy that has some genuinely entertaining moments.

Following this, Mayall went back behind the microphone again for a feature film. This time he lent his vocal talents to the character of Wizard Azbar in *Sindy: The Fairy Princess* animated movie. His character attempts to overthrow the royal family and Sindy must stop him, even if that means marrying the Prince. Mayall delivers some great vocal work with much growling and snarling which enables him to create a truly nasty character. Mayall commented on playing Wizard Azbar: "He's kind of incompetent. I'm good at baddies". More on-camera film work followed when Matador Pictures released the black comedy *Chaos and Cadavers* during 2003. This film charted the story of two newlyweds who, on their honeymoon at a remote country house hotel, are caught up in the Undertakers' Annual Convention. Nick Moran and Keeley Hawes play the newlyweds and a cameo from Mayall stirs things up as he takes a sexual shine to the couple. This performance by Mayall is reminiscent of Richard Richard but with more confidence, energy and spunk.

The same could be said for Mayall's voiceover work as a bird in the short BMI commercial segments that sponsored the London Weekend Weather on ITV. Mayall was one of several British celebrities that provided voices for the segments that also ran on local radio stations. He also popped up on TV advertising *Which?* magazine, in his own unique and crazy style. The kids TV channel Nickelodeon hired Mayall to host their Sunday line-up throughout May. Alongside the usual announcing of what programmes were coming up next, Mayall created little sketches to be shown in-between the programmes where he called himself Merlando the Magician.

Yet another nationwide tour for Mayall and Edmondson with *Bottom Live 2003: Weapons Grade Y-Fronts.* As with the previous tours it sold out theatres up and down the UK across the final three months of the year. The performance at Southend's Cliffs Pavilion was selected as the location to record the DVD release of the show. This tour marked ten years of the Bottom Live shows. It also proved to be the last time Mayall and Edmondson would work together under the guises of Richard Richard and Eddie Hitler.

Mayall had already flirted with the world of ABBA, the Swedish pop band, back in 1993 when his *Rik Mayall Presents...* episode called *Dancing Queen* used the infamous song. This time is was ABBA who were the stars of the video... sort of. ABBA appeared as string puppets for a special compilation video to be shown during the 2004 Eurovision Song Contest semi-finals. The puppets performed a megamix of their hits to a weasel-y record company executive, played by Mayall. Looking unashamedly bored initially, Mayall's sneering face soon turns to joy and he rises from behind his desk to dance along with Dancing Queen. His trousers almost up to his armpits and the zip on his trousers protruding out as he dances around. Shortly after, when his assistant goes against what Mayall says, he gives him a good, hard twist of the balls – classic Mayall move. Much of the dialogue is lines from ABBA songs save the end of the audition where Mayall thanked them for the music but told them No! and then laughed in their faces. It is a cute and funny video that was conceived as the last time ABBA would be seen together, hence the title *Our Last Video.*

Churchill: The Hollywood Years is a film Mayall found himself in along with a lot of his contemporaries from the alternate comedy circuit including: Harry Enfield, Vic Reeves, Bob Mortimer, Phil Cornwell, Steve Pemberton, Miranda Richardson and Sally Phillips. They were all led by Hollywood heartthrob Christian Slater as American G.I. Winston Churchill, who has arrived in England to help the war effort against the Nazi's. While in England, Churchill falls for the beautiful Princess Elizabeth played by Neve Campbell. Mayall's role as Baxter, a military general, instantly conjures the expectation that he will play it very much like his scene-stealing performances as Lord Flashheart in Black Adder series four. However, that is not the case. It is a much more submissive performance. The cocksureness of Flashheart appears briefly however it is soon overthrown when Baxter is taken to task by Churchill and pushed into the Thames. Later, when Baxter is ready to shoot Churchill and is told to stand down he almost veers off into Richard Richard camp territory, but turns it around as he licks his lips at the thought of shooting Churchill in the back as he runs away.

There are classic Mayall moments in the performance but they are toned down. The film itself is uneven in terms of its comedy. One minute it is laugh-out-loud hilarious and then the next it is tumbleweed-across-a-dusty-street embarrassing. It feels like an elongated version of a thirty-minute TV show that can't stretch the jokes to eighty minutes. That's why it is important to note that *Churchill: The Hollywood Years* was written and directed by Peter Richardson, one of the members of *The Comic Strip presents...* troupe. *The Comic Strip presents...* was at its best working in the half hour time frame, but the majority of their longer output struggled to maintain the laughs-per-minute hit rate it needed. *Churchill: The Hollywood Years* struggles with the same problems. At least *Churchill: The Hollywood Years* was released because, in the same year, Mayall's performance as the Vet in British director Ray Brady's horror film *Cold Dark* never materialised, and neither did the film. Very little information exists about this project apart from its own IMDb.com webpage. Even there, only the bare bones information is available. What is known is that, according to two early film posters, it was due to be released in 2004. It was to be a revisionist vampire movie of some description (a tagline on one of the posters said: "forget everything you know about vampyres") This author tried to contact Brady to discover more information but phone calls and emails were never returned. Has *Cold Dark* got past development hell? Has it been filmed? Did Mayall shoot any footage? It is all a very big mystery.

Shoebox Zoo was a fantasy TV series for children produced by BBC Scotland and several Canadian television companies. Its story, about an American girl studying in Edinburgh who is given a mysterious box of toys that come alive in order to track down an ancient magical book, was created by BBC Scotland director Claire Mundell and television director Justin Molotnikov (further development came from Brian Ward and Sarah Dodd). The series was predominately live action apart from when the toys came to life via the means of animation. Its cast list included some high-profile names and faces including Alan Cumming, Bill Paterson, Siobhan Redmond, Peter Mullan and Simon Callow. Mayall provided the voice for Edwin de Wyntor aka Edwin the Eagle, one of the toys that came alive. The voice work for Edwin is much primmer than a lot of Mayall's work. There is still a hootin' and hollerin' occasionally but this character is the self-appointed leader of the Shoebox Zoo and feels he should speak with an authoritative voice, apart from when he gets frightened. While more strait-laced that most of Mayall's voice work it is still undeniably Mayall behind Edwin. There is still that little anarchic twang in the voice. On a behind-the-scenes promotional video, Mayall commented: "You can throw out other bits for the director or the producer, little sort of noises here and there that the animators might like. If you give them a larder full of ideas as well as the actual script that is written it is more liberating that actual film acting. It's so abnormal and weird. That's the kind of stuff I like." The first series was made up of thirteen episodes and ran from September 2004.

One TV job Mayall had never done by this point was presenting. That changed when he fronted the three-part Discovery Channel show *Violent Nation* about how violence used to, and still does, rule Great Britain. Over the three episodes Mayall spoke to leading experts on subjects such as torture, domestic violence and football hooliganism. At times it would tell dark and devious stories from centuries past and at others it would have an air of whimsy, all expertly curated by Mayall and his ability to twist words -

including asking one man about his balls (he was referring to footballs). One stand-out comedy moment occurs when Mayall is taught fencing. He struggles to understand how to hold the sword but makes sure that he puts his full thrust into the motions, Mayall style. It is a shame that no more episodes were ordered as there is something wonderfully entertaining about watching Mayall give educational lessons on historical violence. Ex-Monty Python-er Michael Palin created a whole new career out of presenting travel shows, so it is a great disappointment that Mayall never got to do anything like that as these three episodes display that he could easily have given such light-hearted programmes a little added zing. Director Nick Canner recalls what it was like working with Mayall on *Violent Nation*: "We enjoyed working on the scripts, finding extra gags and losing the worst ones. He was always looking to make it better and would trust me if I felt he wasn't up to scratch during a take. I wanted to make a great film and he responded to that. I learnt a lot about staging a fight on-screen. We blocked out a sequence where he beat up a peasant and he helped (told) me where the best angles would be, which shots we needed for the sequence etc. The result looks genuinely painful (due credit to the stuntman who was being beaten up with a crane). After fluffing a line, his default practice was to swear repeatedly for 20-30 seconds so that the blooper would have a chance of appearing on *It'll Be Alright On The Night* and he could earn, in his words, "200 easy quid". He was also genuinely interested in the people we interviewed along the way, having a knack of making them feel at ease and having a laugh with them."

Fans of Mayall could easily imagine him leading an entire country. He had the brass balls to do something like that even if he didn't know the first thing about what to do - he would give it a ruddy good go. When CITV commissioned an animated series on the King Arthur legend called *King Arthur's Disasters* who else could they pick apart from Mayall?! However, this wasn't your usual Arthurian retelling. This was a twisted spin on King Arthur and his attempts to woo Princess Guinevere through a series of tasks that she sets him. Additional voices were provided by Matt Lucas, Phil Cornwall and Morwenna Banks as Merlin, Sir Lancelot and Guinevere respectively. Yet it is once again Mayall's voice work that stands out.

It is a good, clean, wholesome comedy for very young kids yet it has a slightly surreal Monty Python vibe to it. In an episode titled *The Parchment of Arusella*, as Arthur is trying to ask Guinevere to marry him she suggests he asks her father first but Arthur doesn't quite understand what she means and replies with: "I Have to marry him as well? Very well I shall ask your father although, quite frankly, I'd still rather marry you." The entire two series had a playful vibe to them with some dark undertones designed to engage adults as well as children. Totalling twenty-six episodes over its two series the show was hugely popular with its demographic regularly achieving over 20% of all children viewers and routinely beating whatever was on CBBC at the same time. It was also nominated for a Children's BAFTA in the Best Animation category but lost out to *The Amazing Adrenalini Brothers*, another CITV show. *King Arthur's Disasters* is consistently funny, slightly zany and bags of fun. If you have young children and you want them to understand the brilliance of Rik Mayall then *King Arthur's Disasters* is the place to start.

Mayall's voice work continued as he took part in the animated film: *Valiant*. He was in the company of some of the finest English actors of several generations, all in the form of animated birds. Actors such as Ewan McGregor, John Cleese, John Hurt, Ricky Gervais, Tim Curry, Jim Broadbent, Hugh Laurie, Olivia Williams and Sharon Horgan leant their voices to this British animated film set in 1944 about a pigeon called Valliant who wants to contribute to the war effort. An independent feature film produced by Vanguard Animation and Odyssey Entertainment, it got a huge push across the Atlantic when Walt Disney Pictures picked it up for distribution. While it didn't do the numbers that Disney are used to with their animated features it still brought in a healthy $62 million. Mayall voiced Cufflingk, a Nazi pigeon, who bumbles his way through most of his missions. His voice work is standard fare throughout as he spurts and screams in a clipped German accent. While not the standout in the film it is pretty obvious who voices Cufflingk and there are a couple of moments where you know Mayall was in the vocal booth gesturing with all he is worth.

2005 was the year Mayall finally released his memoirs. However, this was a memoir with a difference. It was billed as semi-autobiographical and those that read the extravagantly titled *Bigger Than Hitler Better Than Christ* soon discovered that Mayall was writing in the third and first person as THE Rik Mayall. It was a unique writing style that perfectly fitted his on-screen persona. It was loud, brash and very flash but in an almost over the top manner. The book's title was a tongue-in-cheek reference to him having a bigger standing than Adolf Hitler and that he was better than Christ because he only died for three days whereas Mayall, after his quad bike accident, died for five days before coming back. While it contained stories of how he came to be one of the greatest comedians the UK had ever witnessed it was difficult to know which parts of the book were genuine and which were flamboyantly exaggerated. Yet this mattered not to his army of fans who flocked to buy the book. Mayall went on a tour around the bookstores of the UK. His signing at Waterstones on London's Oxford Street caused traffic jams as hordes of fans lined around the block to meet him. He eventually left the store after three hours of signing books and taking rude photos.

It had been three years since Mayall appeared on-screen in a character driven piece. His return was for ITV in a comedy-drama called *All About George* written by *Cold Feet* writer Mike Bullen. Mayall played George Kinsey, a husband, son, father and grandfather in the large Kinsey family. "It is very different from anything else I have ever done. There are so many things that are true to life in this series," Mayall commented to *The Stage*. George is the epicentre of the Kinsey family and he has to navigate family problems including affairs, under-age sex and grandmother being kicked out of her home for trying to kill a fellow resident who has a better apartment. Airing on ITV in September 2005, it was billed as a classic sitcom for the whole family to enjoy. Then what the hell was the enfant terrible of alternative comedy doing in it? "You're accusing me of going all sentimental," Mayall told *ITV Teletext*. "I was being asked to play something I haven't played before – a good man. That attracted me." The show forces Mayall to deliver a performance that is almost embarrassingly toned down. There isn't a wink or a nudge or a double-entendre in sight. It is all very safe. An entire series of middle-class people complaining about middle-class problems (what will young Ben Kinsey do without the latest mobile phone?) is a tough watch. Adding one of Britain's greatest comedians into the mix doesn't make it instantly funny, especially if he is given languid dialogue. This is a difficult show to watch as the viewer is left to hope that Mayall may crack a filthy joke or two at any moment. He doesn't. Instead he becomes something that he so very much hated in the early years – a safe, mainstream sitcom actor. *All About George* never made it to a second series as viewers very quickly switched off.

For all his crude and rude work however, Mayall could still provide funny and harmless comedy work that did hit the right note. His voiceover work as the Labrador puppies in the Andrex commercials proved that. So successful were the adverts that a year later Mayall was called back to perform multiple Labrador voices as they all sat around enjoying Christmas dinner. Moreover, the animated TV show *Shoebox Zoo* returned for a second series in October 2005 and Mayall returned to voice the pompous, yet slightly scared, Edwin the Eagle. The story was transposed from Scotland to Denver, Colorado where the story focussed more on Native American mythology. It ran for thirteen episodes on CBBC in the UK and Showtime in the US. A third series was never commissioned.

Mayall's voice-over work for adverts continued to grow in 2005 as he could be found making silly noises and while excitedly narrating adverts for *Horrible Histories* magazine (again) and also their free CD giveaway in special boxes of Cornflakes. He did voice work for Heart 106.2 radio station for their promos of Disney movies *The Aristocats*, *Toy Story* and *Mikey's Twice Upon A Christmas*. Mayall was also the voice of the three UPS adverts that were being broadcast across UK commercial radio stations. If that wasn't enough, Mayall narrated an episode of the BBC 2 children's series *Making Sense of Health* called *Teeth and Eating*. The show aimed to introduce children to the purpose of teeth in humans and animals, the importance of keeping teeth and gums healthy and the need for food & water and a varied diet.

It had been over five years since *The Comic Strip Presents…* had produced a new episode for Channel 4. Peter Richardson rounded up a couple of the old gang for a new episode broadcast on the 28th December 2005 called

Sex Actually. Mayall and Planer appear briefly yet it is left to other talent such as Robert Bathurst, Phil Cornwell, Rebecca Front and Sheridan Smith to try to carry on the alternative comedy torch that The Comic Strip Presents… originally lit twenty three prior. Coming off like a twisted wife-swapping parody of *Notting Hill,* the episode has none of the riotous behaviour that fans had come to expect. It all seemed a little too safe. The new cast hold it together well but there is no energy, no anarchic chaos. Even Mayall and Planer's performances seem subdued.

2006 saw a change of pace to Mayall's voice work in terms of pace and style as he narrated the audio book of *Decline And Fall,* a novel from Evelyn Waugh about an ex-Oxford student who has to slum it as a teacher in a Welsh public school. Mayall continues his interminable pisstaking and pronounced the surname of the character Margot Beste-Chetwynde as "Beast-Cheating" throughout the recording. Mayall also provided the voice for the intergalactic robot in the part live action, part animated corporate advert *BINZ,* produced by Cheshire-based Electromedia. It was aimed at children to encourage them to throw their rubbish in bins (geddit?!). Promotional DVD's were sent out to local Cheshire schools.

Mayall didn't seem the type to go on caravanning holidays (more a sun-kissed beach surrounded by loads of birds), yet he leant his voice to two separate adverts for Welsh caravan companies. Firstly for *Welsh Caravans* and secondly for *Angels Caravans.* These adverts ran on local commercial radio stations in the UK.

By the time the fourth season of the Nickelodeon animated TV series *SpongeBob SquarePants* was in production it had become a worldwide phenomenon. Creator Stephen Hillenburg was lavished with awards left, right and centre. Also, the *SpongeBob SquarePants* movie had been released in cinemas the year before to great acclaim and made buckets of money at the box office ($140 million from a $30 million budget). Episode 10b of season four saw SpongeBob help his friend Sandy with her inventions when the Chimpanzee beneficiaries come calling to check on her work. Mayall voiced the very British Lord Reginald who is forced to try the "incredible back-scratching, hair-combing, nose-picking ukulele tuner." It is a deadpan vocal performance and one that, if you weren't aware of who it was, might pass you by. This was not one of Mayall's standout voice performances. However, somebody at Nickelodeon must have been a fan of *The Young Ones* as not only did Mayall voice one of the three chimps, so too did Nigel Planer and Christopher Ryan. It was an animated Young Ones reunion in chimp form, and at the bottom of the sea.

There was a small *Blackadder* reunion going on in TV advert land when S.C. Johnson & Son's Toilet Duck advertisement campaign hired Mayall to voice the germy General and Tony Robinson to provide the voice for his equally germy side-kick. Another reunion of sorts occurred towards the end of 2006 as Mayall returned to playing Alan B'Stard, only this time on-stage. The show's original writers Marks & Gran modernised B'Stard for a new, younger audience. Mayall first took the show out on the road under the title *The New Statesman – The Blair B'Stard Project*, which ran from April through to July 2006 at a handful of regional theatres. In December of the same year a brand-new Alan B'Stard play arrived at Trafalgar Studios in London's Whitehall, a stone's throw from Downing Street, for a seven-week run. Called *The New Statesman – Alan Bastard's Extremely Secret Weapon*, the show was hailed a triumph. *The Sun* said: "Rik Mayall is brilliant." *The London Evening Standard* proclaimed: "Rik Mayall gets my vote." *The Times* wrote: "Rik Mayall's star power ensures pure apolitical pleasures."

By the mid noughties Mayall had become a master of voice work and in 2007 he lent his voice not once, not twice but seven times to the Belgium/French/Polish/British co-production of *Snow White: The Sequel*. However, this was no Disney-type follow on. This was an animated film aimed at teenagers and beyond with its filthy language and constant nudity. The plot follows what happened to Snow White and Prince Charming after their marriage. The sexual conquests of Cinderella and Sleeping Beauty by Prince Charming are depicted while Snow White is lumbered with a loan shark syndicate of greedy, blackmailing dwarfs. Mayall voiced all seven of the dwarfs – Horny, Grungy, Scumy, Filth, Flunky, Spotty and Metal – with different accents including cockney and scouse. He is clearly having fun with the swearing and his voice work is up to his usual high standards but the film stops short of going full-tilt on the swearing and titillation. Instead it comes across as the type of 1980s animated movie that you would find on the top shelf next to *Fritz the Cat* but is disappointingly nowhere near as X-rated as Bakshi's work. The animation is rough and ready and the English language voice work is excellent but the film suffers for not having the balls to go as filthy as it could have done.

More audio work followed as Mayall's voice appeared in the Children's animated show *Gina's Laughing Gear*, which showcased potential new kids' comedy shows. He voiced Trevor Mullet, a Bond villain-esque owner of an old person's home, in the episode *Stairlift to Heaven*. Alongside him there was voice work from Richard Briars, Una Stubbs and Mark Gatiss. The part is pretty standard fare for Mayall as he crackles and snivels his way through the voice work. Broadcast in March 2007, the show (and the individual cartoon) didn't go past the initial ten episodes aired. At the same time Mayall's voice appeared on the audio version of Claire Freedman and Ben Cort's children's book *Aliens Love Underpants*. He not only narrated the story but also the voices for the aliens.

However, Alan B'stard could not be stopped. Due to the success of the West End run of *The New Statesman – Alan Bastard's Extremely Secret Weapon*, Mayall continued to play the ex-Conservative turned Labour MP from March through to July at selected regional UK theatres.

Two more pieces of voice work opportunities opened up during the year. Firstly, an audiobook of Tony Mitton and Guy Parker-Rees's children's novels *Spookyrumpus* and *Bumpus Jumpus Dinosaurumpus*, narrated by Mayall. Secondly, the audiobook of Ben Elton's *High Society*. The story follows a Labour Party MP (a character Mayall knew how to play) and his pursuit to legalise drugs in the UK. *High Society* could be read as a book about one of the Young Ones who made it big and yet still has that dark, violent and sadistic nature lurking inside.

2008 saw Mayall's name only appear twice in work circles. He narrated the audiobook of Kaye Umansky's children's book *The Silver Spoon of Solomon Snow*. Followed by a decidedly strange and random piece of work to publicise a credit card. Goldfish, the financial services company, decided to let Mayall loose on a three-minute story called *Me and My Goldfish*, written and voiced by Mayall, accompanied by cut-out animation directed by Arno

Salters. The following year he upped his work rate slightly with three pieces of audio work and two TV appearances.

Nutcase Stories appeared on download sites at the start of 2009. It was six episodes about different subjects including magic, wildlife and football. Mayall narrated and provided the voice for the different characters in each episode. It is another entertaining kids' audiobook performance from Mayall, especially when he is channelling Kenneth Williams in one of the episodes. Back on the BBC, this time on BBC Radio 2 for *Galton & Simpson's Half Hour*, Mayall starred alongside June Whitfield in the scripted comedy *I Tell You It's Burt Reynolds*. An entertaining and often hilarious story in which Mayall's character Eric believes he has seen Burt Reynolds and goes to extraordinary lengths to prove it.

For a man who made a huge chunk of his living doing voice work it comes as quite a shock that Mayall's work on the six-part radio series *Bedside Tales* isn't up to his usual high standards. Broadcast in late 2009 on BBC Radio 4, the six episodes feature titles such as *Jimmy*, *Mountain Girl* and *Train to Paris*. This series was co-written by John Nicholson of Peepolykus theatre company and Mayall himself. Though only thirteen minutes in length, each episode feels twice as long due to a below-par Mayall voicing all of the characters in a very shout-y manner.

Mayall had been visually off-screen for nearly four years by the time he made a one-episode appearance in the reboot of *Arthur*, the famous 80s TV series. Episode two of the new series, entitled *In Vino Veritas*, saw Mayall play upper-class gent Maurice, an old school friend of Archie Daley's, who is about to witness the marriage of his daughter. However, he soon discovers that the groom might be in trouble with a loan shark. It is an assured performance from Mayall, who looked trim and dapper in a smart suit. His performance offers a slight hint of comedy but is more serious and stoic. The episode aired on 11th February 2009.

A more substantial on-screen performance came in *Why Didn't They Ask Evans?* An adaptation of Agatha Christie's crime novel that was part of the ITV's *Agatha Christie's Marple* television series. Mayall, with a short crop of hair that blended seamlessly into his greying beard, played it straight. No guffaws or chaotic energy. But behind that façade lurked a creepy guy. During a scene where he administers a sedative to Lady Frances, he demands her to "pop it down" meaning swallow it whole. As she takes the pill, she closes her eyes and the camera moves to Mayall who rather devilishly allows his tongue to poke through his lips in a perverted manner before walking away. It was only a brief role in the episode yet it once again proved that Mayall could, and would, do straight acting.

This streak of straight-acting continued six months later when Mayall appeared in the ITV series *Midsomer Murders* in an episode entitled *The Creeper*. He played David Roper, an alcoholic author who may or may not be associated with the murders. There is a touch of arrogance and sexuality in Mayall's performance. He is the recognizably cocksure Mayall but it is toned down, not through want but more because age was catching up with him and he couldn't careen about like a twentysomething anymore. Instead, he sits and waits for the right moment to be anarchic and wild through the delivery of his dialogue. It is another entertaining drama performance from Mayall. Promotional material issued by ITV included praise for Mayall by his fellow cast members. Actress Jenny Agutter, who also guest starred in the episode as Isobel Chettham, complimented Mayall: "Rik was a joy and great fun to be around. He comes in larger than life from rehearsal onwards and the performance doesn't go down. He is fully of energy and never sits quietly for a moment." John Nettles, who played the lead character of DCI Tom Barnaby, said of his guest star: "Rik Mayall was a complete surprise. You think of all the anarchy but he was surprisingly disciplined and controlled." Mayall had been a fan of Nettles for many years and that is why he took the role. It further appealed to him because "there's a bit of fighting, a bit of being carried upstairs and the promise of working with Jenny Agutter. I was very impressed by how fantastically efficient an organisation it was. I thought I was a wild danger man, but they seemed to take me on quite effortlessly!" The noughties ended with Mayall slowly creeping back onto his old stomping ground of television.

2010s

(*Man Down* people, man… down)

Chris Wade, a musician, writer and filmmaker, commissioned Mayall to narrate his book *Cutey and the Sofaguard* (2010), a surreal story about a nameless anti-hero whose adventures appeared in a dream-like existence. Wade's initial idea for the story came in the strangest of places: "I wrote it in 2008 when I was working at a stationery shop. I'd come up with these random ideas when the shop wasn't very busy. I had this idea of a fella buying a sofa and an armed guard comes with it until he feels you are a good enough owner. I thought it could have a double meaning. He could be his guard in real life until he feels he can leave. Like an imaginary friend who comes to his help when he needs him." Wade self-published the book then months later thought it could make an interesting audiobook: "I approached Rik's agent and they said to send it along as a pdf and he might read it if he gets a chance and to expect an answer in a couple of months. Two days later they got back to me and said he had read it twice already and he wants to do it no matter what."

The expected gusto and swearing aplenty comes to the fore in Mayall's performance of *Cutey and the Sofaguard*. Yet his usual patter is also juxtaposed with a softer, more elegant reading. In another's voice it might be jarring but with Mayall's it sits perfectly. In fact, Mayall's vocal performance of the main character is very similar to his Jackanory work. Cool, calm and collected but also slightly mad and eccentric when needed. *Cutey and the Sofaguard* also offers something not present in other performances from Mayall – the use of multiple regional UK accents. He was already proficient in his Brummie accent thanks to playing Kevin Turvey but there is more to discover about Mayall's vocal prowess in this audiobook. He performs accents including Geordie, Scouse and Yorkshire. Not only are there accents but Mayall can also be heard beautifully rolling his D's on certain words: "men ddddddddroping like flies". His performance as Uncle Archie conjures up images of an old man in a chair reciting his life story while drool spills from the corner of his mouth.

His performance as the Wisdom Twins however is the one that really shines. He makes them so grotesque that they wouldn't be an unexpected presence in a horror film. Wade recalls why Mayall loved voicing the twins so much: "He made them so foul. He saw them as a continuation of Rik from *The Young Ones*. He was tearing into it so much that I had to leave as I was laughing so much". On the surface *Cutey and the Sofaguard* is a silly, humorous audiobook littered with tremendous vocal work from Mayall. Yet scratch beneath that surface and there is a fascinatingly surreal narrative that gets more bizarre the further it goes along. The result is a twisted and heartfelt story centring on the message that we are never alone, even when we think we are. Wade was immensely impressed with Mayall's work on his project: "He saw more depth in it, as a story, than I did. He had taken loads of notes and typed out loads of notes for me. It was ten pages of notes. Finally, when I edited it together, I sat and listened to it and was really moved by it."

Mayall's next project was a complete change of pace. For decades, songs have been released to coincide with great football events. Mainly songs released by English musicians, TV personalities or celebrities have accompanied the Three Lions into the World Cup, and Mayall became one of them. For the 2010 World Cup in South Africa, he released a song called *Noble England*. Much like the English national side it failed miserably and didn't even reach the Top 100 chart. (Author's note: after the death of Mayall in 2014 there was a campaign to get the "lost song" to number one. The track peaked at number seven on the following week's chart).

Meanwhile back on television, the success of Ricky Gervais and Stephen Merchant's *The Office* opened the flood gates for mockumentaries galore. One such mockumentary was *Just For The Record*, a comedic take on the British film industry. Mayall is front and centre in this project as he plays documentary maker Andy Wiseman who attempts to document why a British rom-com collapsed during production by interviewing those involved. It is an interesting idea for a film, and one that certainly is grounded in real-life, but this is a far cry from the work of Christopher Guest (*This Is Spinal Tap, For Your Consideration*). The film looks cheap and isn't funny. It may have British stars galore but it fails to use them to any discernible advantage. The characters rarely appear on-screen together either so it's difficult to understand the dynamics between them, and why the movie fell apart. Mayall slugs his way through but even he can't save this material. One scene features him conducting an interview off-camera.

The sound in this segment has clearly been overdubbed later as it is completely different to the audio for the rest of the scene. *Just For The Record* could have had something very interesting to say about the demise of the British Film Industry but misses every single crucial point it should pick up on. Thankfully, that wasn't the case with Mayall's next project.

This Side of the Afterlife was a short film written by Joe and Adam Horton and Joe Walker. It was also directed by the Hortons. Funded by the UK Film Council as part of the Derby QUAD cinema short film scheme in 2010, it was an eight-minute rhyming fairy-tale about an actor who has the ability to communicate with the dead so decides to set up a side business conducting ghost walks. The venture, however, does not go as he would have hoped. Co-director Adam Horton told *chortle.co.uk* what it was like working with one of his heroes: "[Rik] had comprehensive notes and ideas on how he wanted to deliver certain lines and what he thought his character motivations might be in each scene." This is a dastardly devious voice over from Mayall. One that conjures up thoughts of him in the booth pulling all sorts of mouth shapes when spitting out the rhymes. According to Horton, Mayall delivered a near perfect first take in the vocal booth and that he classed just as his warm-up. Several more run throughs ensued but it was the majority of the first take that made it into the final cut. *This Side of the Afterlife* went on to pick up a nomination at the Raindance Film Festival for Best UK Short.

Mayall was involved in a very special project during 2011. Over 34,000 school children had shared their ideas and drawings with Aardman Animations, who had been commissioned by the Tate Movie Project, to produce a thirty-minute animation movie called *The Itch of the Golden Nit*. The story revolved around 11-year-old Beanie who has to save his parents from the evil Stella and also return the Golden Nit into the sun in-order to save the universe. Mayall's brief voice appearance as President Pinky is a typically crazy performance. Mayall's trademark energy makes his voice work instantly recognisable and yet distinctive. The film was shown on BBC Two on the 2nd July. It also screened around the country during the summer at regional galleries and even made a brief appearance at Vue Cinemas across the UK on the August Bank Holiday. It has not been broadcast since. However, the DVD and book are available to purchase from the Tate website.

Max Kinnings, who had previously ghost written Mayall's autobiography, co-created and scripted an interesting idea for a soap opera called *Soapopolis* for Brunel University. Kinnings and co-creator Professor Steve Dixon envisaged a soap opera where it's storylines would be influenced by fans who could email or text in their preferred future plotlines. Only the pilot of *Soapopolis* was made as sadly it didn't take off as expected. It is a slightly surreal piece of work that would never have sat comfortably with fans of your typical soap opera. For those that grew up on surreal or anarchic comedy however, there is something at the heart of it that could have been an interesting exploration if it had got past that initial episode.

By the time Mayall and Edmondson cooked up a little skit for the BBC's *Let's Dance For Comic Relief* charity TV show, it had been eight years since they last worked together. In this sketch, Edmondson was one of the featured dancers battling to make it through to the final and also raise money for Comic Relief causes. His performance of The Dying Swan (an iconic piece of ballet) was funny from the moment he walked out onto the stage in a pristine white leotard and ruffled skirt. He was void of grace, yet owned the stage as he pirouetted and dipped into his death scene. Just as the dance was about to end Mayall walked on stage and shouted at him: "WHY DON'T YOU JUST DIE ALREADY?" and followed it up with a series of frying pan smashes to the face. Ballet is all about the tender and fluid movements but the legendary comedic duo undercut this to create something anarchic and hilarious. Edmondson made it through to the final where he performed The Dying Swan routine again only this time Mayall dropped a huge 1 tonne weight on him at the end. It was classic Mayall and Edmondson. Sadly, Edmondson didn't win but even sadder was the fact that it would be the last time the duo worked together in public.

In May 2011 the Wells & Young brewery drafted in Mayall to front their new campaign for Bombardier beer. Mayall's character, The Bombardier swaggered into battle, defeated French soldiers and then returned back to base to regal the troops with tales of bravery and romance the ladies, all the while drinking a pint of Bombardier. It was pure Lord Flashheart.

Hilariously, OFCOM, the communications regulator, banned one of the Bombardier adverts for breaching broadcasting rules. The advert in question saw The Bombardier look into the camera and say: "ah, the sweet kiss of summer" followed by a woman appearing from under a blanket on his lap. He turns to her and says: "Hello Summer" the young lady smiles, laughs and then goes back under the blanket. OFCOM believed that the advert "clearly implied that the woman had been performing oral sex on the Bombardier." The alleged sex act in question was seen as being intrinsically linked with the alcoholic drink and as such the advert was found to have breach a Broadcasting Code rule. The advert did go out after 10pm and only on one UK TV station (Dave) but it was still pulled by the broadcaster.

Mayall's dog training skills came in handy in the workplace when he agreed to narrate the CBBC game show *Who Let The Dogs Out?* Over thirteen episodes dogs and their owners had to compete in a series of challenges including skateboarding, dancing and skipping to take home the *Who Let The Dogs Out?* trophy. Mayall's "Wows", "Yikes" and "Blimeys" featured regularly in his energetic voice over work. The show is a lot of fun and is helped by the fact the narrator is equally as excitable as the dogs in the show.

One By One was Mayall's last film shot on English soil. In it he plays a professor called Ernest who has some very different and controversial views on the terrorist attacks in America on 11th September 2001. This was another serious character role for Mayall that proved he could do other types of acting. Whether you buy into the conspiracy theories laid out in the film or not this is an engaging performance. The problem is, the rest of the film is dreadful. Lines such as: "If a picture paints a thousand words then our eyes can see a thousand lies" gives a rough idea as to how self-important the film thinks it is when talking about conspiracy theories. *One By One* was shot in 2011 but not released until 2015. Internet conspiracy theorists suggested this was because the government was trying to supress the film. However, the truth is probably less twisted and is simply that no distributor wanted to release it because of its out-of-date horror clichés and, most importantly, incredibly drab composition.

Channel 4 aired a new, one-off episode of *The Comic Strip Presents...* called *The Hunt for Tony Blair*. Designed as a 1950s noir where Tony Blair is envisioned as a multiple killer and best friend to mafia boss George Bush. The show featured a predominately new cast including Stephen Mangan, James Buckley, Ross Noble and Morgana Robinson. It did also feature a few of the original performers from *The Comic Strip Presents...* such as Robbie Coltrane, Jennifer Saunders and Nigel Planer. Mayall appeared briefly as Professor Predictor, a sort-of Dr Strangelove clone, who is either falling over or pulling faces. Not one of his finer Comic Strip Presents... performances, it has to be said. But then the whole episode is a little flat. Going for Tony Blair's jugular should have been right up the Comic Strip's street, yet this is, on the whole, rather lifeless. Only Stephen Mangan, as Tony Blair, seems to have an understanding of what makes The Comic Strip material so funny.

Shortly after, Mayall appeared as Alan B'Stard on an advert for No2AV early on in the campaigning. The "No2AV" campaign was a political movement to persuade the public not to change the United Kingdom's voting system. The campaign was successful in maintaining the current UK voting system.

Continuing his work on narrating children's books, Mayall voiced audiobooks for three of Craig Green's *Clickety Books* about animals. Green recalls how the project came about: "I had set up a publishing company that was making books and resources for children with speech problems. I had written these stories and to make them work properly we did audio narration CD's. They had been really well received. I just wrote this begging letter to Rik Mayall's people basically saying how all the children would cry if Rik didn't do it [*laughs*]. They said yes and we went into a recording studio in Devon. I was incredibly nervous about meeting Rik in the studio. One day I was on the beach with my children paddling in the water and my phone rang and I answered it and someone said: "I've heard you've got Mr Mayall in the studio next week" and I said "Yes" and they replied: "There will be a bomb!" and I was shocked and said: "What?" and he went: "Only joking! It's me, Rik" and I was so confused. I was laughing and a little bit crying at what was going on [*laughs*]. He went so far beyond what he needed to do with these characters. There is a chicken and he wanted it to be a middle-class hypocrite. We got on really really well."

Mayall's subsequent work on *Errors Of The Human Body* was in sharp contrast to most of the other projects he had taken part in. This was a psychological thriller that first made the rounds at film festivals including The Melbourne International Film Festival, Fantastic Fest in Austin and Frightfest in London. The plot centres on a genetics researcher unwittingly creating a lethal virus and it's jumping off point was discussions between the writer/director Eron Sheean and a scientist he met at Germany's Max Planck Institute of Molecular Cell Biology and Genetics. The film is an eerie, taut thriller that favours a sense of impending dread over jump scares. While Michael Eklund, in the lead role, received the majority of the plaudits (and rightly so), it must be said that Mayall gives an exemplary and quite subtle performance as fellow scientist Samuel Mead. While only in the film briefly it is a performance we are unused to seeing from Mayall. Gone is the anarchy and the chaos which is replaced with intellect and self-importance. *Errors Of The Human Body* is a terrific film that sadly seemed to have passed most by.

A second series of the children's game show *Who Let The Dogs Out?* aired in 2012 with Mayall returning as narrator. Some of the challenges included dogs pushing prams, jumping on trampolines and saving footballs. Mayall's hilarious narration of what the dogs are supposedly thinking during the tasks, lends weight to the argument that Crufts would be so much more fun to watch if it had a crazy narrator.

Mayall's next project wasn't anywhere near as fun to watch. Sometimes a B-movie comes along with such an amazing cast that you think it might just be entertaining and give it the benefit of the doubt. *Eldorado* aka *Highway To Hell* certainly had those credentials when it was released in 2012. It boasted a cast list as diverse as Daryl Hannah, Peter O'Toole, David Carradine, Michael Madsen, Patrick Bergin, Brigitte Nielsen, Steve Guttenberg, Sylvester McCoy, Robin Askwith and Rik Mayall. Written and directed by Richard Driscoll (who had also made *Evil Calls: The Raven*) it was part *Texas Chainsaw Massacre*, part *Blues Brothers*, part *Sin City*, part *A Fistful Of Dollars*, part *Little Shop of Horrors,* part *Cannibal Holocaust*, but all shit! It is like a mad libs of a movie with no one scene directly connecting to the next. Mayall, who pops up briefly as Chef Mario, gets to ham it up spectacularly in a scene where he lip syncs to Verdi's La Traviata opera. It is a gloriously debauched segment as Mayall is covered in blood and is donning a long, curly moustache. It is the only fully watchable scene in the entire film. The rest of it is utter utter garbage. It's not even palatable in a so-bad-it-is-good type way. But the history behind the production is even more bizarre than the film itself.

Driscoll, a horror film director and bit-part actor from Cornwall, bank rolled the film to the tune of £9 million. The film was shot on location in Los Angeles, Las Vegas, London and Cornwall (specifically at his farm where he also raked in cash from his herd of Llamas). Shooting lasted over two years and Driscoll was able to get all of the actors to come to his farm except Hannah who stayed in L.A. The song and dance numbers were lip-synched by the actors as Driscoll had popped down to the local working men's club and got the singers to re-record classic songs such as Aretha Franklin's "Think", Steve Winwood's "So Glad We Made It" and Tammy Wynette's "Stand By Your Man". The bonkers CGI was grafted onto the film by Douglas Shrock, who moved from the US to Cornwall to work on the film at Driscoll's request. However, due to terrible working and living conditions he left (the last straw was possibly when Driscoll tried to put him in a headlock).

When the film was finally finished in 2010, Driscoll submitted a one hundred and fifty-eight-minute cut to the British Board of Film Classification. They rejected it almost immediately citing it as "too strong for an 18 certificate." Driscoll recut the movie by removing thirty minutes and also, bizarrely, re-recording the song and dance numbers. Soon after it transpired that the distributors of the film, Breakdown Films Ltd couldn't get hold of Driscoll. He had put his farm on the market and disappeared. Then in 2011 the Inland Revenue caught up with Driscoll and charged him with Tax Fraud. Amongst his dodgy invoices were ones that suggested Darryl Hannah spent seven days filming in Cornwall (She never left L.A.) and that David Carradine was paid £400,000 for thirteen days of work (The actual footage was taken from Carradine's 2008 TV mini-series Kung

Fu Killer) yet the date on the invoice was two weeks after Carradine died. Driscoll was found guilty of defrauding the Inland Revenue of £1.5 million (the film actually cost just over £1 million to make) and was sent to prison for three years. *Eldorado* (or *Highway To Hell* depending on which cut you are watching) was eventually released straight to DVD in 2012 and included a 3D version.

Things were much more straightforward for Mayall when writer and illustrator Ed Vere commissioned him to narrate three of his children's books (*Bed Time for Monsters*, *Banana* and *The Gateway*) for the *Me Books* iPad app. These three kids' stories are a delight to listen to as Mayall entertains a slightly softer performance in comparison to his usual voice-over work. Mayall then signed on to narrate six children's books by Mike Bennett. They were updated versions of classic tales such as *Aladdin*, *Beauty and the Beast*, *Goldilocks and the Three Bears*, *Sinbad the Sailor*, *The Gingerbread Man* and the *Three Little Pigs*. The audiobooks were produced by One Media Ip Ltd and were released on iTunes and other digital stores on the 4th November 2012. When One Media Ip Chief Executive and Chairman, Michael Infante and writer Mike Bennett met with Mayall to sign the contract a lawyer had to be present to witness the signatures. Infante remembers Mayall started to berate the lawyer, as a joke, saying: "I hate fucking lawyers and quite frankly you are the worst I have ever met. Now fuck off before I have the waiter throw you out." As the lawyer got up to leave Mayall said: "Where are you going? Sit down! Can't you take a joke? Or is that reserved for when you write your bills?". The audiobooks were eventually adapted into short-form animated movies called *Short Tails and Tall Stories*.

Thirty years after its first official broadcast, *The Comic Strip Presents…* decided to go back to the beginning with a new episode. The original Famous Five were back in for a forty-five-minute episode called *Five Go To Rehab* that aired on Channel 4 on 7th November 2012. The famous children's characters, now grown-up, are brought back together again for one last hurrah in leafy Dorset. Only this time old age, racism, sexism and gangsters are in their everyday lives. Possibly the last ever time the original gang would appear together under The Comic Strip moniker. While fun to see the return of these characters, the episode lacks the cutting-edge humour of the original Famous Five episodes. Occasionally it breaks out into classic Comic Strip alternative comedy but it is few and far between. Mayall's fleeting appearance as a gangster is without any real merit. Simply going through the motions without any real energetic dialogue it is a waste of a character and one of the original performers. Only Edmondson and Saunders have entertaining moments as their cutesy, cuddly façade soon slips to reveal inner turmoil and hatred. On the evidence of this episode alone it seemed like a comedy show that was stuck in its own rut. It was exactly the type of comedy show *The Comic Strip Presents…* hated when they first started out. The original Comic Strip gang gave TV so much great alternative comedy over the years that it was sad to see them go out with a whimper like *Five Go to Rehab*.

Following this, Mayall once again teamed up with Craig Green, who brought on-board his best friend from school, Dominic Vince to co-write a six-part audio series called *The Last Hurrah* about an immortal, sherry drinking snowman called Elton. Mayall loved working on the series and said: "It is one of the very few chances in one life to legitimately and deliberately behave as a total and absolute cunt. So that's why I'm doing it." Green discusses how *The Last Hurrah* came about: "At university I did an M.A. in creative writing and I wrote this story about an alcoholic snowman who was living in Suburbia and utterly bored. A really really sad piece, which everybody hated. I told Rik about it during this long car journey and we started riffing on it. Then we agreed to meet up again to talk about it some more. We had this really long afternoon in a pub in Parsons Green where we just role played it. He had no self-awareness, or total self-awareness, as he was leaping out of his seat ad-libbing all these scenes. I brought Dominic [Vince] in, who is my oldest friend from school, to write it and Rik added some material. It was amazing. Vince remembers what it was like working with Mayall on the scripts: "I think we had about twenty-five drafts. We had regular meetings going over and over the scripts. If there were any insults of metaphors Rik would always say 'Come on, let's think of a better one. What can you put in there that is funnier than that?'. Occasionally the new scripts didn't always meet Mayall's high standards as Green found out: "I remember re-drafting a page of script and getting it back and one of the pages had a neat pencil line through it and a word that just read 'shit' [*laughs*]. There was no packaging with the criticism. He took it so seriously."

Mayall's delivery of Elton's line's is gleefully rambunctious as he shouts and slurs hilarious lines like: "I want lots of fucking prawns and don't shrimp on the cost", "I don't have any nerves, I am a snowman you gobshite" and the crude yet brilliant moment where he calls the ghost writer a cunt, to which Eager Ed, the interviewer, says "sorry?" as if he hasn't heard Elton. Elton replies with a deliciously witty response of "You interrupted me… I was saying cunt..ries like Spain and… errr… East Germany…" Mayall's energy cascades out of the speakers (or headphones depending on how you are listening to it) and crashes into your earholes like a foul tsunami. There is no escaping it and there was no holding back from Mayall in his performance as Green discovered while watching him in the vocal booth: "He would do these monologues and he would be sweating and he would be hammering these monologues at full volume. I've never seen anything like it. He was absolutely exhausted by the end of it." *The Last Hurrah*'s unapologetic exercise in letting Mayall off the leash and going full tilt rude and crude is its winning hand. "He always said that Elton The Snowman was his last great character" recalls Green "He said 'this is one for the fans'." For the fans it indeed is. It is for everyone who grew up watching his wild anarchic ways in *The Young Ones* or *Bottom* or *The New Statesman*. Who else would delight in saying the phrase "Bastard snow cunt" but Mayall?! *The Last Hurrah* debuted during September 2012 on download and there was also a limited run of CD's. The CD's proved so popular that Green and Vince had to produce a second run.

A second series was discussed and Vince had begun to write it during the recording of series one: "I wanted him to have more input on series two. I wanted to write with him. I deliberately stopped myself writing the last episode of series two and it has still not been written because he died before it could be recorded." *The Last Hurrah*'s legacy lived on after Mayall's death when BBC Radio 4 got in touch to request an edited version they could play out on his birthday as a sign of remembrance. Episodes one and two were edited especially for the BBC. "He never wanted it to go to the BBC" Vince recalls: "He felt you couldn't say the word 'cunt' on

BBC Radio. I didn't edit out 'cunt' for BBC Radio. That was our birthday present for him."

After his well-received debut on *Jonathan Creek* back in 1998 it was unsurprising to find Mayall back for a second go around of playing the wheelchair-bound Detective Inspector Gideon Pryke for the Easter special *The Clue of the Savant's Thumb*. The show had been off the air for three years before returning with this special in 2013. While Creek and his sidekick Joey Ross, played by Sheridan Smith, continue their inoffensive, light-hearted puzzle-solving again, sadly this time Mayall's Pryke seems to have little to do. There is still the odd flash of one-upmanship against Creek but it's all a little bit wasteful and as such Mayall lacks the edge he displayed in his previous appearance in the episode *The Black Canary*. This outing wasn't that well received by critics and fans alike however over eight million people still tuned in to watch it on the 1st April.

A few months later, during the summer of 2013, a four-minute animated short appeared on Channel 4 as part of their Random Acts on-going series. This short was called *Don't Fear Death*. It was produced by Birmingham-based animation studio Dice Productions and Mayall lent his voice to the piece, energetically spitting out all the advantages of being dead: "You'll never have to waste one more single, soul-crushing hour in your mindless, dead-end job." Mayall barrels through the voice over at great speed but still maintains a certain vigour in his voice. It is a crazy yet enjoyable short that really pushed Mayall to the top of his voice acting ability.

With Mayall appearing more and more on TV, it seemed that the Riknaissance was picking up pace. None more so than a new comedy show that returned Mayall to his anarchic best.

"Eventually… I fucked her against that wall"

They say everyone has a doppelganger. Another person who looks almost identical to themselves even though they are unrelated. Legend suggests that coming face-to-face with your doppelganger is a warning of your forthcoming death. In some circumstances however, meeting your doppelganger can bring about unique ideas, collaboration and friendships in your personal or professional life. Certainly, that was the case with British comedian Greg Davies because for years the average person on the street had been telling him he looked a lot like Rik Mayall. Not exactly like Mayall, more the lanky love-child of Dr. THE Rik Mayall: "It happened in my late 20s/early 30s the first-time people started saying 'you look like him'. I was a huge fan of his and I think I just fucking morphed into him." But Davies wasn't a comedian during his 20s and 30s, he was a school teacher, unhappily teaching drama to uninterested children. "I was lost at sea. I wasn't happy where I was in life. In my 20s I was a huge drinker. We'd go out at weekends and get absolutely shitfaced," Davies commented years later. He would try and make his friends laugh to alleviate the stress and boredom of his day job. Eventually, he found himself gigging on the stand-up circuit. Within two years he was making enough money to finally quit teaching and become a comedian full-time. After hugely successful appearances on TV shows *The Inbetweeners* and *Cuckoo*, and a UK-wide sell-out stand-up tour called *Firing Cheeseballs At A Dog*, Davies started to write his own sitcom. Using elements of his stand-up show as part of the narrative Davies began to formulate a show based, largely, on his own life as a school teacher and his inability to be a grown-up. The show was called *Man Down*, based on the fact Davies character – Dan – would always man down instead of man up in emotional situations. Davies also injected the idea that whatever happened to Dan was always his fault: "He's a nice man but he always makes the wrong decisions."

When it came time for casting *Man Down*, Davies pulled in fellow stand-up comedians Roisin Conaty and Mike Wozniak to play his friends Jo and Brian respectively. Gwyneth Powell was cast as Dan's mum. She had been acting since the late sixties but was best-known as the strict headmistress Mrs McClusky in children's TV show, *Grange Hill*. If you are going to make a show about a teacher then why not include one of the most iconic British television teachers' ever to play your mother? "All the characters are quirky, even the ones who appear to be quite normal, like the mother – there's a quirkiness about her," Powell said in the Channel 4 press kit.

The dream list for the actor to play Dan's dad, the psychopathic yet loving man of the house, was a small list. It consisted of one name – Rik Mayall. As Davies was writing the series with his co-writers Stephen Morrison and Sian Harries they would joke that Mayall would play his father: "Of course he will, that's what must happen," Davies told *Chortle.co.uk*, "Then he said 'Yes' and I couldn't fucking believe it." So, a joke that had percolated for years, of Mayall and Davies looking alike and possibly being related, was finally going to be included as the plot in a real show. "I was first attracted to the part through Greg Davies, who I've always admired and thought was great… because he is," Mayall said in an interview before the show aired "Then the pilot came up last year, and I had a spare week and he was looking for a psycho to attack him, so I thought this looks lovely." He couldn't help but bring up the fact that he and Davies look alike either: "Plus, of course, he is my love child – as many people are aware – we look like each other." Dan's dad was based on Davies real father: "My dad wasn't a psychopath. He didn't physically attack me, but he did constantly wind me up." One prank saw Davies Sr. hide in a bush for two hours waiting for Greg to return from the pub so he could jump out at him. Then there was the time Davies introduced his first girlfriend to his dad he said to her: "You know I used to have to wash his bollocks for him?" Davies Sr had a scar on his neck after an operation to remove an enlargement of the thyroid gland. Never once did he admit it was from that operation. He religiously told his kids it was from a shark attack off the coast of Wales. Davis pointed out to *The Express*: "Our family were very quick to laugh at each other," and Mayall commented that: "This character is 'very Rik Mayall' and it's what the punters would expect, as I think the essence of my work is that I've always taken the mick out of myself." Mayall was perfect casting.

The first meeting between Mayall and Davies saw the legendary anarchic comedian saunter up to his Man Down colleague, give him a soft hug and whisper in his ear "Comrade." That wasn't the only time that Davies was taken aback by Mayall. In one scene, the Dad refused to flush a shit in his son's toilet, creating a huge stench that filled the entire flat. Mayall pulled Davies aside and said to him: "Greg, can you tell me what my motivation is for me going into your toilet and taking a massive shit?"

"It's just for a laugh Rik," Davies replied.

"There must be more to it. What does it say about the relationship between father and son?" Mayall enquired.

Davies managed to blag his way through and give Mayall a reason why his dad would do that, something more profound than "just to have a massive shit."

Filming took place around Reading, Watford and South Oxhey during the summer months of 2013. As Davies' character, Dan, is a teacher the show needed a school to film in. Sandhurst School in Berkshire was selected. Mainly because Davies had that school in mind while writing the show as that was the school he used to teach at. It was fitting that he returned to the school where he was "lost at sea" to play a heightened version of himself: "I was at that school for about seven years so it felt like some sort of therapy to go back and film in that place where I was unhappiest" he told *Chortle.co.uk*.

Channel 4, who commissioned the series, broadcast the first episode of *Man Down* on the 18th October 2013. Critical response was mixed. *Time Out* said: "Ageing *'The Young Ones'* fans will love it." While *The Telegraph* scathed: "*Man Down* was a big let-down." Its viewership plateaued at around the one million mark for the first series (the first episode opened to 1.83 million viewers). Renewed for a second series, then a third and a fourth, also Christmas specials, *Man Down* continues to be popular up to this day. It has a loyal set of fans who tune in every week to see what antics Dan and his friends get up to. It is a testament to Davies that he has created a premise that results in a show that everybody involved in seems to be having a brilliant time making it. It helps that Davies can call on his own experiences, whether it be from his teaching years or the countless times his dad played a joke on him, to further fuel this show about a delta male. While the fictional Dan has nobody he can really turn to in those trying times, Davies was incredibly lucky to have his father there as a source of encouragement and inspiration: "He was hilarious. I can't think of anybody who's made me laugh as much."

Father/Son casting can be a tricky thing to get right. They two actors don't necessarily have to look alike or even act alike, it just must be believable that they are related. In the case of Davies and Mayall for *Man Down* it goes beyond that to the point where it does look and feel like they are <u>father and son</u>. As Davies stated at the time of casting, they do look a lot alike but on screen there is also a clear emotional and physical connection.

Their relationship is central to everything that the adult Dan is trying to break away from yet can't because he still loves his dad and his dad still loves him. The actors convey this in a unique and aggressive way. Dan may be the enfant terrible of the show but where did he get that attitude from? Why does he think it is acceptable to behave like that? And who continues to push his buttons to make him act out? Psychologists could have a field day analysing the crazed relationship between Dan and his dad. There is, however, no psychoanalyzing in the show and instead we are treated to endless slapstick gags that usually culminate in Dan being injured in one way or another: nipple bitten by a horse, being pushed into a Christmas tree, fighting his Dad, who is dressed as a bear, in the street, to name just a few.

Herein lies the brilliance of the show: Davies as creator and head writer doesn't take all the best comedic lines. He spreads them around the main cast and is happy for the punchline to end up being a gag about his character. Conaty, Wozniak and Powell deliver hilarious dialogue in their own style imbuing the show with several different interpretations of the scripted comedy. All of them contribute significantly to the over-arching comedic aspect of the show. It is, however, Mayall who contributes the most. He is back to his scene-stealing best in *Man Down*. Every single moment he is on-screen is a joyous and rambunctious moment. Even the way he walks into a room is funny. When he cocks his eyebrow and gives that little devilish grin from the corner of his mouth, you know it is all about to kick off in a very special, and painful, way.

The heart of the anarchic Mayall of thirty years ago still beats under the character but the non-stop energy is sadly missing. However, it has been replaced with calculating comedy. This comedic performance still seems to be full of energy but actually isn't as Mayall is mainly standing still or walking in and out of a room. The way Mayall performs even the slightest of gags is reminiscent of the slapstick old days alongside Edmondson. This time the butt of the jokes is Davies and not Mayall (as was the way in *Bottom* etc). It takes a very confident lead actor to not only work with a scene-stealer like Mayall but to also encourage him to be the centre of every scene he appears in. Not enough praise is given to Davies in that regard.

This show also gave Mayall a rebirth. After years of voice-overs, TV bit parts and occasional B movies *Man Down* brought Mayall back to the masses. Mayall's older fans lapped up the show in droves and it brought new, younger viewers to his work. It truly was the renaissance of Rik Mayall.

Tragically, shortly before filming began on series two of *Man Down* the news came of Mayall's untimely passing. This put the show on hiatus as Davies and his writers scrambled to re-write the first four episodes that had already been signed off. If that wasn't sad enough, Davies' real father passed away shortly after Mayall, and as the father in *Man Down* was loosely based on him it was a double-whammy for Davies to deal with. The show, somehow, had to address the death of the father on-screen. But how do you write a heartfelt and emotional tribute in a slapstick sitcom? The answer came in *Man Down*'s Christmas special of 2014. While the episode is about establishing a new character, Auntie Nest played by Stephanie Cole, it is top and tailed with two touching scenes of first Mum, and then later Dan, looking at a framed picture of Dad. This is after the dog has pushed Dan into the Christmas tree. Harking back to when his Dad did the same thing in series one. "We felt his loss, all of us did, particularly in the stuff we filmed in the house because we associate that particularly with him. He had a couple of cracking scenes there," Davies reminisced to the *Radio Times*. There is also a beautifully-written scene towards the end of the episode where Mike explains to Dan that his Dad pulled these pranks on him because he saw him not as his son but as his best friend. It is a genuinely touching scene and one that, whilst clearly written for the show, had more than a touch of personal emotion for Davies.

Man Down returned Mayall back to the summit of TV situation (and slapstick) comedy. It wasn't his show and his screen-time throughout the whole first series was less than twenty minutes. Yet nobody could fail to cry tears of laughter at every single scene he featured in. The pure, unadulterated chaos that he brought to the show was a joy to behold. It helped that Davies's work was also from the Mayall school of comedy – energetic and completely self-deprecating. They were two peas in a pod, and that is why they worked so well together. They were happy to let the other lead if it meant they got the bigger laugh. What hi-jinx those two would have got upto in future series, we will never know. What we do know is that *Man Down* allowed the audience to witness the comedy of Mayall in contemporary setting and it was utterly, utterly hilarious.

Stephen Morrison (writer/actor – Community Support Officer): I had co-written the pilot and it had faded away and then when it was announced that Rik was going to be on it I thought it was going to be brilliant. My first reaction was that it was going to be a project I wasn't involved in. Then I was again, which was wonderful.

Matt Lipsey (director): The approaches were made and one thing leads to another and we find ourselves in a room together. We are not going through casting, this is Rik. There is a direct offer if ever there was one [*laughs*].

Gwyneth Powell (actor - Mum): When I was offered the show I was in South Africa and they wanted to arrange a morning's rehearsal the morning I flew back home. I had not slept much on the plane and I had to share the car back to the rehearsal room with Greg [Davies], who said: "Oh, have you worked with Rik before? He is a force of nature." He kept saying it over and over. I sort of went cold and I thought I'm not going to be able to cope with the energy levels of this guy. We had a really productive morning, laughed a lot. I kind of fell in love with him. It was a joy after that. He was such the perfect gentleman.

Morrison: They sit the principal actors in the centre [of the writers' room] and we had to go around and say our name and star sign. The way they do these icebreaker things. Star signs aren't funny. Nobody can make it funny. But Rik did and I thought it was amazing. He said Pisces in the most vicariously filthy way that he got the whole room laughing.

Lipsey: He was fascinating, absolutely fascinating. He comes in with everything from an anarchic stance. If there was a method involved then he would spit on it. We'd shoot from the hip, that is where he would like things to be. When it came to discussing the finer points of stuff he would brush past it. He would just look at the script and go: "Well, it's funny. That's what we will do." Which is exciting and refreshing, but also slightly scary because there are details that you do need to go through.

Morrison: He used to be obsessed with the script. He would constantly be asking why this is happening or why that is happening. To the point of irritation. I was thinking; "fucking hell mate, it's too late for that because we are shooting it."

Lipsey: What we would end up with was I would play a game of compromise with him. Which, to his credit, he was prepared to do. He would say to me: "Look, I'll do it your way. It is wrong but I'll do it your way. As long as I can do it my way as well." The truth is that sometimes he was right and sometimes I was right. To his credit, he turned around a couple of times and said: "Do you know what? Your way was better."

Powell: He had this supreme confidence. It was big and it was confident. The rest of us just followed in the wake. The only thing that buoyed my confidence was that Greg had specifically chosen us because we were icons of his childhood. Me for Grange Hill and Rik for The Young Ones. He had never done anything before so his first thoughts on casting were to go back to his childhood and people he liked on the television, and it worked. It gave me a bit more confidence in working with Rik.

Lipsey: I can remember standing in the bedroom of Greg's character's flat with him [Mayall] and a bucket containing several gallons of water & leaves that he is supposed to spill over Greg. We sort of ended up having a shouting match. Him going: "Look! I'm just going to do this!" and I said: "No, no, no. We have to do the count." I was in the middle of my number count when he just launched in and threw the bucket over Greg [*laughs*]. No harm done and it was even more spectacular in terms of Greg's reaction because it happened when he didn't expect it to.

Powell: There was an episode in the first series where Greg is supposed to be taking up running and I tell Rik he is going running and we both start to laugh, and we laugh and laugh and laugh and laugh. We couldn't stop laughing actually. It worked brilliantly on-camera but we were exhausted by the end of the scene because we had got into a fit of laughing.

Morrison: My trailer was next to his. Something went wrong with the temperatures and it was in the summer and we were in blazing hot caravans and we were joking about being in [TV show] *Tenko* together. That was a good laugh.

Powell: He wasn't afraid of putting his arm around you. It was natural. We both were very relaxed in believing that we were a happy couple and Greg's parents. He was charming with everybody. The crew all loved him. The drivers loved him. Sickening really isn't it?! [*laughs*]

Morrison: There was a runner on-set and it was his first job. He was about seventeen and he was blushing at anything & everything. Rik had spotted this and he said to him: "I need you to do something for me. I need you to go online and find out how to make a nuclear bomb" and he said "I don't think that is in my remit." Rik replied: "I'm the talent and you're the runner. I want you to do that." The guy went off and then someone asked Rik why did it and he said: "He is shy. He needs a project to come out of his shell" and, sure enough, he came back with all these printouts. Within three or four days the young lad was chatting and laughing. I think Rik had seen an uncomfortable kid and decided he needed to help him. It was so lovely.

Powell: We were very excited that we were being recommissioned for a second series. We were just about to start and then… the awful blow. A double whammy for poor Greg as his own dad died soon after Rik. It was a tragedy in every way. We didn't think, initially, that we would be able to do a second series. To lose somebody of Rik's stature and such a huge part of the show… it did look like it would be a one series.

Morrison: We were writing the second series and had written scripts that were hilarious for him.

Powell: The first episode of the second series started in a difficult way for my character because we were leaving to hear the will read out and there was a picture of Rik on the set which I had to pick up and look at before I left. I actually did burst into tears. I didn't have to act that bit. It really was very emotional for all of us.

Lipsey: Greg told me how he was going to approach it [The dad's death]. I said that it sounded perfect and it was. It was brilliantly done.

Morrison: We got Mark Hamill on the show in the third series. He was in the area doing Star Wars, but the only reason we got him was because he was a massive Rik Mayall and Bottom fan. He just wanted to know everything. Mark Hamill was obsessed with Rik.

Lipsey: Rik gave us a run for our money. It was like the Tasmanian Devil had come through your house and you are left with the aftermath, slightly reeling and slightly breathless but also going: "WOW!" It was a fairly profound experience and pretty damn wonderful. I can't think of anyone comparable in my thirty years of experience.

Powell: He loved wearing this cap & bells because he was jingling about on-set and pulling faces and making everybody laugh. That first series with Rik was very special. We had lots of scenes where we had to laugh together and that was pretty easy. I remember it being an absolute joy.

Morrison: The last time I spoke to him was really haunting. I walked off and he was chain-smoking. He had his script and as I was walking away, he shouted: "Steve! You're lucky in this show. Because you get to play a cunt!" I burst out laughing and he went straight back to his script.

Mayall's witty and hilarious voice-overs returned for the third series of CBBC's *Who Let The Dogs Out?* This time dogs took on challenges that ranged from shopping to skating and onto disappearing, all presided over by new Judges Ashleigh Butler and her dog Pudsey, winners of 2012's *Britain's Got Talent.*

Over in Ireland comedian Andy Quirke had convinced TV network RTÉ to greenlight his *Damo and Ivor* characters in a new TV series. The two characters originally appeared as part of the satirical late-night TV show *Republic of Telly* and managed to score a hit single in the Irish charts with "Everybody's Drinkin'", a musical parody. The commissioned RTÉ TV show would continue Quirke's Irish stereotype comedy as he played both Damo Whelan and Ivor Itchdaddy: brothers who were separated at birth, one raised by a wealthy family and the other raised by his maternal Grandmother. When it came to casting the father, Alastair there was only one person Quirke had in mind – Rik Mayall. However, Quirke and his co-writer Jules Coll thought he was "out of their league" in terms of getting him to appear: "We were even chasing the dream. We thought, 'that's completely out of our league'. We were struggling a bit to cast his father and we said, 'Here, we'll just go for it'." he told *The Independent.* Mayall agreed almost instantly and flew over to Ireland a few days before to talk to Quirke and Coll about the character "He goes into a massive amount of detail, I had never seen anyone do that before, he was a pro."

Mayall appeared in the first two episodes of series one as Alastair Itchdaddy. His performance is one of awkwardness for the viewer. Mayall appears to play it halfway towards his work in *Filthy, Rich & Catflap* but also adds in a smidgen of Alan B'Stard. The problem is that those two characters do not mix and as such the character of Alastair is a bit of an annoyance. Mayall flits between accents that include posh cockney, working-class Essex and a touch of Irish lilt. It makes for a bizarre accent and his portrayal of the character is quite reserved when actually he should be loud and brash. Despite this, the show did find its audience from the first episode when it aired in September 2013. It regularly pulled in 215,000 viewers per episode and became one of RTÉ Two's highest viewed shows.

Quirke said of working with Mayall "He's the only person I'd ever met where I thought 'That's who I want to be when I'm older'."

2014 saw the release of a Dutch film called *De Ontsnapping* (renamed *The Escape* for English language territories). It is the story of Julia, who runs away from her Dutch family to find a new life, and love, in The Algarve. It is a Dutch Shirley Valentine, if you will. Mayall played the landlord Eddie (no surname given, but presume it wasn't Hitler). Dressed in a cream linen suit, a cravat and a Panama hat, Mayall reverts back to the performance he found fame with – slightly devious, sexual and initially full-on while also going on the back foot whenever anybody fully confronts him. It's plays out a little bit as though Richard Richard moved to Portugal and got a job but kept the Hammersmith lothario in his veins. He appears in just two scenes as he shows Julia to a house overlooking the sea. Mayall rounds off his performance by quoting Shakespeare's Macbeth but not before telling two dwarves to "Fuck off!". It seems he had a good time on set as behind the scenes footage shows Mayall larking about and acting up to camera.

In May Mayall returned to the voice-over booth. Only this time it was to record dialogue for the band Magic Eight Ball's latest album called *The Last of the Old Romantics*. Singer Baz Francis told *catonthewall.net* how Mayall became involved: "I contacted his agent and began negotiations with her, which included sending them our first album. To my delight, they both loved it – so I was then asked to send a script to them." Mayall's narration appears on three of the sixteen tracks. His pronunciation is exceptional as he gives it a bit of extra Mayall zip with: "Well then, shall we proceed? Mmmmm?" and signing off on the track "On The Days That You Wish You Could End It All" in typical Mayall pisstaking by saying: "Well, they are a nice enough bunch of guys but that Baz really is a complete and utter cunt."

After Mayall's naughty performance reading of George's Marvellous Medicine on *Jackanory* back in 1986 it was only right that he would feature in a modern-day adult spin on *Jackanory* called *Crackanory* on the TV channel Dave. Reading Tony Way's story *The Weatherman* about a man who finds he can control the weather Mayall said: "I'm pleased to have been in both *Jackanory* and *Crackanory*." This reading was typical Mayall, letting his inner rude boy run riot in a setting where he was free to do so. Even before he uttered one word the camera panned across to him and he was gleefully smiling with his middle finger up and in-front of his mouth. As he slowly, methodically and energetically told the story, Mayall wriggled and shifted in the leather chair. He leaned in… and then out. He wagged his finger and flapped his hands. He over-emphasized certain words ("Glooooooomy Sunday") and calmly spoke others ("He said a cheery 'Hello' to his portrait of Michael Fish"). This was Mayall at his storytelling best. As he delivers his last line Mayall cocks his head to one side and raises his right eyebrow, as the camera pans away, as if to say "You've just been seduced by THE Rik Mayall", and the viewers had. When it was broadcast on Wednesday 24th September the episode drew an audience of nearly 400,000 people. However, most viewers tuned in because that would be the last time they would ever see new material from Mayall.

THE PEOPLE'S POET IS DEAD!

There are some people who you naturally assume will live forever, especially in the entertainment industry. Cher has been around forever and will continue to be around long after most die, she is possibly immortal. Ditto Betty White and Ellen DeGeneres. Keanu Reeves hasn't aged a day and neither has Snoop Dogg. Oprah Winfrey simply changes her hair every decade to make it look like she is aging, but secretly she isn't. These and a few other entertainers are going to outlive everyone. Rik Mayall should have been on that list as well. He had already beaten death once, why would the Grim Reaper come calling again? Also, didn't the hooded figure with the scythe know that he was dealing with Dr. THE Rik Fucking Mayall? A man who enriched countless people's lives whether you met him in person or simply enjoying watching his work.

On Monday 9th June 2014, at his home in South-West London, Richard Michael Mayall died. He was 56 years old.

On Tuesday 10th June 2014, a nation mourned. Mayall's death made the front page of the national newspapers including *The Daily Telegraph*, *The Guardian*, *The Times*, *The Independent*, *The Daily Mail*, *The Daily Express* and *The Daily Star*. The *Metro* newspaper simply led with: "RIP Rik". *The Mirror* also went with: "R.I.P. Rik." *The Sun*, never one to miss a pun headline, wrote: "R.I.P. Rik, You Were A Funny B'Stard." Scotland's *Daily Record* said: "Forever A Young One." ITV's 10 o' Clock news led with Mayall's death, stating: "The world of comedy has been shocked by the unexpected death of Rik Mayall." BBC News called him: "One of the leading British comedians" when reporting on the tragic news. Mayall, even in death, was continued to be a pioneer. When did a comedian, an alternative comedian at that, make the front pages of the newspapers and the opening segments of every news show after their death? Probably none. Even much-loved actors/actresses didn't make as much noise in death as Mayall did.

He would have absolutely loved it. His face was plastered all over TV and the newspapers. Tributes came in on social media from far and wide. Friend and co-writer Ben Elton said: "I owe him so much, he changed my life utterly." Co-star of *The Young Ones* and *Filthy, Rich & Catflap* Nigel Planer commented that Mayall was "Inspirational, bonkers and a great life-force." Singer Cliff Richard stated: "I was thrilled when he used me in

Young Ones." Fellow *Comic Strip* star Dawn French said: "He was honestly one of the funniest people ever, a breathtakingly funny man and a beautiful guy." Social media was awash with grief and tributes too. Actor/comedian David Walliams wrote: "I am heartbroken that my comedy idol growing up Rik Mayall has died. He made me want to be a comedian." Co-star in *Blackadder* Stephen Fry put: "Simply distraught to hear of the death of Rik Mayall. An authentic comedy genius and a prince among men." Eric Idle, star of *Monty Python*, wrote: "Very sad to hear of the passing of Rik Mayall. Far too young. A very funny and talented man." Comedian Bob Mortimer described what had happened when he last met Mayall: "Last time I saw him he grabbed my crotch and said, 'Not eaten yet then?' So sad. Funniest man of his generation." The tributes were never ending, from celebrities to the average person on the street, Mayall was loved by all.

One heart-breaking statement stood out more than any other. His best friend of forty plus years and his comedy partner Adrian Edmondson wrote: "There were times when Rik and I were writing together when we almost died laughing. They were some of the most carefree, stupid days I ever had and I feel privileged to have shared them with him. And now he's died for real. Without me. Selfish Bastard."

Mayall's funeral took place on Thursday the 19th June at St George's Church, Dittisham, Devon. It was a private affair with around one hundred and forty family and friends gathering to pay their last respects to the comedy legend. Those in attendance included Ruby Wax, Peter Richardson, Alexei Sayle, Alan Rickman, Ben Elton, Nigel Planer, Dawn French and Jennifer Saunders. Adrian Edmondson was one of the pallbearers. Much like the man himself, his funeral was no by-the-book standard service. Laughter, cheers and clapping were the order of the day. Ending with the playing of Van Morrison's classic song *Brown Eyed Girl*.

In honour of his passing, Mayall's long forgotten World Cup song from 2010 *Noble England* was suddenly re-awakened by DJ Jon Morter. Having previously steered Rage Against The Machine's *Killing In The Name Of* song to the top of the charts at Christmas 2009, Morter wanted to repeat that feat with *Noble England*, saying that it would be a "great thing for Rik's memory." The campaign saw the song finally become a hit by charting at

No. 7 on the week of Mayall's passing. Also, in the days after Mayall's death an online petition was started requesting Hammersmith Council install a bench on the traffic island where the opening credits of *Bottom* was shot after the original one had been removed years previously. The campaign was orchestrated by Jamie Bird, a fan and long-time friend of Mayall's, who explained why it was so important to have a memorial to him: "The reason I did the bench was because for years, every single time we passed that little traffic island, Rik would always mention that bench and how it actually made him a little sad that it was no longer there because it was a 'bloody icon of a monument to a great British comedy' and that it shouldn't have been taken away. He really missed that bench. When he passed, I couldn't process it, I didn't handle it very well and the bench suddenly popped back into my mind and I latched on to it."

The petition gained thousands of signatures within the first few days and Hammersmith Council eventually, after several months, announced they would be erecting a new bench in honour of Mayall. It was unveiled on the 14th November 2014 in a ceremony that brought not only Mayall's family and friends together but also fans from all over the UK. The plaque that sits in the middle of the bench has several lines of wording including Mayall's five mantras to live by "Equality, Opportunity, Wisdom, Freedom and Love." It also has a heartfelt sign-off dedicated to his wife, that simply reads: "Barbara: Love IS the answer." The plaque was designed by Jess Horton who was a huge fan from a really young age: "When Jamie gave me the opportunity to donate and design the plaque, it was the perfect way to give something back to Rik. It was an honour and a pleasure to provide something that can be enjoyed by all of his fans. He deserves that." Bird recalls a heartfelt note left on the bench by a fan: "Someone left some flowers there and I'll always remember what was in that card, it read 'Thank you for putting this bench here and decorating it, it makes me laugh on the way to school and even though I've been going through a hard time at school, this makes me smile."

Another tribute to Mayall was unveiled on the side of Harlow's Playhouse theatre. A 6ft high piece depicting Mayall wide-eyed and excited was painted by street artist David Nash aka Gnasher. Harlow Council's Emma

Toal commented to the BBC: "Rik grew up in a village just on the outskirts of Harlow and local people are proud that Rik is nationally associated with the town. We felt if we could help recognise the joy he brought to so many people we should do something. The final result is absolutely stunning and a fitting tribute to a man who made millions laugh." The bench in Hammersmith and the mural in Harlow were two ways of remembering the comedy legend and ensuring his legacy would continue for future generations.

Matt Lipsey (director – *Man Down*): He had a very different take on anarchic comedy. It was his unwillingness to conform. He had an extraordinary way of doing it.

Steve Morrison (writer – *Man Down*): Genre defining, almost sort of Dadaist. A genre defining physical comedian.

Gwyneth Powell (Actress – *Man Down*): I think his genius was in the fact he was a one-off. He was really a one-off. There wasn't anybody like him.

Tony Fingleton (writer – *Drop Dead Fred*): I think he brought comedy to a level of madness that had a great sense of reality to it. I think he changed comedy in many ways especially in England. Rik was very physical and that was what was wonderful about him.

Ate de Jong (director – *Drop Dead Fred*): I think his legacy is that he could show you other ways of thinking are possible and that people who thought differently didn't have to be condemned.

Serena Gordon (actress – *The New Statesman*): He liked crossing barriers. He liked pushing everything to an extreme. Rik grabbed life by the neck and shook it.

Geoffrey Sax (director – *The New Statesman*): I think he encouraged younger comics to push the boundaries. To be brave. He was fearless.

Maurice Gran (co-creator – *The New Statesman*): His legacy is 90% of what's on BBC Two, BBC Three and Channel 4 because, along with Ben Elton, he created *The Young Ones* and that changed comedy. I've seen people on TV and stage shows who channel him and just rip him off. There is a pantheon of comedy Gods, in terms of performers, and then there is Rik pissing on them.

Laurence Marks (co-creator – *The New Statesman*): He was a man who took everything to the edge, and sometimes almost over it. His whole personality was 'how close to the edge can I go before falling down?'

Chris Wade (Writer – *Cutey and the Sofaguard*): The thing that is missing from comedy now, and Rik had this, is the ability to laugh at yourself. He was always the butt of his own jokes. There is a magic to his stuff that will make him a legend. People will always be influenced by him.

Dominic Vince (writer – *The Last Hurrah*): It is a big legacy. He was very warm and very sincere, and always making you laugh.

Craig Green (writer – *The Last Hurrah*): His legacy is characters that could only be played by Rik. You can hear a sentence from him and it is unmistakably Rik.

Nick Canner (director – *Violent Nation*): A truly unique writer and performer who deserves to be alongside the best in the pantheon of British comedy.

Piers Ashworth (writer – *Rik Mayall presents… The Big One*): I think Rik is, without question, the face of that second generation of English comedy. The first being Monty Python, but the next generation of English talent was… *The Young Ones* kicked it off as that was a new kind of comedy. Rik was at the cutting edge of that brand of comedy.

Simon Wright (producer – *The Comic Strip Presents… Mr. Jolly Lives Next Door*): He changed the landscape of comedy. Not single-handedly but he absolutely was at the forefront of it.

Sandy Johnson (director – *The Comic Strip Presents... Bad News Tour*): He will always be remembered as a beautiful, funny man. He was an incredible energy.

Roger Slowman (actor – *Bottom*): I think his legacy is that he moved television comedy on from Monty Python and into the 80s and took it on another stage. There was something edgy about what Rik did and what *The Young Ones* did and what *Bottom* did, and I think his legacy is that he was at the centre of that.

Rupert Bates (actor – *Bottom*): He was a gift to... just how to be. If you've got something then get it out there and he did that. A man in the right place at the right time.

Helen Lederer (actress – *Bottom*): Rik represented the beginning of an exciting era. One that was new anarchic and genuine. He was both an individual and a team player with a unique talent. And may I respectfully share my time with him was so, so special.

Jon Plowman (producer – *Bottom*): I think his legacy is he never grew old. So, our memories of him are of a young to middle age person who brought huge comic energy. He was bloody good.

Andy de la Tour (actor – *Bottom*): A one-off. A unique comic performer. Which is why he was so successful.

Mark Lambert (actor – *Bottom*): He had as much influence on comedy as punk did on music.

Carla Mendonca (actress – *Bottom*): He was a man of excess. Everything was huge. He was so bright and his comedy timing was impeccable.

Norman Lovett (actor – *The Young Ones*): His legacy is making many people very happy not just with his performances but also being a very kind person.

Michael Redfern (actor – *The Young Ones*): He had something about him that was different from everyone else. He really was a one-off.

Christopher Ryan (actor – *The Young Ones*): He helped move comedy on. He was warm and funny. He shared his humour and sense of fun with everybody. He opened his arms and let it all out.

Paul Jackson (director – *The Young Ones*): On a technical level he left an arrogant, overly confident way of portraying a character that has become part of the comic cannon. In terms of the spirit of the man, I hope he has been an inspiration to generation after generation of young performers to say 'Just bloody do it.' He never compromised.

Alexei Sayle (actor – The Young Ones): He was exceptional. You think about what a massive star he was and because he never gave interviews and because he didn't live that celebrity lifestyle, he was kind of an underground act. He was an enigma really.

Lloyd Peters (friend and 20th Century Coyote founder): He was always the star. He was the star because his confidence was unflappable. He celebrated ego in a way that was exhilarating to watch. His performances foreshadowed the end of the alpha male. He showed that the game was up.

Mike Redfern (friend and 20th Century Coyote member): His legacy is on two levels for me. His ability to perform in the here & now is a legacy. His other legacy to me personally is that he is my oldest, dearest friend and I say that in the present tense… I miss the arse off him.

Alexie Sayle wrote in his autobiography *Thatcher Stole My Trousers* that "What Rik liked to do most, once he'd built up a body of work, was to watch tapes of himself on TV. He did not watch these tapes in any sort of analytical way but rather he viewed them as a devoted fan of Rik Mayall. As Rik watched Rik he would laugh with the wholehearted enjoyment of somebody who had not seen the material before. With anybody else this could have seemed narcissistic but with Rik the pleasure he took in seeing himself on TV seemed so innocent that it was charming."

Words and phrases that have described Mayall through the years: Pioneer, inspiration, God-given talent, larger than life, anarchic, crazy, bold, magnetic, multi-talented, sexy, energetic, unpredictable, legend and phenomena.

Above all others, there is one word that stood out: Genius.

Rik Mayall: Comedy Genius.

Acknowledgements

Thank you to Richard Michael Mayall for being incredibly funny and serving as an inspiration for millions of us.

Thank you to all the interviewees who feature in this book. Your time and willingness to talk to me is hugely appreciated.

Also thanks to all the managers, agents and lawyers who said "Yes" and scheduled time with their client(s).

My personal thanks go to the following people who aided me with this book: Chris Wade, Pip Ellwood, Oliver Double, Cat Park @ Ten Letter PR, Daniel Hatton, Leonard Sultana, Simon Thompson and Sam, Damian, Mark & Michael at Copyright Repro Ltd.

This book would not have been possible without the love and support of the following three people:

Helen Cox. Thank you for agreeing to be my editor again after the mamoth task of my previous book. Your constant feedback pushed me to be a better writer. Thank you once again.

My partner, Samantha. It's very difficult to put into words how much you mean to me. So I'll just say: Thank you and I Love You.

My Mum. You took me to see the first Bottom stage show when I was way too young and it fills me with a great sense of pride that we saw every single Bottom live show together. I think the show made us laugh more than anything else. You are a true inspiration and an amazing mum. Thank you for always being there. Love you.

About the Author

Mark Searby is a film critic, broadcaster and author. He is the resident film critic on BBC Radio's Suffolk and Northampton and also Phoenix FM. He has written for numerous media outlets including: Heat Magazine, MTV, New Empress Magazine, Entertainment Focus, Film Stories magazine and An Englishman in San Diego. Mark has written and presented video retrospectives on movies such as *Serpico*, *The Three Faces of Eve* and *The 'Burbs*. He is also a seasoned interviewer and has conversed with film industry figures such as Mark Millar, Ben Wheatley, Michel Gondry and many more. Mark's previous book – *Al Pacino: The Movies Behind The Man* – was an in-depth look at the films of the iconic actor and featured over fifty exclusive interviews.

Before becoming obsessed with movies, Mark was a DJ for many years. He travelled around the UK appearing at numerous bars and nightclubs including Ministry Of Sound, The Dogstar and Sugar Hut Brentwood.

Mark can be found following, and being regularly disappointed by, his favourite football team Nottingham Forest. He is huge addict of the TV show The Wire and will tell anyone & everyone that it is the greatest TV show of all time. He is also an avid collector of limited edition movie memorabilia.

More information about Mark can be found on his website: www.marksearby.com

He can be found on Twitter: @Mark_Searby

Bibliography

Books

Barnes, Jennifer. *Television Opera: The Fall of Opera Commissioned for Television.* Boydell Press, 2002.

McCall, Douglas. *Monty Python: A Chronology, 1969-2012*, 2d ed. McFarland, 2013.

Mayall, Rik. *Bigger Than Hitler Better Than Christ.* 2005

Peters, Lloyd. *The Roots of alternative comedy – the alternative story of 20th Century Coyote and Eighties Comedy. Comedy Studies Journal*, volume 4 2013 – issue 1.

Roberts, J.F. *The True History of the Blackadder.* Arrow, 2013.

Sayle, Alexei. *Thatcher Stole My Trousers.* Bloomsbury. 2016

Wilmut, Roger and Rosengard, Peter. *Didn't You Kill My Mother-In-Law?* Methuen. 1989

Websites

The Internet Movie Database. *IMDB.com, Inc*
< https://www.imdb.com/>
Rik Mayall Interviews and Articles Archive.
< https://rikmayallinterviews.wordpress.com/>
MayallOnline
<http://rik-mayall.com/mayallonline/>
Movie Locations
<http://www.movie-locations.com/index.php>

Webpages

Bate, Gema. "Young Ones actor Rik Mayall, a former Worcester schoolboy who grew up in Droitwich, dies aged 56" *Worcester News.* 9 June 2014.
<https://www.worcesternews.co.uk/news/11266087.young-ones-actor-rik-mayall-a-former-worcester-schoolboy-who-grew-up-in-droitwich-dies-aged-56/>

Palmer, Martyn. "How We Met: Rik Mayall and Adrian Edmondson" *The Independent*. 20 February 1994.
<https://www.independent.co.uk/arts-entertainment/how-we-met-rik-mayall-and-adrian-edmonson-1395270.html>

Shenton, Mark. "Remembering Rik Mayall: One of the oddest and most fun interviews I've Ever Done" *The Stage*. 10 June 2014.
<https://www.thestage.co.uk/opinion/2014/remembering-rik-mayall-one-oddest-fun-interviews-ive-ever-done/?login_to=https%3A%2F%2Fwww.thestage.co.uk%2Faccounts%2Fusers%2Fsign_up.popup>

"Tributes paid to Droitwich comedian Rik Mayall" *Droitwich Advertiser*. 10 June 2014.
<https://www.droitwichadvertiser.co.uk/news/11268089.tributes-paid-to-droitwich-comedian-rik-mayall/>

Cohen, Dave. "What I learned from Rik Mayall" *Chortle*. 12 June 2014
<https://www.chortle.co.uk/correspondents/2014/06/12/20379/what_i_learned_from_rik_mayall>

Dastor, Sam. "Letter: Rik Mayall's courage in Cell Mates" *The Guardian*. 16 June 2014
<https://www.theguardian.com/tv-and-radio/2014/jun/16/letter-rik-mayall-cell-mates>

"Rik Mayall stars in £4m campaign for Bombardier beer" *The Drum*. 12 May 2011.
<https://www.thedrum.com/news/2011/05/12/rik-mayall-stars-pound4m-campaign-bombardier-beer>

Lowther, Ed. "No! Rik Mayall's political campaigns" *BBC News*. 11 June 2014.
<https://www.bbc.co.uk/news/uk-politics-27781756>

"New campaign: Andrex" *Campaign Live*. 22 November 2006
<https://www.campaignlive.co.uk/article/new-campaign-andrex/605859>

Solomons, Jason. "London was chaotic for filming" *The Guardian*. 20 August 2009.
<https://www.theguardian.com/film/2009/aug/30/john-landis-american-werewold-london>

Bell, Chris. "Eldorado: The bizarre story of the worst movie ever made" *The Telegraph*. 23 January 2017.
<https://www.telegraph.co.uk/films/0/eldorado-bizarre-story-worst-movie-ever-made/>

Roy, David. "One in a million: Rik Mayall in One By One" *Irish News*. 3 July 2015.
<http://www.irishnews.com/arts/2015/07/03/news/one-in-a-million-rik-mayall-in-one-by-one-154938/>

"Jakes Journey: Partially found CBS pilot; 1988" *Lost Media Wiki*
<https://lostmediawiki.com/Jake%27s_Journey_(partially_found_CBS_pilot;_1988)>

"10 more promising TV pilots that weren't picked up" *Vulture*. 10 February 2012
<https://www.vulture.com/2012/02/10-more-promising-tv-pilots-that-werent-picked-up/>

Kimberley, Nick. "Virtual Reality: the battle between technique and technology" *The Independent*. 14 February 1994.
<https://www.independent.co.uk/arts-entertainment/virtual-reality-the-battle-between-technique-and-technology-nick-kimberley-on-television-opera-1394131.html>

Hanks, Robert. "Those days are over: After the police, Stewart Copeland sets himself up as a composer" *The Independent*. 7 October 1993.
<https://www.independent.co.uk/arts-entertainment/music-those-days-are-over-after-the-police-stewart-copeland-set-himself-up-as-a-composer-robert-1509126.html>

"When we were rich: Horse Opera and the decline of British Public Broadcasting" *Mediolana*. 18 October 2012. <https://mediolana.wordpress.com/2012/10/18/when-we-were-rich-horse-opera-and-the-decline-of-british-public-broadcasting/>

"No-one tells a story like Jackanory" *BBC Press Office*. 1 October 2006. <http://www.bbc.co.uk/pressoffice/pressreleases/stories/2006/11_november/01/jackanory_history.shtml>

Chen, Anna. "Rik Mayall RIP: when I met Rik. Briefly." *Madam Miaow*. 10 June 2014. <https://madammiaow.blogspot.com/2014/06/rik-mayall-rip-when-i-met-rik-briefly.html>

"Rik Mayall's forgotten police drama Wolcott to receive a DVD release" *The Guardian*. 11 August 2015. <https://www.theguardian.com/tv-and-radio/tvandradioblog/2015/aug/11/rik-mayalls-forgotten-police-drama-wolcott-to-receive-a-dvd-release>

Bowles, Rachel. "Rik Mayall interview: Jonathan Creek, Bottom, Hooligan's Island & more" *Den of Geek*. 28 March 2013. <https://www.denofgeek.com/tv/rik-mayall/25014/rik-mayall-interview-jonathan-creek-bottom-hooligans-island-more>

Lampert, Nicole. "As he returns to TV in a Jonathan Creek special…" *The Daily Mail*. 22 March 2013 <https://www.dailymail.co.uk/femail/article-2296997/As-Rik-Mayall-returns-Jonathan-Creek-special-tells-chum-Ade-Edmondson-pulled-latest-project-.html>

Marcus, Laurence & SRH. "Murder Rooms: The Dark Beginnings of Sherlock Holmes" *Television Heaven*. 9 January 2019 <https://televisionheaven.co.uk/reviews/murder-rooms-the-dark-beginnings-of-sherlock-holmes>

Wylie, Ian. "Midsomer Murders: Rik Mayall" *Life of Wylie*. 25 January 2010 <https://lifeofwylie.com/2010/01/25/midsomer-murders-rik-mayall/>

"Midsomer Murders: The Creeper. Cast interviews" *midsomermurders.org* <http://midsomermurders.org/creeper5.htm>

Sweeney, Tanya. "Damo & Ivor: The comic birth of very different identical twins" *Irish Times*. 19 September 2014. <https://www.irishtimes.com/life-and-style/damo-ivor-the-comic-birth-of-very-different-identical-twins-1.1929751>

Finn, Melanie. "Andy Quirke reveals he doesn't know what to do without Rik Mayall for series two of Damo & Ivor" *independent.ie*. 11 June 2014 <https://www.independent.ie/entertainment/television/tv-news/andy-quirke-reveals-he-doesnt-know-what-to-do-without-rik-mayall-for-series-two-of-damo-ivor-30346283.html>

Furness, Hannah. "Rik Mayall reads a final bedtime story" *The Telegraph*. 10 September 2014. <https://www.telegraph.co.uk/culture/tvandradio/11088502/Rik-Mayall-reads-a-final-bedtime-story.html>

Dean, Will. "Crackanory, Dave, review: All hail Rik Mayall, the much missed king of manic comedy" *The Independent*. 25 September 2014. <https://www.independent.co.uk/arts-entertainment/tv/reviews/crackanory-tv-review-all-hail-mayall-the-much-missed-king-of-manic-comedy-9754170.html>

Plunkett, John. "Rik Mayall's last TV appearance draws 400,000 to Dave's Crackanory" *The Guardian*. 25 September 2014 <https://www.theguardian.com/media/2014/sep/25/rik-mayall-last-appearance-dave-crackanory>

"King Arthur's Disasters" *Toonhound*. <http://www.toonhound.com/disasters.htm>

"Western Animations / King Arthur's Disasters" *TV Tropes*. <https://tvtropes.org/pmwiki/pmwiki.php/WesternAnimation/KingArthursDisasters>

Gran, Maurice. "I knew he'd would be a perfect B'Stard" *The Daily Mail*. 9 June 2014. <https://www.dailymail.co.uk/news/article-2653402/I-knew-hed-perfect-BStard-MAURICE-GRAN-writer-The-New-Statesman-created-mesmerising-Rik-Mayalls-dream-role.html>

"Films based in Minnesota" *Minnesota Fun Facts.*
<https://www.minnesotafunfacts.com/minnesota-in-mass-media/film/>

De Morgan, Grace. "26 Years On, 'Drop Dead Fred' Is Way Darker Than You Remember" *Junkee.* 25 May 2017. <https://junkee.com/drop-dead-fred-dark-review/106434>

Harrison, Mark. "Looking Back at Drop Dead Fred" *Den of Geek.* 15 August 2016. <https://www.denofgeek.com/uk/movies/drop-dead-fred/42685/looking-back-at-drop-dead-fred>

Collins, Andrew. "I came so close to madness" *Chortle.* 27 August 2013. <https://www.chortle.co.uk/interviews/2013/08/27/18564/i_came_so_close_to_madness>

"Greg Davies on Man Down, the death of Rik Mayall and losing his real father" *Radio Times.* 1 June 2015 <https://www.radiotimes.com/news/2015-06-01/greg-davies-on-man-down-the-death-of-rik-mayall-and-losing-his-real-father/>

Stephenson, David. "Comedian Greg Davies on his role in Man Down: I delight in pushing the character". *The Express.* 24 May 2015 <https://www.express.co.uk/showbiz/tv-radio/579261/Greg-Davies-Man-Down-interview>

"Greg Davies interview" *comedy.co.uk.* 25 October 2013. <https://www.comedy.co.uk/tv/man_down/interview/greg_davies_2013/>

"Rik Mayall interview" *comedy.co.uk.* 25 October 2013. <https://www.comedy.co.uk/tv/man_down/interview/rik_mayall/>

"Rik Mayall remembered at private funeral service" *Hello!* 19 June 2014. <https://www.hellomagazine.com/celebrities/2014061919473/rik-mayall-mourned-at-private-funeral-service/>

Horton, Adam. "Rik Mayall: His Genius and Generosity" *Huffington Post.* 20 June 2014. <https://www.huffingtonpost.co.uk/adam-horton/rik-mayall-his-genius-gen_b_5509679.html?guccounter=2>

Coates, Anne. "The Itch of the Golden Nit". *Parenting Without Tears.* 1 July 2011.
<https://www.parentingwithouttears.com/articles/itchofthegoldennit>

Brown, Mark. "Catherine Tate and David Walliams star in crowdsourced Tate Movie Project". *The Guardian.* 23 June 2011.
<https://www.theguardian.com/film/2011/jun/29/tate-movie-project-golden-nit>

Image Credits